Workplace Violence

Workplace Violence
Issues, trends, strategies

edited by

Vaughan Bowie, Bonnie S. Fisher and Cary L. Cooper

 Routledge
Taylor & Francis Group

LONDON AND NEW YORK

First published by Willan Publishing 2005
This edition published by Routledge 2011
2 Park Square, Milton Park, Abingdon, Oxon OX14 4RN
711 Third Avenue, New York, NY 10017

Routledge is an imprint of the Taylor & Francis Group, an informa business

First published 2005

ISBN 10: 1-84392-134-0 (hardback)
ISBN 13: 978-1-84392-134-9 (hardback)

British Library Cataloguing-in-Publication Data

A catalogue record for this book is available from the British Library

Typeset by GCS, Leighton Buzzard, Bedfordshire
Project managed by Deer Park Productions, Tavistock, Devon

Contents

List of tables and figures

Tables

Figures

Acknowledgements

This book is dedicated to all those who have suffered from the physical or psychological abuse of others at work and to the researchers and advocates who have devoted their expertise and energies to these issues so to improve the safety of workers everywhere.

Vaughan Bowie would like to acknowledge the support provided by the College of Social and Health Sciences and the Social Justice and Social Change Research Centre at the University of Western Sydney Australia which enabled him to devote his full time attention to the development and production of this book.

Bonnie Fisher thanks her husband, Nicolas Williams who is a labor economist, for answering endless questions about labor markets and supporting her research that focuses on workplace violence.

Cary Cooper acknowledges Diane Lamplugh for all the work she did to highlight workplace bullying in the UK.

Notes on editors and contributors

Vaughan Bowie has had a career in the human services for over 30 years. He currently lectures at the University of Western Sydney Australia to youth workers, social workers, psychologists, nurses, police, lawyers and others, and provides in-service training to a range of health, welfare and youth organizations across Australia. He is the author of the book *Coping with Violence* (1996) and has written a number of book chapters and journal articles on workplace violence. He has become increasingly involved in issues related to workplace violence, non-abusive organizational change, workers' compensation and occupational health and safety.

Jennifer L. Burnfield is a doctoral student in Industrial-Organizational Psychology at Bowling Green State University (USA), specializing in research on occupational health psychology. Her current research focuses primarily on the study of the antecedents, consequences and multi-dimensional measurement of workplace incivility. As co-principal investigator of a pilot grant sponsored by the National Institute for Occupational Safety and Health's Education and Research Center, Ms Burnfield is examining the antecedents of incivility experienced by hospital nurses to inform future intervention efforts.

Adrian N. Carr is Associate Professor and Principal Research Fellow in the interdisciplinary School of Applied Social and Human Sciences at the

University of Western Sydney, Australia. Dr Carr is a member of a number of editorial boards, including *International Journal of Organisation Analysis*; *Journal of Management Development*; *Administrative Theory and Praxis*; *Global Business and Economics Review* (founding editorial member); *Policy, Organisation and Society* and *Journal of Organizational Change*. Dr Carr's areas of research interest are critical social psychology, psychoanalytic theory, critical theory, postmodernism, ethics, dissent in organizations and the management of change.

Jennifer H. Childress is a Faculty Lecturer/Retention Specialist at Northern Kentucky University in the Department of Political Science and Criminal Justice. Her research interests include criminal justice systems theory, the effects of race and gender in the application of law, police discretion and workplace violence. She has published perspectives in *Policing: An International Journal of Police Strategies and Management* (for which she served as Assistant Editor, 2003–4) and has co-authored a chapter on the Whiskey Rebellion for the five-volume set, *America's Famous Crimes and Trials*.

Cary L. Cooper is Professor of Organizational Psychology and Health, Lancaster University Management School and Pro Vice Chancellor (External Relations) at Lancaster University. He is the author of over 100 books (on occupational stress, women at work and industrial and organizational psychology), has written over 400 scholarly articles for academic journals, and is a frequent contributor to national newspapers, TV and radio. He is currently founding editor of the *Journal of Organizational Behavior* and co-editor of the medical journal *Stress and Health* (formerly *Stress Medicine*). Professor Cooper is also the President of the Institute of Welfare Officers, Vice President of the British Association of Counselling, an ambassador of The Samaritans and Patron of the National Phobic Society.

Ståle Einarsen is Professor of Work and Organisational Psychology at the University of Bergen, Norway, and acts as Director for the Bergen Bullying Research Group. He is a licensed clinical psychologist with a PhD in psychology from the University of Bergen, and a pioneer in the field of bullying at work. He has published extensively in the field of organizational psychology, particularly on topics related to leadership, psychosocial work environment and bullying at work. His work has appeared in the following journals *Violence and Victims*, *Violence and Aggressive Behaviour, European Journal of Work and Organisational Psychology, British Journal of Guidance and Counselling, Creativity Research Journal* and *International Journal of Manpower*.

Bonnie S. Fisher is a Professor in the Division of Criminal Justice and Senior Research Fellow at the Center for Criminal Justice Research at the University of Cincinnati. Her current research is on the extent and nature of workplace violence and risk factors associated with the victimization of college women and older women. She is currently the co-editor of the *Security Journal*.

Carol S. Fullerton is Research Associate Professor in the Department of Psychiatry, Uniformed Services University of the Health Sciences, and Scientific Director of the Center for the Study of Traumatic Stress. Dr Fullerton, widely published in the areas of post-traumatic stress disorder and the psychological effects of traumatic events, is the editor or co-author of *Bioterrorism: Psychological and Public Health Interventions* (Cambridge University Press 2004); *Terrorism and Disaster: Individual and Community Mental Health Interventions* (Cambridge University Press 2003); *Mental Health and Mass Violence: Evidence Based Early Psychological Intervention for Victims/Survivors of Mass Violence* (National Institute of Health Publication No. 02-5138, 2002) and numerous other publications.

Paula L. Grubb is a Research Psychologist in the Organizational Science and Human Factors Branch at the National Institute for Occupational Safety and Health. Her research interests include workplace violence, bullying and psychological aggression, racial/ethnic discrimination and health disparities, traumatic stress, supervisory best practices, organization of work and job stress. Her current research focuses on developing intervention and evaluation strategies for workplace psychological aggression and bullying, as well as examining workplace violence and psychological aggression policies and organizational decision-making. Dr Grubb is a member of the Federal Interagency Task Force on Workplace Violence Research and Prevention.

Charmaine Hockley is an international workplace relationship consultant. She has been a researcher in the field of workplace violence since the mid-1980s, conducting a series of studies to establish the extent, nature and impact of workplace violence on primary and third-party victims, including family members. She has published and spoken extensively on the topic nationally and internationally. Her book *Silent Hell: Workplace Violence and bullying* is based on 15 years of researching violence among nurses in their formalized working relationships. Dr Hockley divides her time between writing, lecturing, researching and public speaking on workplace relationships, nursing, and management issues from her business base in Strathalbyn, South Australia.

Helge Hoel is a lecturer in Organizational Psychology in the Manchester Business School at the University of Manchester. A Norwegian by birth, he came to Britain in 1991 to study Human Resource Management and Industrial Relations. Prior to taking up his post as lecturer, he was working together with Professor Cary Cooper (then UMIST) undertaking the first nationwide survey of workplace bullying. Dr Hoel has published a number of articles, books and book-chapters on the issue of bullying and harassment for academics and practitioners.

Vittorio Di Martino is an international consultant specializing in health and safety at work, enterprise development and organizational wellbeing. He was responsible for the programmes on stress and violence at work at the International Labour Organisation, Geneva, from 1988 to 2001. He is currently a Visiting Fellow in Employment Policies at the University of Bath and Senior Research Fellow at the School of Management, University of Manchester.

Diane Myers has her master's degree in psychiatric nursing from Yale University and is in private practice as psychotherapist, trainer, consultant and author with over 25 years' experience in trauma and disaster mental health. She has worked in over 35 major disasters, including the Oklahoma City bombing and the World Trade Center attacks. She has authored three books and over 100 publications, training videos and training manuals. She serves as faculty for numerous training institutions and consults and teaches internationally, specializing in psychological impacts and mental health interventions with disaster and terrorism.

Corinne Peek-Asa is a Professor in the Departments of Occupational and Environmental Health and Epidemiology at the University of Iowa, College of Public Health, and the Director of Science for the Iowa Injury Prevention Research Center. Her current research interests include epidemiology of violence in the workplace, domestic violence, injuries from natural disasters, evaluation of injury prevention programs and injury surveillance. Among many other professional affiliations, she serves on the Study Section for the National Center for Injury Prevention and Control and the Board of Directors for the Iowa Center for Agricultural Safety and Health.

Charlotte Rayner is Professor of Human Resource Management at Portsmouth Business School in the UK. She has been involved in research into bullying at work since the mid 1990s when she completed the first major UK survey for the BBC. She has continued to research this topic, including a set of surveys for Britain's largest trade union, UNISON, in 1997 and 2000. She has recently co-authored *Workplace Bullying: what we know, who is to blame and what can we do?* (with Cary Cooper and Helge Hoel).

Rashaun K. Roberts is a Research Psychologist in the Division of Applied Research and Technology, Organizational Science and Human Factors Branch at the National Institute for Occupational Safety and Health. Dr Roberts' current research at NIOSH focuses on the contributions of structural and psychosocial variables to the emergence of psychological aggression in the workplace and on understanding the implications of psychologically aggressive behaviours for occupational safety and health. As a member of the Federal Interagency Task Force on Workplace Violence Research and Prevention, she is collaborating to develop NIOSH's research agenda in these areas.

Naomi G. Swanson is head of the Work Organization and Stress Research group at the National Institute for Occupational Safety and Health (NIOSH). Along with Dr Steven Sauter of NIOSH, she was involved in some of the initial research in the USA examining the relationship of organizational factors to non-fatal workplace violence. She is currently participating in research examining the relationship between workplace stressors and depression, the assessment of work organization interventions designed to improve worker health and wellbeing, and the assessment of workplace violence programs and practices.

Ros Thomas grew up in South Africa and moved to Geneva, Switzerland, in 1989 where she lives with her family. While in South Africa she qualified with an MA in Clinical Social Work from the University of Witwatersrand where she taught in the Department of Social Work. She lectures in psychology and counselling at Webster University Geneva and is the co-director of the Master of Arts in Counseling Program. Until she returned to her studies in 2002 she ran a private clinical practice in Geneva.

Robert J. Ursano is Professor of Psychiatry and Neuroscience and Chairman of the Department of Psychiatry at the Uniformed Services University of the Health Sciences, Bethesda, Maryland. He is also Director of the Center for the Study of Traumatic Stress, and editor of *Psychiatry*, the distinguished journal of interpersonal and biological processes. Dr Ursano is an internationally recognized disaster psychiatrist who provides leadership to government, healthcare and public health, industry and academia on disaster preparedness and response, and the mental health effects of trauma. He has over 200 publications in this field.

Nancy T. Vineburgh is Assistant Professor, Department of Psychiatry, Uniformed Services University of the Health Sciences (USUHS) in Bethesda, Maryland and Director, Office of Public Education and Preparedness, Center for the Study of Traumatic Stress (CSTS). Ms Vineburgh is a recognized expert in health communications encompassing television, radio and print journalism, and community and employer-based health and mental health initiatives. She is the Co-Principal Investigator of a research study, *Workplace Preparedness for Terrorism*, funded by the Alfred P. Sloan Foundation. She is a member of the Washington School of Psychiatry, the American Public Health Association, the Employee Assistance Professionals Association and Employee Assistance Society of North America.

David F. Wee has over twenty years of experience in the field of crisis intervention and disaster mental health. He is an Instructor, California State University Hayward, Social Work Department; Adjunct Faculty, California Specialized Training Institute, Governor's Office of Emergency Services; Field Instructor, University of California Berkeley, School of Social Welfare; and Instructor, UC Berkeley Extension. He provides training in emergency management, crisis intervention, disaster mental health, terrorism and workplace safety. He is a Program Supervisor at City of Berkeley Mental Health, Berkeley, California.

Monica T. Whitty is a lecturer at Queen's University Belfast in the School of Psychology. She lectures in social psychology, qualitative methods and cyberpsychology. Monica is well published in the areas of cyber-flirting, internet relationships, misrepresentation online, internet privacy and surveillance in the workplace. Her work is regularly cited in the media.

Barb Wigley has an undergraduate degree in health sciences, two post-graduate degrees, in business (organization consulting and change) and in development studies, and is currently writing her doctoral thesis exploring the culture and dynamics of international humanitarian and crisis-oriented organizations. After many years as a clinician and then manager in the public health and community sector in Australia, she moved into management and organizational consulting and sessional teaching at La Trobe University in Melbourne. Barb currently works as a consultant with the United Nations, based in Geneva.

Dieter Zapf is Professor for Work and Organizational Psychology at the Johann Wolfgang Goethe-University Frankfurt. He has a diploma in psychology and a degree in theology, with a PhD from the Free University of Berlin. He has published extensively in the field of organizational psychology and especially on issues such as human-computer interaction, emotion work, stress at work and bullying in the workplace. He is also associate editor of the *European Journal of Work and Organizational Psychology*.

Chapter 1

Introduction: new issues, trends and strategies in workplace violence

Vaughan Bowie, Bonnie S. Fisher and Cary L. Cooper

This book is the second in a series on workplace violence published by Willan Publishing. The first volume, *Violence at Work: causes, patterns and prevention*, set a high standard in research and scholarship which we hope has been rivalled by the many excellent chapters found in this second volume. The concluding comments of *Violence at Work* identified new and emerging types of workplace violence, including, among others, domestic violence spilling over into the workplace, cyberstalking, violence against peacekeepers and international aid workers and violent organizational cultures as key areas for further research and scholarship. This second book has taken up this challenge and includes a number of chapters on these topics.

As we developed the desired directions and content of this volume there emerged a number of key distinguishing themes that we hoped to see represented. These features included 1) an emphasis on an integrated and comprehensive typology of workplace violence, 2) a focus on new and emerging issues in workplace violence, 3) the inclusion of terrorism within a framework of workplace violence, 4) an emphasis on the 'human services' element within responses to terrorism and related incidents, and 5) an international focus from a number of expert contributors. We believe that we have been able to begin addressing these key distinguishing features in the ways outlined below.

An integrated and comprehensive typology of workplace violence

In this opening chapter we outline an integrated and comprehensive typology of violence at work. Most current texts on workplace violence are not based on an integrated typology that allows a comprehensive response to the various types of workplace violence. Current strategies outlined in such existing texts tend to focus mainly on criminal violence, client violence on staff or bullying and often leave out a whole range of equally damaging workplace violence incidents. Few books that we are aware of currently include terrorism as a type of workplace violence.

Previously Bowie (2002) outlined an expanded typology of workplace violence that included organizational violence and terrorism as types of work-based aggression and violence. In the earlier typology terrorism was originally included as a type of external/intrusive workplace violence that can include:

- **Those pursuing acts of terrorism using violence**. This may occur in incidents of plane hijackings, assassinations or bombing of embassies. The recent terrorist attacks in New York and Washington, DC in 2001 and Bali in 2002 clearly illustrate the possibility of such violence occurring within a workplace.

- **Those protesting in a violent way against an organization's policies or practices**, such as multi-nationals which pollute the environment or exploit third-world countries, or abortion clinics that may terminate pregnancies. Recent anti-globalization rallies and protests have also illustrated the possibility of such violence impacting on people at work or on their way to and from work. Such 'single issue' events could be interpreted as terrorist actions.

However, though terrorism would generally be seen as external events that intrude into the workplace, there is also the possibility that violent terrorist events may be planned and executed within organizations by disgruntled workers, religious or political zealots or alienated clients or patients and not just by external perpetrators.

Similarly, countries and organizations may also be involved directly in developing and/or supporting terrorist actions against other countries, organizations or individuals. For example, there has been a long history of the CIA training and supporting terrorist groups in South and Central America (Barkan and Snowden 2001) and more recently the USA and Britain training the Taliban to fight against the Soviet Union. State-sanctioned terrorism could include ethnic cleansing and genocide (Martin 2004).

Thus, since 2002 this typology has continued to be developed to include the various forms of type 1–4 of workplace violence outlined in Table 1. We have decided to include this revised and expanded typology here to provide a framework to aid readers of this volume in further understanding and integrating the range of workplace violence issues. A number of the following authors also use this typology as a basis for identifying the particular forms of workplace violence that they are addressing.

New and emerging issues in workplace violence

This book also examines some of the key issues around violence at work that have emerged in the new millennium, including the events of September 11 and other terrorist-related incidents. This book fills a void in much of the current literature dealing with terrorism and workplace violence by identifying terrorism incidents as being an extreme form of workplace violence. This important nexus is often overlooked or misunderstood and this book attempts to spell out this link in more detail.

Table 1.1   Expanded workplace violence typology

Type 1: external/intrusive violence
- Criminal intent by strangers
- Terrorist acts
- Protest violence
- Mental illness or drug-related aggression
- Random violence

Type 2: consumer-related violence
- Consumer/clients/patients (and family) violence against staff
- Vicarious trauma to staff
- Staff violence to clients/consumers, including terrorist acts

Type 3: relationship violence
- Staff-on-staff violence and bullying, including terrorist acts
- Domestic violence and sexual harassment at work
- Third-party violence

Type 4: Organisational violence
- Organizational violence against staff
- Organizational violence against consumers/clients/patients
- Organizational violence against other organizations or communities
- Organizationally condoned or sponsored terrorist acts

This volume also addresses some key emerging and controversial issues. Among the timely issues the contributors focus on are: staff who abuse those in their care, domestic violence spilling over into the workplace, violence against aid and humanitarian workers, and organizations who are themselves abusive to their staff and service users as well as oppressive of their surrounding communities.

Human services responses to terrorism

This volume goes beyond the current major emphasis on equipping 'primary responders' (e.g. police, fire, ambulance, etc.) to react to terrorist risks and related workplace violence incidents. Attention is specifically given to the 'secondary' responders such as human services workers, managers, human resources staff, unions, occupational health and safety professionals, humanitarian aid workers and media staff. A number of chapters outline how organizations can train and support such staff to help themselves and others operate in a non-oppressive manner in a much more globally unstable work environment.

An international focus on workplace violence

This volume provides the international perspectives of the first volume with contributors from Australia, the United States, England, Northern Ireland, Switzerland, Germany and Norway. Most of the chapters call upon an international body of cross-disciplinary scholarship and research from these countries, while others focus on relatively new areas of research in Africa, the Middle East and Europe.

We conclude this chapter by giving the reader a 'taste' of the issues addressed in each chapter. A cursory glance at the table of contents may give the impression that this volume contains a number of diverse topics with little interrelationship apart from the five key themes outlined above. Such an impression may lead the discerning, time-poor reader to pick and read only chapters that address their particular interest or areas of expertise. Such a selective approach, however, may miss the integrative theme woven throughout the chapters. This common theme is that of the proactive role organizations can play in preventing, managing or exacerbating work-related physical and psychological violence.

SECTION I

National and International Trends and Responses to Workplace Violence

Chapter 2

A cross-national comparison of workplace violence and response strategies

Vittorio Di Martino

This chapter provides an overview of the evolution of workplace violence from a purely personal issue into an organizational, societal and eventually a cross-national one around the world. Di Martino identifies a number of key issues that arise from this cross-national perspective. These issues include 1) the influence of different perceptions and cultural backgrounds on the identification of this phenomenon, 2) the increasing awareness of workplace violence in developing countries, 3) the growth of psychological violence and the emergence of mass physical violence as key elements in workplace violence, and 4) the emerging awareness of the economic 'cost' of violence at work. In the light of these emerging issues the chapter outlines the current initiatives in place at an international level to manage and prevent workplace violence. Di Martino concludes this chapter by briefly outlining further key responses needed at a cross-national level to begin to address this issue of workplace violence.

Chapter 3

Organizational factors and psychological aggression: results from a nationally representative sample of US companies

Paula L. Grubb, Rashaun K. Roberts, Naomi G. Swanson, Jennifer L. Burnfield and Jennifer H. Childress

In this chapter Paula Grubb and her colleagues describe the role of higher-level work organization contextual factors such as structure, organization type and policies in effecting two pervasive manifestations of psychological aggression at work – those of bullying and incivility. They explore this issue through data obtained from a nationally representative National

Organizations Survey of US companies that provides an overview of the extent of reported workplace aggression. A unique feature of this present investigation is that the workplace itself is the unit of analysis, not the experiences of individual employees. This survey also provides an overview of policies and programmes in place at these organizations at the time of the reported psychological aggression. The authors then examine how organizations that reported bullying and incivility in the previous year were different in terms of organization structure, policies and programmes, and quality of worklife factors compared to those that had not reported these forms of workplace aggression. They conclude by discussing the implications of these findings for current and future research and practice.

Chapter 4

Reforming abusive organizations

Charlotte Rayner

Rayner tackles two types of internal abuse at the organizational level. The first type of internal abuse is that of interpersonal abuse or what Rayner calls 'Negative Interpersonal Behaviour' (NIB). The second type of internal abuse is organizational abuse or what Rayner identifies as 'Negative Organizational Behaviour' (NOB). Such abuse occurs where systems and processes directly fail to support, undermine or otherwise cause harm to employees. The first part of this chapter focuses on describing what NIB is and outlines reforms that may address NIB. The latter part of the chapter identifies how the organizations might themselves be abusive through NOB and outlines strategies to prevent or minimize such behaviours.

SECTION 2

Identifying and Responding to At-Risk Groups

Chapter 5

Staff violence against those in their care

Charmaine Hockley

Staff violence against those in their care is one of the last of the taboo areas being revealed as a form of workplace violence. In this chapter Hockley examines the paradox that those whose key responsibility is to provide and promote an environment in which the human rights, values, customs and spiritual beliefs of those in their care are respected, should sometimes also be potentially capable of violent acts against those who are committed to their care. Hockley examines the phenomenon of violence by staff against those in their care from the ethical and legal perspectives expected of a health professional. The chapter covers core issues of the typology of workplace violence in healthcare settings, the concept of staff-initiated violence, the victim's and perpetrator's profile, causes and methods, and finally strategies to manage this emerging category of workplace violence.

Chapter 6

Domestic violence and the workplace: do we know too much of nothing?

Bonnie S. Fisher and Corinne Peek-Asa

Fisher and Peek-Asa begin their chapter by exploring the known scope of domestic violence and related incident in the workplace in the United States. They then examine statistics showing that domestic-related homicide, sexual and physical assault, and stalking are increasingly spilling over into the workplace. They go on to identify further research demonstrating that domestic violence diminishes productivity and morale for the victim, perpetrator-employee and co-workers, while increasing healthcare costs for employers and, ultimately, undercutting profits. Fisher and Peek-Asa then analyse key current recommendations for reducing the threat and incidence of domestic violence within the workplace. They conclude their chapter by discussing the gaps in our knowledge about these issues, with a particular focus on the gaps in the identification and prevention of and response to domestic violence by employers and their organizations.

Chapter 7

Caring for those who care – aid worker safety and security as a source of stress and distress: a case for psychological support?

Ros Thomas

Ros Thomas firstly considers within the context of humanitarian aid work the issue of the often largely forgotten aid workers themselves and then outlines the security issues including workplace violence that they face in the 'field'. Thomas further raises awareness of the potential mental health issues resulting from aid work under conditions of war and terrorism and how best to manage these. The chapter concludes with suggestions for practical steps that organizations can tailor to provide support systems that meet the mental health needs of their aid staff before, during and after returning from work in the field.

Chapter 8

Not off the hook: relationships between aid organization culture and climate, and the experience of workers in volatile environments

Barb Wigley

In this chapter Barb Wigley argues that an humanitarian aid organization's culture, climate and dynamic has a greater impact upon aid worker experience than events and incidents that arise directly as a result of their working environment. This organizational climate in turn has a major influence on employees' ability to cope with the violence and trauma they face as part of their work role. The chapter commences with an exploration of aid agencies' organizational culture and considers some of the factors at various levels that help define and mould such humanitarian organization cultures. Drawing from her qualitative and quantitative research, Wigley explores some of the ways in which the organizational culture is experienced by aid workers, especially as it relates to leadership and incident-related stress. Finally, drawing from current organizational research, effective organizational interventions and strategies are outlined to help aid organizations modify their culture, climate and dynamic in such a way as to help staff cope more effectively with the violence and trauma they frequently face as part of their routine.

SECTION 3

Terrorism: A New Type of Workplace Violence

Chapter 9

Organizational violence: a trigger for reactive terrorism

Vaughan Bowie

In this chapter Bowie outlines from the research literature the varying types of terrorism and the sources and triggers of such violence. He further examines the ways in which organizational cultures and work practices may stimulate social and community conditions that provide breeding grounds for cultural, political and religious resentments. Bowie then outlines how such resentments in turn could trigger reactive terrorist feelings and action. He offers insight into the important direct role that trans-national organizations may play in providing such a 'fertile ground' for reactive terrorism to thrive and expand. Bowie concludes by outlining some strategies to identify, minimize and break such a nexus between workplace violence and reactive terrorism.

Chapter 10

Preparing, training and supporting human service workers to respond to terrorist events

David F. Wee and Diane Myers

Wee and Myers focus on how we equip human service workers to respond to terrorist events in the workplace. Most literature about responding to terrorist events focuses on first-line responders such as police, paramedics and firefighters involved in the immediate response to establish safety, extinguish fires, locate and treat the injured, recover the dead, establish and maintain the crime scene, and begin the investigation. Human service responders have a different focus of responsibilities as their job entails providing compassionate, humane and effective support services to both victims and first-line responders, possibly for an extended period of time. This chapter provides guidance for management and for human service teams responsible for providing a human service response to workplace violence and terrorist events. The authors outline ways of preparing, training and supporting human service workers for terrorist events, with a particular emphasis on preventing compassion fatigue and burnout in the human service workers themselves.

Chapter 11

Workplace preparedness and resiliency: an integrated response to terrorism

Nancy T. Vineburgh, Robert J. Ursano and Carol S. Fullerton

This chapter by Nancy Vineburgh and her colleagues addresses the new role that workplace health professionals can play in managing the consequences of terrorism. The authors acknowledge that a number of organizational barriers to terrorism preparedness may exist within any one workplace. Such barriers include 1) an organizational focus on operational matters rather than human continuity, 2) corporate barriers that inhibit the collaboration and coordination vital to facilitating employee preparedness, and 3) employee and employer opposition to being engaged in preparedness activities. This chapter addresses these three organizational barriers through an Integrated Workplace Resiliency Model, which combines a strategy for moving organizations in the direction of terrorism planning and preparedness and a health promotion approach to educate leaders, managers and employees about disaster and terrorism preparedness. The authors integrate some basic principles of disaster mental health that should be part of a terrorism response training curriculum for workplace professionals responsible for this task into the educational approach.

SECTION 4

Bullies at Work

Chapter 12

Workplace bullying: individual pathology or organizational culture?

Ståle Einarsen, Helge Hoel, Dieter Zapf and Cary L. Cooper

Ståle Einarsen and his colleagues provide a comprehensive overview of research results relating to the very nature and causes of bullying at work. The authors begin with a focus on the key characteristics of the phenomenon; that is, a situation where an employee is exposed to frequent negative treatment at work, for a long period of time, in a situation where they find it difficult to defend themselves, leading to a severe victimization process of the targeted employee. They build upon these characteristics to discuss two different but not necessarily mutually exclusive rationales as to why bullying occurs within the work environment: the role of individuals and the role of the organization.

Chapter 13

Cyber-harassment in the workplace

Monica T. Whitty and Adrian N. Carr

This chapter by Monica Whitty and Adrian Carr explores the growing issue of electronic bullying in the workplace with a particular focus on cyberstalking and cyber-terrorism. They commence the chapter by highlighting the still developing nature of our understanding and definitions of cyber-harassment. They turn our attention to how the more severe forms of harassment, cyberstalking and cyber-terrorism are affecting workplaces. Building from these perspectives, they formulate a theory on how to better manage cyberspace within our workplaces based upon object relations theories as developed by Winnicott, Bollas and Klein. Key to their theory about how to more ably manage cyberspace is the understanding that we will develop more effective solutions for dealing with these types of workplace violence if we conceptualize what comprises cyberspace and the relationships workers have with this space.

SECTION 5

Future Directions

Chapter 14

Where to from here? Countering workplace violence in the new millennium

Vaughan Bowie, Bonnie S. Fisher, and Cary L. Cooper

This final chapter identifies some of the key common issues and strategies arising from the previous chapters as well as outlining some of the emerging trends and research concerns around workplace violence.

We hope that this book with its diverse range of topics will appeal to a broad range of occupational groups, businesses and organizations. One of our main goals is to develop theoretical and practical knowledge relevant to addressing effectively the safety from violence of a range of occupations, including human services workers, managers, human resources staff, unions and occupational health and safety professionals, and emerging at-risk groups such as humanitarian aid workers, United Nations personnel and media staff. We believe that this particular goal will be achieved in the following chapters. At the same time we are sure this volume will also be of interest to academics and students in the fields of human resources, work and organizational psychology, and occupational health and management, as well as government and non-government planners and policy makers.

We hope you find this book valuable and interesting. We encourage feedback on this volume, including any new and emerging issues that perhaps could be addressed in future volumes.

Section 1

National and international trends and responses to workplace violence

Chapter 2

A cross-national comparison of workplace violence and response strategies

Vittorio Di Martino

Long considered exclusively as a personal or inter-personal issue, workplace violence is now progressively gaining momentum and recognition as an organizational issue as well as becoming a community and societal concern and, eventually, a leading cross-national issue within the international arena.

This chapter provides an introduction to the evolution of workplace violence from a purely personal issue into one of an organizational, societal and cross-national form. The chapter goes on to identify a number of key issues that are emerging from the cross-national character of this phenomenon. These include the impact of different perceptions and cultural backgrounds on the identification of this issue, the increasing recognition of workplace violence in developing countries, the expanding occurrence of psychological violence, and the emergence of mass physical violence. The final issue examined is that of the growing awareness of the economic 'cost' of violence at work. In the light of such emerging issues, the chapter outlines the current initiatives at an international level to prevent and manage workplace violence. The chapter concludes with a brief outline of further key responses needed at a cross-national level to begin to address this issue.

From a personal to a cross-national issue

The growing recognition and evolution of the issue of workplace violence has not been an easy process. A large part of the literature in this area still only focuses upon the risk factors associated with individual aggressive and self-destructive behaviour, leaving aside the organizational or social aspects of workplace violence. The search for a profile of the perpetrator and of the victim of workplace violence has attracted disproportionate attention and often poisoned the field with stereotypes leading to discrimination and abuse.

In the last decade, however, consideration has been increasingly given to the organizational and societal dimension of organizational workplace violence. A growing body of evidence has shown how organizational factors greatly influence the risks of violence (Chappell and Di Martino 2000). Such organizational and societal dimensions are further addressed by many chapters within this book.

An example of an organizational issue that may impact upon levels of workplace violence is when workload is excessive or unevenly distributed, creating situations that may bring about a violent reaction from workers. Similarly, large queues and excessive waiting time, sometimes for no apparent reason, could instigate client violent behaviour. A related effect may arise from inadequate provision of training. Beliefs about the inadequacy of health and safety measures and the organization's ability to protect its employees against violence (for example, by having insufficient staff present) may in themselves be related to fear and expectations about becoming a victim of violence.

In a broader context, the types of inter-personal relationships, the managerial style, the level at which responsibilities are decentralized and the general culture of the workplace must also be taken into consideration. A participatory working environment, for instance, where dialogue and communication are extensively exercised, may help defuse the risks of violence. In contrast, an increased risk of threats and fear of becoming a victim of violence is found in situations where there is a lack of harmony within a work group and where there is little or no support from fellow-workers.

A further related major concern gaining increasing attention is community and societal issues linked to the emergence of workplace violence. Widespread restructuring through decentralization and rationalization is having a profound effect on conditions of work and employment. These processes may be accompanied, although with differing intensity from country to country and from situation to situation, by downsizing, layoffs, freezes or cuts in salaries, heavier workloads and a faster pace of work, longer hours of effective work, less comfortable shifts and unsocial hours, more subcontracting, and more temporary and occasional work. These are all recognized potential stressors and may eventually lead to a climate of violence driven by uncertainty, growing exasperation and vulnerability.

Violence in society, instability, negative culture and values, widespread injustice and discrimination are growing causes of concern. Several studies strongly hint at direct inroads of societal problems into the workplace, with violence as one of the major issues (Di Martino 2002b). Violence in general, and workplace violence in particular, have thus become major community and societal problems with the same relevance as alcohol, smoke, drugs and HIV/AIDS.

A cross-national issue by now, violence at work is increasingly recognized as a major strategic problem attracting growing attention from the media and the public in practically all countries, as well as from the international bodies operating in this field. Being a reflection of the process shown above, the cross-national dimension of workplace violence should not be considered in isolation but valued and dealt with in connection with the other dimensions of the phenomenon as highlighted in the figure below.

A number of important elements have contributed to the emergence of workplace violence as a cross-national issue. These include the globalization of workplace violence, the widespread recognition of psychological violence and the emergence of mass physical violence in the workplace.

The globalization of workplace violence

Violence in the workplace is to be found in both developing and industrialized nations, although the information from developing countries about such violence is frequently limited, episodic and ill-defined. For a long period a 'forgotten' issue, workplace violence in developing countries is increasingly emerging as a priority area of concern. Evidence is still limited and scattered, often anecdotal, but a new picture is emerging, one that reveals the importance of the phenomenon in all countries.

What we are witnessing, particularly in developing countries, is most probably only the tip of the iceberg. Situations of workplace violence are frequently hidden by other critical issues that may divert attention, while

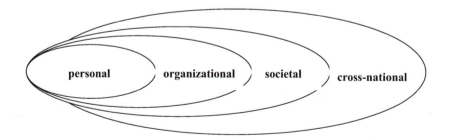

Figure 2.1   The dimensions of workplace violence

heavy under-reporting seems to be the norm rather than the exception. Some of these key critical issues are as follows.

Different perceptions and cultural backgrounds can contribute to a different understanding and evaluation of the various situations. Behaviours that would not be condoned in one country may be accepted or tolerated in another. Such differences in approach may eventually lead to distorted representations of the reality, whereby countries with better awareness of the problem are statistically 'penalised' *vis-à-vis* countries with more limited attention to the phenomenon of workplace violence. However, despite the fact that concepts and definitions are loaded with cultural significance, it would appear that a general, common understanding of workplace violence is emerging that includes physical, psychological and sexual violence at work.

In the area of sexual offences, cultural perceptions and traditions can play a major role in describing and proscribing such behaviour. In many countries rape and sexual harassment both in society and at the workplace are not only widespread but in most cases associated with deeply ingrained stereotypes of behaviour based on gender roles. Because of the traditional perception of women as objects of sexual desire, and their subordinate role in society and in the family, their sexual victimization is often seen as part of the normal order of things. In a number of cultures, the very inclusion of sexual harassment at work within the definition of workplace violence is questioned.

In addition, special attention needs to be given in developing countries to violence consisting of unjust or grossly unfair treatment at work. Such treatment results in serious offence to the dignity and decency of employment and the life of the workers and their families. Forcing someone to perform more than his or her regular work assignment without payment; making an employee do what he or she has no capacity to do; providing low salaries in the public and private employment sectors; indecent work conditions; and the coexistence of multiple types of work contracts to do the same work for different salaries are all examples of such violence. Problems of gaining access to justice, and the fear of reprisals for complaining about abusive work conditions, further exacerbate this kind of violence.

The picture of global workplace violence that progressively emerges is a most dramatic and disturbing one. In the United States, the Bureau of Labor Statistics (BLS) Annual Survey of Occupational Injuries and Illnesses found that 23,694 workplace assaults and violent acts occurred in 2001 (BLS 2001). According to the Bureau of Justice Statistics (BJS) National Crime Victimization Survey (NCVS), between 1993 and 1999 there were an average of 1.7 million violent workplace victimizations per year (BJS 2001).

Table 2.1 Average annual number, rate and percent of workplace victimization by type of crime, 1993–99

Crime category	Average annual workplace victimization	Rate per 1,000 persons in the workforce	Percent of work- place victimization
All violent crime	1,744,300	12.5	100
Homicide	900	0.01	0.1
Rape/Sexual assault	36,500	0.3	2.1
Robbery	70,100	0.5	4.0
Aggravated assault	325,000	2.3	18.6
Simple assault	1,311,700	9.4	75.2

Sources: Homicide data are obtained from the Bureau of Labor Statistics Census of Fatal Occupational Injuries. Rape and sexual assault, robbery, aggravated assault and simple assault data are from the National Crime Victimisation Survey (NCVS).

The research findings which are available across a range of industry sectors in Australia indicate that around 10 per cent of Australian workers may be subject to bullying and 2 per cent to physical violence from supervisors or colleagues at any one time, although there may be significant variations between industry sectors (Mayhew and Chappell 2001).

In Japan more and more disputes concerning violence at work are brought to the courts for conciliation or decision. The number of cases that underwent counselling totalled 625,572 in the period from April 2002 to March 2003. Of these, 5.1 per cent, or almost 32,000, were related to harassment and bullying (Japan Ministry of Health, Labour and Welfare 2003). The number of these disputes appears to be on the increase. The Tokyo Labour Bureau has set up labour consultation centres at 21 locations in Tokyo to provide information on methods of resolving disputes and on how to contact dispute-settlement institutions. A total of 51,444 requests for consultations were sent in between April and September 2003, of which 9.6 per cent concerned bullying and harassment (The Japan Labor Flash 2003).

Workplace violence in developing countries

The above data confirm that all types of violence persist in industrialized countries. In developing countries the magnitude of the phenomenon, especially in respect of more vulnerable workers such as women, immigrants and children, is of particular concern. The information that follows, from the 2003 report of the UN Commission on Human Rights, is merely indicative of the gravity of a problem that is present in many more countries than those mentioned below (UN Commission for Human Rights 2003).

Côte d'Ivoire is primarily a destination for children trafficked to work as plantation and other agricultural labourers, as mine workers and as domestic servants, under conditions in some cases approaching involuntary servitude. Many of these children are trafficked from neighbouring countries such as Mali. An estimated 15,000 Malian children between the ages of 9 and 12 have been sold into forced labour on cotton, coffee and cocoa farms in northern Côte d'Ivoire over the past few years; an even greater number have been pressed into domestic service. Organized networks of traffickers deceive the children and their families into believing that they will be given paid jobs outside their villages. They are then sold to plantation owners for sums ranging between US$20 and 40 (14,500 and 29,000 CFA francs). The children reportedly are forced to work 12 hours per day without pay, and are often abused physically.

Some seven million foreigners work in Saudi Arabia, many of them from India, Egypt, Indonesia, Pakistan, the Philippines and Bangladesh. Conditions are particularly difficult for the estimated one million women who are employed as domestic workers, a job category not covered by Saudi labour law. Over 19,000 women domestics fled from their employers in 2000, a Labour Ministry official acknowledged in April 2001, citing mistreatment, non-payment of wages and other grievances.

Abuse of foreign domestic workers is also a growing problem in Malaysia. Abuse can take the form of beating, overworking, withholding the salary, malnourishment, and denial of contacts with family. A survey of the English-language newspaper media conducted between September 1997 and September 1998 by the Women's Aid Organization (WAO) revealed some of the attitudes which lead to abuse and mistreatment of foreign domestic workers. They are often portrayed as promiscuous and flirtatious, and belonging to an inferior culture which might influence negatively the hosting family (Women's Aid Organization 1998).

In Ukraine, women's groups reported widespread sexual harassment in the workplace, including coerced sex. Apart from the law that prohibits forced sex with a 'materially dependent person', which applies to employees, legal safeguards against harassment are reportedly inadequate.

In Kuwait, rape and sexual assault by male employers and male co-workers is of concern, particularly for foreign domestic servants. The local press devotes considerable attention to the problem, and both the police and the courts have taken action against employers when presented with evidence of serious abuse.

In Ethiopia there have been reports of the large-scale employment of children, especially underage girls, as hotel workers, barmaids and prostitutes in resort towns and rural truck stops. Social workers note that young girls are prized because their clients believe that they are free of sexually transmitted diseases.

The full recognition of psychological violence

While the existence of personal physical violence at the workplace has always been recognized, the existence of psychological violence has long been underestimated and is only now receiving due attention. Such psychological violence includes bullying and mobbing. Both mobbing and bullying involve offensive behaviour through vindictive, cruel, malicious or humiliating attempts to undermine an individual or group of workers. These persistently negative attacks on their personal and professional performance are typically unpredictable, irrational and unfair.

The original conceptual distinction between bullying (primarily referring to situations of individual harassment) and mobbing (primarily covering situations of collective harassment) is now giving way to a conceptual assimilation of these two terms. Most researchers now make no distinction between bullying and mobbing with regard to the number of perpetrators or targets involved. One may argue that even if a distinction was accepted, the psychological processes involved appear to be the same.

This progressive assimilation of mobbing and bullying does not mean, however, that the two terms are used interchangeably worldwide. In some countries, such as Germany or the European Nordic countries, the term 'mobbing' is the prevalent one, while for the same type of behaviour the word 'bullying' is used in Australia, Britain and Ireland. Even in countries with their own terms (such as *harcèlement moral* in France, *acoso* or *maltrato psicológico* in Spain and Latin America, *coacção moral* in Portugal or *molestie psicologiche* in Italy), the two English terms, particularly mobbing, are becoming increasingly popular.

The growing importance of psychological violence within the workplace is further confirmed by more recent international research. In the European Union, the European Foundation's third European Survey on Working Conditions indicated that in 2000, 2 per cent of workers were subjected to physical violence, 2 per cent to sexual harassment and 9 per cent to intimidation/bullying. As shown in Figure 2.2, while physical violence was decreasing in the period 1996–2000 and sexual harassment was stable, psychological violence was on the increase (Paoli and Merllié 2001).

Extensive cross-national research carried out in 2003 in the health sector across seven countries (Brazil, Bulgaria, Lebanon, Portugal, South Africa, Thailand and Australia) showed that high levels of both psychological violence and physical violence were present in all the countries under

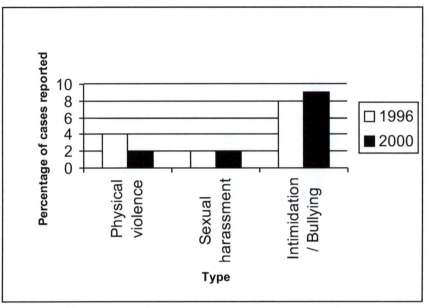

Figure 2.2   Violence at work: trends
Source: European Foundation 1996, 2000

consideration. In Bulgaria 7.5 per cent of the respondents reported having been physically attacked in the previous year; in Brazil 6.4 per cent; in Lebanon 5.8 per cent; in Thailand 10.5 per cent; and in South Africa up to 17 per cent in the public sector.

The major new finding of the study was, however, the widespread presence of psychological violence in health sector workplaces, with verbal abuse at the top of the list. In Brazil 39.5 per cent of the respondents had experienced verbal abuse in the last year; 32.2 per cent in Bulgaria; 60.1 per cent in South Africa; 47.7 per cent in Thailand; 40.9 per cent in Lebanon; and up to 67 per cent in Australia.

The second main area of concern was that of bullying and mobbing, which had been experienced by 30.9 per cent in Bulgaria, 20.6 per cent in South Africa, 10.7 per cent in Thailand, 22.1 per cent in Lebanon, 10.5 per cent in Australia and 15.2 per cent in Brazil. In the past, bullying or mobbing were not recognized or acknowledged in the developing world. The results of these cross-national studies have unveiled for the first time the worrying dimension of these two forms of psychological violence both in the developing world and in countries in transition (Di Martino 2002b).

The emergence of mass physical violence

In the last decade an increased recognition of the importance of psychological violence has often been accompanied by a decline in attention to physical violence. However, in more recent years attention to the issue has been renewed by dramatic episodes of mass physical violence, making this form of violence a priority issue at cross-national and international levels.

According to official statistics there were 643 workplace homicides in the US in 2001, one of the lowest figures recorded in the last 20 years. However, these statistics exclude the victims of 11 September 2001. The total dead and missing numbered 2,995: 2,752 in New York City, 184 at the Pentagon, 40 in Pennsylvania, and 19 hijackers. Many of these dead and missing were people at work: 319 firefighters, 50 police officers, 35 plane crew, 36 civilian employees at the Pentagon, as well as hundreds of people working for the many financial and commercial companies operating within the World Trade Center. If these figures are taken into account, 11 September appears as the most deadly act of violence at work ever, and 2001 the record year for the number of workplace homicides (September 11, 2001 Victims website 2004).

On 19 August 2003 a terrorist bombing attack on the United Nations (UN) offices in Baghdad killed at least 23 people. A later bombing at the International Commission of the Red Cross (ICRC) office on 27 October 2003 killed at least 12 people, including two local staff. Many of the dead and injured were from the international community, in Iraq to provide humanitarian assistance or help in the reconstruction effort. This particular issue is examined in more detail by Wigley and Thomas in later chapters in this book.

The tragedy at the Columbine High School in Littleton, Colorado, where, on 20 April 1999, 14 students and one teacher were killed in yet another school shooting has, again, highlighted the dramatic importance of the problem.

The economics of workplace violence

The traditional response to workplace violence, centred on the mere enforcement of regulations, has been shown to be quite limited in many working situations, including the small/micro, informal and virtual workplace. However, it is becoming increasingly recognized that workplace violence is detrimental to the functionality of the workplace and that any action taken against such a problem should be considered an integral part of the organizational development of a sound enterprise.

Much of this anti-violence response would in any case be needed to develop a healthy competitive enterprise, thus making the violence-conscious manager a 'smart' manager. Attention has, therefore, increasingly focused on the socio-economic costs of violence and harassment at work. These costs are now being quantified, showing the magnitude of the negative impact of these problems on the efficiency and performance of enterprises. The introduction of an economic dimension in organizing the response to violence and harassment is proving a powerful weapon in effectively addressing these problems.

Violence at work not only has an immediate impact on the victim, but also expands in progressively larger ripples, affecting other people directly or indirectly involved, as well as the enterprise concerned and the community (McCarthy 2004). This effect explains why the cost of violence at work has often been underestimated. It is only in recent times that experts have started quantifying the multiple and massive costs of such violence (WHO 2004). Here, the emphasis is on direct, indirect and intangible costs.

- *Direct costs* include accidents, illness, disability, death, absenteeism and turnover.

- *Indirect costs* include reduced job satisfaction, reduced morale, reduced commitment, reduced efficiency, reduced performance and reduced productivity.

- *Intangible costs* include those related to the negative impact on company image, creativity, working climate, openness to innovation, knowledge building and continuous learning. These are intangible assets essential to the competitiveness of new people-centred enterprises whose development is totally incompatible with the presence of stress and violence at work.

In the US the average financial cost to employers of a serious violent incident in the workplace is estimated to be $250,000, while more frequent, less severe incidents are estimated to cost the employer as much as $25,000 per incident; the total cost to US employers per year for workplace violence has been estimated at $4.2 billion (Philbrick, Sparks, Hass, Arsenault 2003). Biddle and Hartley studied the cost of homicides in the workplace in the US and calculated an annual cost of approximately $970 million, including the loss of earnings of victims extrapolated to the age of 67 (Biddle and Hartley 2002). The relative importance of some of the factors impinging on these costs is shown in Table 2.3.

Data from the European Union indicate a very significant correlation between health-related absences and violence at work. As shown in Figure 2.3, 35 per cent of workers exposed to physical violence were absent from

Table 2.2 The impact of violence at the workplace, United States, 1996

Impact	Per cent of respondents
Increased stress	22
Other	19
Increased fear	18
Decreased worker trust	11
Lower productivity	10
Decreased morale	9
Increased absenteeism	3
Increased staff turnover	3

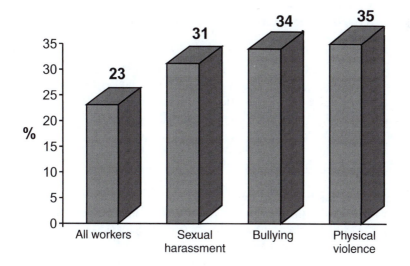

Figure 2.3 Absenteeism in per cent over the last 12 months (1996)

work over the previous 12 months, as well as 34 per cent of those exposed to bullying and 31 per cent of workers exposed to sexual harassment, compared to an average of 23 per cent among workers in general (Paoli 2000).

Sheehan *et al.* have estimated that, overall, bullying costs Australian employers between six and thirteen billion dollars (Australian) each year when both hidden and lost 'opportunity costs' are included. These

Table 2.3 The cost of workplace bullying in a British local authority

Replacement costs	£7,500
Absence	£6,972
Cost of disciplinary process (hearing/solicitor)	£3,780
Head office personnel	£2,600
Witness interview costs	£1,200
Investigators' time for grievance investigation	£2,110
Corporate officers' time (including staff welfare)	£2,100
Local management line-management time	£1,847
Total costs (minimum)	£28,109

Source: Einarsen, Hoel, Zapf and Cooper 2000

Australian costings were based on a conservative estimate of impact prevalence (usually the midpoint of the range of impact results). At an individual case level, they estimated that the total cost of each case of bullying for each employer was at least $16,977 (Sheehan, McCarthy, Barker, Henderson 2001, McCarthy 2004). However, in Australia a Queensland Supreme Court judgement awarded almost $550,000 in damages to a plaintiff in April 1998. The case concerned the abuse by her manager of a sales manager and features coordinator on a north Queensland newspaper (Oberhardt 1998).

Based on a typical case of workplace bullying in a British local authority, the costs to the organisation were calculated and are illustrated in Table 2.3.

Altogether it has been estimated by a number of reliable studies that stress and violence possibly account for approximately 30 per cent of the overall costs of ill-health and accidents, accounting for 0.5–3.5 per cent of GDP per year (Hoel, Sparks and Cooper 2000). McCarthy (McCarthy and Mayhew 2004) takes this actuarial process even further by outlining not only the personal and organizational costs but also the social, economic, political and cultural costs and consequences of workplace violence.

A cross-national response to workplace violence

In the light of these current and emerging issues, let us now look at some of the key international responses to workplace violence.

International regulation and guidance

The concern expressed about violence at work, and the call for action voiced by public authorities, enterprises and workers, is now being transformed into specific initiatives. Guidelines have been issued by governments, trade unions, special study groups, workplace violence experts and employers' groups that address many aspects of the problem. A growing number of enterprises are also introducing violence-prevention programmes that include an increasing participation by workers and their representatives in their development and implementation. Laws and regulations are becoming targeted with greater frequency and accuracy to deal with the problem of violence at work, and new collective agreements are being signed by the social partners in this area. The search for ways of ensuring a violence-free workplace is becoming a major policy issue and a concern for the international organizations operating in this sector. Outlined below are some key current cross-national responses to violence at work.

In 2002 the inter-relationship between occupational stress and violence at work was the object of a special study within the context of a joint programme by the International Labour Office (ILO), the International Council of Nurses (ICN), the World Health Organization (WHO) and Public Services International (PSI) to develop sound policies and practical approaches for the prevention and elimination of violence in the health sector. This study identified negative stress as a cause of violence at work. The more negative stress that is generated the greater the likelihood of violence, up to the most extreme forms such as burnout, suicide and homicide. The connection is not, however, an automatic one. The vast majority of people under severe negative stress – and this happens to everyone at times – do not become perpetrators of violence. It is usually the combination of stress with a number of additional factors, such as alcohol abuse, that triggers violence at the workplace. While the relationship stress/violence is usually mediated, the relationship violence/stress is direct and straightforward. In practically all cases violence, including minor acts, generates distress in the victim with long-lasting, deleterious effects on their health (Di Martino 2003).

In the context of the same programme a series of issue papers and country case studies on workplace violence covering Brazil, Bulgaria, Lebanon, Portugal, South Africa, Thailand and Australia were produced together with a synthesis report on workplace violence in the health sector (Di Martino 2002b).

Framework guidelines for addressing violence in the health sector were also produced in 2003 (ILO/ICN/WHO/PSI 2003). Further guidance was provided in October 2003 by a Meeting of Experts held at the ILO in Geneva for the adoption of a code of practice on workplace violence in services sectors and measures to combat this phenomenon. The new code identifies the roles and responsibilities of governments, employers' and workers' organizations, and the public, customers and clients. Through the processes of identification, recognition, assessment, recording and notification of violence and stress in services sectors, the code lays the foundations for risk assessment, prevention, reduction, management and coping strategies to address these problems. It concludes with an emphasis on the development of policies on occupational violence and in services sectors, through dialogue and cooperation between the social partners, training, continuous improvement, and joint assessment, monitoring and evaluation of workplace policies and practices (ILO 2003).

Intensive action has also been undertaken by the ILO at the interface between violence, drug abuse, alcohol abuse and HIV/AIDS, issues that are closely linked. A first response to such issues was provided by the ILO with a new training package – SOLVE – in 2002. This package is designed to offer an integrated workplace response to the problems of drugs and alcohol, violence, stress, tobacco and HIV/AIDS that often manifest themselves together in the workplace. The package also introduces an innovative approach whereby workers' health, safety and wellbeing become integral parts of the economic sustainability and organizational development of enterprises. By directly linking health and safety issues with managerial and developmental issues, the project offers the tools for immediate, self-sustained policy and action in the workplace to reduce and eliminate the above problems (Di Martino, Gold and Schaap 2002).

In 2003 another training package – Youth, Sport and Protection (YSP) – was produced by the ILO to address addiction, violence, HIV/AIDS, child labour and social exclusion among young people through sport and labour opportunities. The place where people, particularly young people, meet to practise sport is a privileged and, in many cases, the ideal venue in which to address these concerns. Young people gather there spontaneously to do something they like in the spirit and values of sport. This greatly encourages the emergence of partnership and team spirit; social inclusion and the recognition of diversity; the sharing of positive attitudes; healthy lifestyles; increased participation; and awareness of social issues. This location is also the place of work for coaches and other sport operators who are the proponents of these values and deliver them to young individuals and athletes practising sport. Some of these young people will eventually themselves become sport professionals and will make their passion for sport a job. All others will find their entry into the world of work greatly facilitated by bringing with them such values and skills that are increasingly recognized as essential professional assets within the sporting world. Expressly targeted to this unique workplace, the package addresses workplace violence by linking the values and practice of sport with personal development, safety and health issues, cost effectiveness, employment creation and local development (Di Martino, Di Cola and Schenk 2004).

In 1996 the World Health Organization, at its 49th World Health Assembly, adopted a Resolution that – in recognizing the serious immediate and long-term implications for health and psychological and social development that violence represents for individuals, families, communities and countries – declared violence to be a leading worldwide public health problem. As requested in the Resolution, a plan of action for progress towards a science-based public health approach to violence prevention was presented to, and approved by, the WHO Executive Board in January 1997. The plan highlights the dramatic dimensions and consequences of violence, including violence at work, and indicates priorities and means of action to deal with the problem (WHO 1997).

Further WHO action in this area led, in 2002 to the production the *World Report on Violence and Health*. The report is directed at raising awareness about the problem of violence globally, making the case that violence is preventable, and highlighting the crucial role that public health has to play in addressing its causes and consequences (WHO 2002). Following the launch of the *World Report on Violence and Health*, a Global Campaign for Violence Prevention was launched. The objectives of the campaign are to raise awareness about the problem of violence, highlight the crucial role that public health can play in addressing its causes and consequences, and encourage action at every level of society. The campaign serves as the main platform for implementing the recommendations of the *World Report on Violence and Health*. A wide array of activities is being conducted in the context of the campaign. More than 30 governments have already organized national launches or policy discussions of the *World Report on Violence and Health*. Resolutions endorsing the report and calling for its implementation have been passed in a number of policy fora such as the World Health Assembly, the Commission on Human Rights and the African Union.

In recent years EU action in the area of workplace violence has intensified with important new initiatives in the field. Workplace violence is now a topical and priority issue within the Union. In 1999 the Advisory Committee on Safety, Hygiene and Health of the European Commission set up an *ad hoc* group on prevention of violence at work, prompted by the new Article 13 in the EC Treaty, introduced in 1999 by the Amsterdam Treaty, which enables the council to take appropriate action to combat discrimination based on sex, racial or ethnic origin, religion or belief, disability, age or sexual orientation. In 2001, the European Parliament stressed the need for interventions tackling harassment in the workplace to be made a priority, particularly bullying and sexual harassment (European Parliament 2001)

The European Parliament made a statement that:

> Calls on the Member States, with a view to counteracting bullying and sexual harassment at work, to review and, if appropriate, to supplement their existing legislation and to review and standardise the definition of bullying;
>
> urges the Commission to consider a clarification or extension of the scope of the framework directive on health and safety at work or, alternatively, the drafting of a new framework directive as a legal instrument to combat bullying and as a means of ensuring respect for the worker's human dignity, privacy and integrity; emphasizes in this connection the importance of systematic work on health and safety and of preventive action. (p. 3)

In 2000 and 2002 two directives were adopted, the first applying to all situations of racial harassment, the second referring specifically to sexual harassment at work:

- The Council Directive 2000/43/EC (June 2000) implements the principle of equal treatment between persons irrespective of racial or ethnic origin; and

- The June 2002 Directive amending Council Directive 76/207/EEC implements the principle of equal access for men and women to employment, vocational training and promotion, and working conditions.

The abovementioned directives are only the beginning of more intensive legislative intervention. Various EU bodies have reiterated the need for further action in the area of workplace violence, including regulatory action. In its Communication 'Adapting to change in work and society: A new Community strategy on health and safety 2002–2006' the European Commission has stressed the need to adapt the legal framework to cover the emerging psycho-social risks:

> The increase in psycho-social problems and illnesses is posing a new challenge to health and safety at work and is compromising moves to improve wellbeing at work. The various forms of psychological harassment and violence at work likewise pose a special problem nowadays, requiring legislative action. Any such action will be able to build on the acquis [acquisition] of recently adopted directives rooted in Article 13 of the EC Treaty, which defines what is meant by

harassment, and make provision for redress. The Commission will examine the appropriateness and the scope of a Community instrument on psychological harassment and violence at work. (p. 12)

Along similar lines, the European Commission's Advisory Committee on Safety, Hygiene and Health Protection at Work, in its 'Opinion on Violence at the Workplace' adopted on 29 November 2001, calls for the issuing by the Commission of guidelines in this area:

The Commission should therefore draft guidelines based on the definition of the phenomenon in all its various forms and on its inclusion among the risk factors that employers are obliged to assess under the terms of the framework directive. A model for the assessment of the specific risk as part of the overall assessment would therefore be useful. (p. 2)

The Commission's action has been complemented by that of the EU specialized agencies competent in this area. In 2002 the European Foundation for the Improvement of Working and Living Conditions issued a report on violence and harassment in the workplace. The report identifies the different forms and patterns of violence and harassment in the workplace in the EU and describes the recent upsurge in activity and initiatives with respect to violence and harassment within the legal arena, with new legislation addressing these problems enacted or in the pipeline in a number of countries. It also presents evidence of adverse effects on individuals, organizations and society, and assesses the potential financial costs. Finally, it analyses the factors that may contribute to and cause physical and psychological violence, and reviews a variety of good practices with respect to preventing and managing violence and harassment at work (Di Martino, Hoel and Cooper 2002a).

The high road to a cross-national response to workplace violence

Against this background a number of key issues around workplace violence are emerging that deserve special attention. These include:

- The recognition of the global nature of workplace violence crossing all countries, sectors and occupations.

- The recognition of workplace violence as one of the major threats to public health and the world of labour.

- The recognition of both physical and psychological violence and their intrinsic inter-relationship at work.

- The recognition of the gender dimension of workplace violence, affecting both men and women.

- The recognition of the special impact of violence on vulnerable workers.

- The recognition that only part of workplace violence is disclosed and that a large part of it is still undisclosed.

In tackling these issues a series of key responses appear particularly important. These include:

- Enhancing awareness of the need to tackle the problem of violence at work.

- Identifying situations at special risk, while recognizing that each one is unique.

- Tackling workplace violence not just as an individual issue but also as an inter-personal, organizational and environmental one.

- Tackling workplace violence as an immediate and strategic issue at the same time.

- Approaching in a combined way the socio-economic dimension of workplace violence.

- Approaching workplace violence in a participative way.

- Approaching workplace violence in a preventive, systematic and targeted way.

- Stressing the importance of cross-national initiatives in this area.

- Stressing the need for linking such initiatives to business and managerial goals at enterprise level.

A 'high road' response such as this that is able to combine the different responses highlighted above to combat workplace violence into an overall win-win response is progressively emerging. It is based on the progressive integration of cross-national guidance and regulation with workplace initiatives to combat workplace violence. By directly linking regulatory action with managerial and developmental issues, this response offers the tools for immediate action in the workplace to reduce and eliminate workplace violence.

As shown in Figure 2.4, cross-national policies and regulations would provide a favourable framework in which such initiatives can be developed and would be accompanied by guidance on the best ways to concretely tackle workplace violence. This would allow for a natural process of proliferation of such initiatives that is largely based on the replicability of best practices and leads eventually to their full establishment and self-sustainability.

Workplace initiatives would in turn provide the necessary feedback to revise and improve cross-national policies and regulations on a permanent

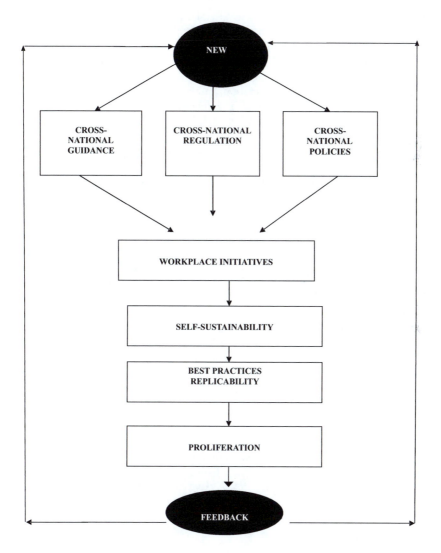

Figure 2.4 A cross-national response to workplace violence

basis. A positive cycle can thus be activated that develops from inside the workplace to progressively expand independently of the mechanics of short-term influences and forced intervention. How we trigger this cycle is the great challenge we currently face.

References

Biddle, E. and Hartley, D. (2002) 'The cost of workplace homicides in the USA, 1990–1997' in *Injury Prevention and Control*, 6th World Conference, pp. 421–2, Montreal: Les Presses de l' Université de Montreal.

Chappell, D. and Di Martino, V. (2000) *Violence at work*, ILO, Geneva.

Di Martino, V., Hoel, H. and Cooper, C., (2002a) *Preventing violence and harassment in the workplace*, European Foundation, Dublin.
www.eurofound.ie/publications/EF02109.htm

Di Martino, V. (2002b) *Synthesis report on workplace violence in the health sector*, ILO/ ICN/ WHO/PSI, Geneva.
http://www.ilo.org/public/english/dialogue/sector/papers/health/violence-ccs.pdf

Di Martino, V. (2003) *Workplace violence in the health sector, Relationship between work stress and workplace violence in the health sector*, ILO/ICN/WHO/PSI, Geneva.
http://www.ilo.org/public/english/dialogue/sector/papers/health/stress-violence.pdf

Di Martino, V., Di Cola, G. and Schenk, R. (2004) *YSP – An action-oriented training package to address addiction, violence, HIV/AIDS, child labour and social exclusion among young people through sport and labour opportunities*, ILO/IOC.

Di Martino, V., Gold, D. and Schaap, A. (2002) *SOLVE Training Package – Managing Emerging Health Problems at Work – Stress, Violence, Tobacco, Alcohol, Drugs, HIV/ AIDS*, ILO.

Einarsen, S., Hoel, H., Zapf, D. and Cooper, C.L. (eds) (2000) *Bullying and emotional abuse in the workplace. International perspectives in research and practice*, London: Taylor and Francis.

European Commission's Advisory Committee on Safety, Hygiene and Health Protection at Work, in its 'Opinion on Violence at the Workplace', adopted on 29 November 2001.

European Commission Communication 'Adapting to change in work and society: A new Community strategy on health and safety 2002–2006' (COM (Brussels) 11.03.2002, 118 final).

European Parliament's Resolution on Harassment at the Workplace 2001/2339.

Hoel, H., Sparks, K. and Cooper, C. (2000) *The cost of violence and stress at work and the benefits of a violence- and stress-free working environment*, UMIST.

ILO (2003) *Code of practice on workplace violence in services sectors and measures to combat this phenomenon*, Geneva.
http://www.ilo.org/public/english/dialogue/sector/techmeet/mevsws03/mevsws-cp.pdf

ILO/ICN/WHO/PSI (2003) *Framework guidelines for addressing violence in the health sector*, Geneva.
http://www.ilo.org/public/english/dialogue/sector/papers/health/guidelines.pdf

Japan Ministry of Health, Labour and Welfare
http://www.jil.go.jp/jil/bulletin/year/2003/vol42-07.pdf#statis_4

The Japan Labor Flash No.5, 1 December 2003
http://www.jil.go.jp/foreign/emm/bi/5.htm

Mayhew, C. and Chappell, D. (2001) Internal' Violence (or Bullying) and the Health Workforce, Taskforce on the Prevention and Management of Violence in the Health Workplace, Discussion Paper No.3, The University of South Wales, December.

McCarthy, P. (2004) 'Costs of Occupational Violence and Bullying' in McCarthy and Mayhew, *Safeguarding the organisation against violence and bullying: an international perspective*, Palgrave Macmillan: Hampshire UK.

McCarthy, P. and Mayhew, C. (2004) *Safeguarding the organisation against violence and bullying: an international perspective*, Palgrave Macmillan: Hampshire UK.

Oberhardt, M. (1998) 'Worker awarded $550,000', *The Courier-Mail*, 24 April.

Paoli, P. (2000) *Violence at Work in the European Union – Recent Finds*, European Foundation for the Improvement of Living and Working Conditions, Dublin, December.

Paoli, P. and Merllié, D. (2001) *Third European survey on working conditions 2000*, European Foundation for the Improvement of Living and Working Conditions, Dublin, 2001.
http://www.eurofound.eu.int/publications/files/EF00128EN.pdf

Philbrick, Jane Hass, Sparks, Marcia R., Hass, Marsha E. and Arsenault, Steven (2003) 'Workplace violence: The legal costs can kill you', *American Business Review*, January.

September 11, 2001 Victims website
http://www.september11victims.com/september11victims/STATISTIC.asp

Sheehan, M., McCarthy, P., Barker, M. and Henderson, M. (2001) 'A model for assessing the impacts and costs of workplace bullying', paper presented at the Standing Conference on Organizational Symbolism (SCOS), 30 June to 4 July 2001, Trinity College, Dublin.

Society for Human Resource Management, (1996) *Workplace Violence Survey 1996*, Alexandria, Virginia.

UN Commission for Human Rights, 59th session, Report of the Special Rapporteur on violence against women, its causes and consequences, Ms Radhika Coomaraswamy, Addendum 1 – International, regional and national developments in the area of violence against women 1994–2003.

US Bureau of Justice Statistics (BJS) Special Report, December 2001, NCJ 190076, *National Crime Victimization Survey Violence in the Workplace, 1993–99* by Detis T. Duhart.
http://www.ojp.usdoj.gov/bjs/pub/pdf/vw99.pdf

US Bureau of Labor Statistics (BLS), *Number of nonfatal injuries and illnesses R27*, detailed source by selected events or exposures.
http://www.bls.gov/iif/oshwc/osh/case/ostb1182.pdf

WHO Executive Board, 99th Session, Provisional Agenda Item 13, 'Prevention of violence', Document EB99/INF. Doc/3, 7 January 1997, Geneva.

WHO (2004) *The economic dimensions of interpersonal violence*, Geneva.

WHO (2002) *World Report on Violence and Health*, Geneva.
http://www.who.int/violence_injury_prevention/violence/world_report/wrvh1/en/

Women's Aid Organization, *The Growing Problem of Foreign Domestic Worker Abuse in Malaysia*, WAO, 1998.
http://www.wao.org.my/research/fdw.htm)

Chapter 3

Organizational factors and psychological aggression: results from a nationally representative sample of US companies

Paula L. Grubb, Rashaun K. Roberts, Naomi G. Swanson, Jennifer L. Burnfield and Jennifer H. Childress

Introduction

Background

Workplace psychological aggression has emerged as an important organizational issue, particularly in the UK and Europe where investigators spearheaded initial research efforts. In the US, however, workplace psychological aggression has received less emphasis, as the focus has been on high-profile workplace shootings and homicides spotlighted in the media (Baron and Neuman 1996; Keashly and Jagatic 2003). It is only during the past decade that US researchers have focused on non-fatal, non-physical forms of workplace violence (Cole, Grubb, Sauter, Swanson and Lawless 1997).

History

Landmark data from the National Institute for Occupational Safety and Health (NIOSH) ranked homicide as the third leading cause of death at work for all workers in the US, and as the leading cause of workplace death for women (NIOSH 1992; NIOSH 1995; Jenkins, Layne, and Kisner 1992; Jenkins 1996). This pioneering work spurred substantial research activity aimed at delineating the risk factors for workplace violence, at-risk industries, and potential prevention and intervention strategies for reducing worker homicides and traumatic injury due to workplace assaults.

Workplace violence was found to be clustered in occupational settings such as the retail trade and service industries (NIOSH 1995). Taxicab drivers had the greatest risk of homicide on the job, whereas workers in community services, healthcare and retail were at increased risk of non-fatal assaults. Risk factors identified for fatal and non-fatal assaults included working alone or at night, dealing with the public, exchanging money, and delivering goods and services. The suggested prevention strategies included environmental controls (e.g. good lighting, increased visibility, separation of workers from customers/clients, key card access), administrative controls (e.g. staffing plans, work practices, policies and procedures, etc.) and behavioural strategies such as conflict resolution training (NIOSH 1995).

Non-fatal workplace violence

Although these initial studies of workplace violence broadened their definition to include more subtle forms of non-fatal violence such as threats, the main thrust of the research was still aimed at preventing homicides and physical assaults.

Similarly, the National Crime Victimization Survey (NCVS) indicates that during the time period 1993 to 1999, an average of 1.7 million people per year were victims of violent crime while working or on duty in the United States (Bachman 1994; Duhart 2001). Of those victimizations, roughly 900 work-related homicides (0.1 per cent) occurred each year (Duhart 2001). The majority of victimizations while on the job, however, were non-fatal, with an annual average of 1.3 million (75 per cent) of these incidents being simple assaults (i.e., attacks without weapons resulting in no injury or minor injury), while an additional 19 per cent were aggravated assaults (Duhart 2001). While the incidence of simple assaults was high, only 41 per cent were reported to the police.

Northwestern National Life Insurance Company (1993) conducted a survey on workplace fear and violence among 600 civilian workers and found that non-fatal workplace violence such as physical attacks, threats and harassment was pervasive in the US. According to this study, 15 per cent of the workers surveyed had been physically attacked while on the job at some point during their working lives, 21 per cent had been threatened with physical harm on the job, and 19 per cent were harassed on the job. As with the NCVS data, the majority of victims did not report the incident to anyone. In the Northwestern National Life survey, victims of violence or harassment were also more likely to report stress-related conditions such as depression and insomnia, that they felt their productivity was reduced, and that they were likely to change jobs. Interestingly, non-victims were also affected, with 21 per cent of workers reporting that the fear of harassment or violence on the job resulted in adverse mental or physical health outcomes, reduced productivity, turnover intent, and absenteeism.

Cole, Grubb *et al.* (1997) conducted more in-depth analyses of the Northwestern National Life data and their findings indicated that work climate factors such as co-worker support and work group harmony were salient predictors of threats, harassment and fear of becoming a victim of violence at work. This was the first study to suggest that both work climate and structural aspects of the job might be important in promoting non-fatal workplace violence.

Psychological aggression as a form of workplace violence

Studies of non-fatal workplace violence found that actual physical violence has a relatively low base rate in most organizations, and that non-physical acts of aggression such as verbal threats and harassment are commonplace in work organizations. The umbrella term 'psychological aggression' refers to a wide range of victimizing, humiliating, undermining, harassing or threatening behaviours that emerge in the context of interpersonal relationships in the workplace.

These more prevalent 'low intensity' forms of violence, while not necessarily immediately traumatic, have been shown to lead to a number of negative outcomes for both employees and the organization, such as burnout, job dissatisfaction, intention to leave the organization, and physical and psychological symptoms, as well as financial costs to the organization related to sick leave, lost productivity and even potential litigation (Cortina, Magley, Williams and Langhout 2001; Pryor 1987). It has been hypothesized by some researchers that these more subtle acts of aggression can escalate to physical violence in a spiral of uncivil behaviours (Andersson and Pearson 1999). Therefore, preventing these types of aggression could potentially also decrease some sources of physical workplace violence. Such preventive efforts require an understanding of the causes of psychological aggression.

Although relatively little is known about the etiology of workplace psychological aggression, several classes of antecedents have been suggested: (1) individual factors (e.g. personality characteristics of victims or perpetrators), (2) social factors (e.g. perceptions of injustice, climate for hostility); and (3) work organization (e.g. task-specific stressors, organizational structure) or environmental factors (e.g. noise). (Einarsen 2000; Hoel, Rayner and Cooper 1999; Neuman and Baron 2003).

The purpose of this chapter is to describe the role of higher-level work organization factors (e.g. structure, organization type, policies) in two pervasive manifestations of psychological aggression at work: bullying and incivility. We will present results from the National Organizations

Survey (NOS), which surveyed a national sample of US workplaces, to explore the contextual factors that might facilitate bullying and incivility in the workplace. These findings are then used to offer implications for research and practice.

Terms and definitions

Expanding the concept of workplace violence beyond overt physical attacks has led to a variety of definitions, terms and workplace behaviours falling under the general rubric of workplace psychological aggression (Barling 1996; Keashly and Jagatic 2003; Neuman and Baron 1998; Robinson and Greenberg 1998; Snyder, Chen, Grubb, Roberts, Sauter and Swanson 2004). Research on this topic can be found under mistreatment (Tepper 2000), harassment (Brodsky 1976), abuse (Richman *et al*. 1999), counterproductive work behaviour (Chen and Spector 1992), bullying and mobbing (Zapf, Einarsen, Hoel and Vartia 2003) and incivility (Andersson and Pearson 1999).

Definitions of workplace aggression differ in terms of intentionality, perpetrators, intended victims, actions and consequences (Snyder *et al*. 2004). Most definitions of aggression include both physical and non-physical actions (e.g. Baron and Neuman 1996), and some stipulate that there must be an intent to harm either the individual or the organization (Baron and Neuman 1998).

In the European literature, frequency, duration and power structure are critical definitional components; there must be a persistent pattern of aggressive behaviours over time (Einarsen, Hoel, Zapf and Cooper 2003), and this definition has become the standard. In the US, however, there is considerable latitude in defining various types of psychological aggression, and no consensus among researchers as to which definitional elements are crucial (Keashly and Jagatic 2003). This lack of cohesiveness among US researchers has made it difficult to build a systematic body of literature, with the limited crosstalk between disciplines hindering progress in the area of psychological aggression.

Nature and extent of psychological aggression

Regardless of definitional difficulties and varying labels, research indicates that most hostile behaviour at work is indirect, passive and verbal in nature (Keashly and Jagatic 2003), and may include talking behind someone's back, silent treatment, social isolation, exclusion, undermining, belittling and so on. These behaviours are typically described as 'lower forms' of workplace violence, although, as Keashly and Jagatic (2003) point out, assigning degrees of severity to aggressive behaviour can be a complex issue, as some investigators have found that ratings of severity of some physically abusive behaviours were similar to those of some emotionally abusive behaviours, or that there was some degree of overlap.

In US workplaces it has been shown that psychological aggression is widespread. Keashly and Jagatic (2000) reported that 59 per cent of respondents who participated in a statewide survey conducted in Michigan reported that they had experienced at least one type of emotional abuse at the hands of co-workers, and that 27 per cent reported being mistreated by a co-worker in the past 12 months. European research on bullying suggests that estimates of the frequency of bullying depend very much upon how one asks the question (Zapf, Einarsen, Hoel, and Vartia 2003), with more stringent estimates coming from studies in which the definition has strict criteria. As mentioned above, the European literature specifies that frequency, duration and power are crucial components in defining bullying, i.e., there must be a persistent pattern of abuse aimed at a particular target over time, rather than isolated incidents, for the behaviours to be considered bullying (Einarsen, Hoel, Zapf and Cooper 2003). The formal definition of bullying in the European literature is as follows:

> Bullying at work means harassing, offending, socially excluding someone or negatively affecting someone's work tasks. In order for the label bullying (or mobbing) to be applied to a particular activity, interaction or process it has to occur repeatedly and regularly (e.g. weekly) and over a period of time (e.g. about six months). Bullying is an escalating process in the course of which the person confronted ends up in an inferior position and becomes the target of systematic negative social acts. A conflict cannot be called bullying if the incident is an isolated event or if two parties of approximately equal 'strength' are in conflict. (Einarsen *et al.* 2003, p. 15)

In European studies using these criteria, estimates are that between 8 and 10 per cent of employees have been bullied.

Some studies of psychological aggression have found that supervisors or managers are often identified as the aggressors (Keashly, Trott and MacLean 1994), and others have reported that co-workers are most often the source of workplace aggression (Cortina *et al.* 2001; Neuman and Baron 1997). There have also been instances of 'upward bullying' reported where a subordinate is the identified aggressor (Keashly, Hunter and Harvey 1997). It is important to note that most studies on workplace psychological aggression, such as incivility, have focused primarily on aggression within the organization, but in some occupations, external customers are the most common sources of verbal abuse (e.g. Grandey, Tam and Brauburger 2002). Thus, employees can potentially receive mistreatment from multiple constituents.

Impact

Workplace psychological aggression has been shown to impact the individual, with some studies finding increased symptoms of depression, anxiety and psychosomatic complaints in those who are victimized (Einarsen and Mikkelsen 2003). These symptoms have also been found in cases where individuals witnessed others being victimized in the work environment (Rogers and Kelloway 1997). Psychological aggression has also been found to negatively impact work organizations. It has been associated with absenteeism, higher turnover rate, reduced productivity, and litigation costs (Hoel, Einarsen, and Cooper 2003).

Organizational factors and psychological aggression

Some studies conducted in Europe have identified linkages between organizational variables and psychological aggression. For example, organizational size and type have been investigated in relation to bullying. However, findings have produced a somewhat mixed picture with some studies finding higher rates of bullying in larger, more bureaucratic organizations, while other studies have indicated a higher prevalence of bullying in small and medium-sized companies (Hoel et al. 2003). Further, some European studies have shown that bullying is more common in the public sector (Hoel and Salin 2003), while others have shown that bullying is more prevalent in the private sector (Einarsen and Skogstad 1996). In addition to structural variables, work organization factors such as role conflict and role ambiguity have been shown to be associated with bullying (Einarsen, Raknes and Matthiesen 1994).

In the US, Baron and Neuman (1998) have hypothesized that organizational changes such as job insecurity, cost-cutting and social change (e.g. increased diversity) are associated with workplace aggression in general. It has also been suggested that conflict between workers may increase as more of the workforce begins working in self-directed teams (Hoel and Salin 2003), and that enforced teamwork may provide a substrate for aggression, particularly if there is team competition for limited rewards (Hoel and Salin 2003; Zapf, Dormann and Frese 1996). Further, psychological aggression has been associated with communication problems, lack of involvement in the decision-making process, work environments where employees are unable or hesitant to express their views, and poor psycho-social climate (Keashly and Jagatic 2000; Vartia 1996). Cortina et al. (2001) found that an organizational climate that fostered fair inter-personal treatment was negatively correlated with incivility.

The present study

To date, studies of organizational factors and psychological aggression have gleaned information from the perspective of those victimized in the workplace. In the US, there have been some studies of psychological aggression that involved data collection from workers, but very few of these studies have obtained representative samples. Even less information has been collected on policies and programs in US companies that might address aggressive behaviour in the workplace.

A unique feature of the present study is that the workplace itself is the unit of analysis. This approach elicits information about the organization that cannot necessarily be ascertained from individual employees. This national survey of US companies provides a snapshot of the extent of workplace aggression and an overview of policies and programmes in place at these organizations.

In the present chapter we focused on the two most common types of psychological aggression: bullying and incivility. We examined how organizations that reported bullying and incivility in the past year differed from those that did not report these forms of workplace aggression in terms of organizational structure, policies and programmes, and quality of worklife indicators.

Method

Background

The National Organizations Survey III (NOS III; Kalleberg, Knoke, Marsden, and Spaeth 1994) is a nationally representative sample of US organizations in which the unit of analysis is the workplace itself. This survey was conducted by the National Science Foundation, The National Institute for Occupational Safety and Health, and the Commonwealth Fund to investigate the nature of policies and benefits, and the structure of companies throughout the US. The survey was administered by the National Opinion Research Center (NORC), and is a follow-up to the 2002 General Social Survey (GSS; Davis, Smith, and Marsden 2002), which is a nationally-representative survey of the non-institutionalized US population aged 18 and older.

Survey procedure

The NOS III sample was based on information from the 2002 GSS. Half of all household respondents from the 2002 GSS interviews were asked to provide contact details for their place of employment. For each of these organizations, a key informant was identified within the company who could best provide the data required (e.g. a human resources professional, company owner, etc.).

Data collection ran from October 2002 to May 2003. The unadjusted response rate was 59 per cent (N = 516 organizations). The adjusted response rate was 62 per cent (adjusted for all cases that were not located, or were duplicates of another physical location). For this particular study, only those cases that provided valid answers to the bullying and incivility items were retained.

Survey development

A convenience sample of Chicago-area employers representing firms of varying sizes, industries and types of ownership was used by NORC to pre-test the questionnaire. The final version of the questionnaire was made into a computer-assisted telephone interview (CATI) for self-employed persons and a paper-and pencil survey for all other businesses. NORC supported telephone interviewers by setting up a telephone number management system (TNMS) and CATI. Survey administration time was approximately 55 minutes.

Survey measures

Basic descriptive information about the companies was collected in the core section of the questionnaire. This included information about organizational structure, the company's primary business and corporate policies. A module was added which contained specific queries about workplace violence and psychological aggression, and policies and procedures related to violence and aggression. At the time the survey was administered there were no available measures of bullying and incivility at the organizational level of analysis, therefore all items were developed for the present study.

Psychological aggression measures

The definition of bullying used in this study was a broad one, utilizing concepts found in the US and European literature. The terminology in the present study reflects an attempt to capture some of the essential features found in the precise European definition, to include US influences, and to be appropriate for the time constraints and nature of the NOS III. Bullying was assessed by the item 'How often in the past year has bullying occurred at your establishment, including repeated intimidation, slandering, social isolation, or humiliation by one or more persons against another?' Key informants responded on a 4-point scale: 1 (never), 2 (rarely), 3 (sometimes) and 4 (often).

Likewise, the definition of incivility was a general one, incorporating facets of other US definitions of the concept. Incivility was assessed by the item 'How often in the past year has incivility occurred at your establishment, such as acting rude or discourteously?' Informants responded on a 4-point scale: 1 (never), 2 (rarely), 3 (sometimes) and 4 (often).

Structural characteristics of organizations
Key informants indicated the number of employees at their establishment. This variable was used to assess organizational size. The responses were recoded into four broad size categories: very small (1–9 employees), small (10–49 employees), medium (50–249 employees) and large (250 or more employees). These organization size categories were based on the distribution of responses. Data were also collected regarding type of industry, profit or not-for-profit status, and union or non-union status. Industry data were taken from the 2002 GSS household respondents' answer to an item about the industry in which they were employed at that time.

Organizational programmes and policies
Responses were coded as 0 = 'no' and 1 = 'yes'. For violence and aggression programmes, the item was 'Has [establishment name] ever offered any of the following kinds of training specifically on workplace violence?' Specific items under violence training programmes were seminars/workshops on general workplace violence risk factors and specific prevention strategies, hands-on or classroom training in conflict resolution or de-escalation techniques, and hands-on training in restraint of disruptive persons or management of disruptive behaviour. Sexual harassment training programmes and diversity training were assessed with the questions 'Is there sexual harassment training for managers at [establishment name]?' and 'Is there a diversity training programme for managers at [establishment name]?'

Organizational policies
General policies were assessed by the item 'Does [establishment name] currently provide [policy]?' Responses were coded as 0 = 'no' and 1 = 'yes', except as noted. Information was elicited about whether or not

employees worked in teams, whether or not teams made decisions about task assignments or work methods, did teams meet at least once a month to solve work-related problems, did teams choose their own leaders, and on schedule flexibility for starting/quitting times.

Regarding violence and aggression policies, respondents were asked if their workplaces had documents describing policy about workplace violence, and whether or not job candidates were required to take psychological tests prior to being hired to determine if they were at risk for committing acts of violence in the workplace.

Quality of worklife outcomes

Quality of worklife indicators were assessed by dichotomous items (0 = 'no' 1 = 'yes') asking whether or not their organization was committed to avoiding layoffs, whether or not there had been formal complaints of sexual harassment in the past 12 months, whether or not there had been formal complaints of racial discrimination in the past 12 months, whether or not there had been formal complaints of age discrimination in the past 12 months, and whether or not there had been formal complaints of disability-based discrimination in the past 12 months. Other indicators examined were whether or not the organization strove to improve employee wellbeing and whether or not it offered skills useful to its employees (both items rated on a 4-point Likert-type scale ranging from 1 [strongly disagree] to 4 [strongly agree]). Respondents were also asked about how much choice their employees had concerning the best way to accomplish their assignments (1 = no choice, 2 = small amount, 3 = moderate amount, 4 = large amount, and 5 = complete choice) and how closely employees were supervised as they did their work (1 = no supervision, 2 = small amount, 3 = moderate amount, 4 = large amount, and 5 = complete supervision). Key informants were also asked to rate the general relationship between managers and employees at their workplace (on a scale from 1 = very poor to 5 = very good).

Results

Frequency and correlates of bullying and incivility

Based upon the distribution, bullying responses were dichotomized into 'no' (response category 'never') and 'yes' (responses of 'rarely', 'sometimes', and 'often' collapsed into one category). The same strategy was used for dichotomizing incivility. In all analyses 'no' = 0 and 'yes' = 1.

As can be seen in Table 3.1, the majority of companies (75.5 per cent) reported no bullying in the past year. Overall 24.5 per cent of the companies

Table 3.1 Number and percentage of organizations indicating some degree of bullying and incivility during past year

	Frequency	Percent
Bullying		
Never	373	75.5
Rarely	86	17.4
Sometimes	27	5.5
Often	8	1.6
Total	494	
Incivility		
Never	194	39.4
Rarely	168	34.1
Sometimes	110	22.4
Often	20	4.1
Total	492	

Organizations with missing data on particular survey items (i.e., unable or refused to answer question, question not asked by interviewer) were not used in the analyses. Bullying and incivility responses were both dichotomized into 'no' (response category 'never') and 'yes' (responses of 'rarely', 'sometimes', and 'often' collapsed into one category). In all analyses 'no' = 0 and 'yes' = 1.

reported some degree of bullying in the past year. The distribution for incivility ranged across the response scale with 39.4 per cent of the organizations reporting no incidents of incivility in the past year, and 60.6 per cent reporting some level of incivility. This suggests that incivility is a more common form of psychological aggression than is bullying in US organizations. Perhaps this is because incivility is associated with more ambiguous intentions to harm and is not necessarily characterized by repetitive mistreatment towards others. In addition, because bullying often involves power issues, it may not be as relevant a concept for aggression from external customers as is incivility.

Table 3.2 shows the inter-correlations among bullying, incivility, structural characteristics of organizations, organizational programmes and policies, and quality of worklife indicators. Bullying and incivility were significantly correlated with one another (.43), but not so strongly as to be considered redundant concepts. Both variables correlated with structural factors of organizations, programmes/policies and quality of worklife outcomes. These relationships will be discussed in the following sections.

Table 3.2 Inter-correlations among psychological aggression variables, programmes/policies and quality of worklife outcomes

Variable	Bullying	Incivility
Bullying	–	–
Incivility	**.43****	–
Structural characteristics of organizations		
No. employees (organization size)	**.43****	**.38****
Type of industry: product/service	.01	-.03
For profit/not-for-profit	**.29****	**.18****
Union	**.25****	**.16****
Organizational programmes		
Seminars on violence risk factors	**.29****	**.27****
Training in conflict resolution	**.29****	**.26****
Training on restraint of disruptive persons	**.27****	**.20****
Sexual harassment training	**.27****	**.34****
Diversity training	**.23****	**.22****
Organizational policies		
Work in teams	**.19****	**.15****
Teams make assignments	.10	.10
Monthly team meetings	**.16****	**.19****
Teams choose leaders	.05	.07
Flexible schedule	**−.13****	−.22
Violence policy/documents	**.29****	**.33****
Dispute resolution process	**.28****	**.30**
Sexual harassment complaint procedure	**.30****	**.34****
Pre-employment psych. testing	−.01	.01
Quality of worklife		
Commitment avoid layoffs	.08	**.15****
Sexual harassment complaints	**.40****	**.25****
Racial discrimination complaints	**.39****	**.19****
Age discrimination complaints	**.25****	**.12****
Disability discrimination complaints	**.36****	**.17****
Improve employee wellbeing	.01	−.03
Useful skills	.07	.05
Choice accomplish assignments	−.06	**−.17****
Amount supervision	.03	**.15****
Pos. emp./mgmt relations	**−.19****	**−.21****

Note: Significant correlations are in bold type. Sample size ranges from 235 to 515 based on missing data. **Correlation is significant $p < .01$.

Structural characteristics of organizations reporting bullying and incivility

Frequencies and percentages of bullying and incivility were reported across the levels of the organizations' structural characteristics in Table 3.3.

When interpreting the percentage within each industry category reporting bullying and incivility, it is important to note that the number of organizations in some of the categories is low (e.g. mining = 0; agriculture, forestry, fishing = 1 per cent of sample; construction = 6 per cent of sample; transportation and public utilities = 5 per cent of sample). For example,

Table 3.3 Structural characteristics of organizations in the sample and the percentage of organizations within these structural categories reporting bullying and incivility in past year

Structural category	% Sample	% within structural category reporting bullying	% within structural category reporting incivility
Size of organization			
(Number of employees)			
Very small (1–9 employees)	40	8	37
Small (10–49 employees)	20	22	72
Medium (50–249 employees)	19	27	72
Large (250 or more employees)	21	57	85
Type of organization			
For profit	70	17	55
Not for profit	30	44	74
Union	21	46	76
Industry type			
Agriculture, forestry, fishing	1	50	83
Mining	0	0	0
Construction	6	22	59
Manufacturing	12	32	56
Transportation and public utilities	5	8	60
Wholesale/retail trade	16	23	64
Finance, insurance and real estate	5	38	57
Services	48	24	63
Government	7	26	46

Note: N = 507. n = 121 companies reported bullying; n = 298 companies reported incivility

50 per cent of organizations in agriculture, forestry and fishing reported bullying and 83 per cent reported incivility. However, these organizations represent only 1 per cent of the total sample. Services represented the largest percentage of industries in the entire sample, with 24 per cent of organizations in the service industry reporting bullying and 63 per cent of companies in the service sector reporting incivility. The wholesale/retail trade accounted for 16 per cent of the total sample, and 23 per cent of those organizations reported bullying and 63 per cent incivility. There was no significant difference between organizations reporting bullying and incivility and those that did not in terms of industry type. This is likely because the two largest industry categories both include occupations that involve working with customers (retail, service), which would be expected to experience incivility due to customer social stressors, and the remaining nearly 50 per cent of the industries did not represent large enough categories of industries to make an adequate comparison with the service and wholesale/retail industries.

There was a linear relationship between organization size and both bullying and incivility. Fifty-seven percent of large organizations (250 or more employees) reported bullying in the past year and 85 per cent of large organizations reported incivility, in comparison to 8 per cent of very small organizations (1–9 employees) reporting bullying and 37 per cent reporting incivility. Organizations reporting bullying tended to be not-for-profit, $F(1, 491) = 46.10, p < .0001$, with 44 per cent of those in not-for-profit organizations reporting bullying as compared to 17 per cent of for-profit companies, and those organizations with bullying were also typically unionised, $F(1, 487) = 33.26, p < .0001$, with 46 per cent of unionized organizations in the sample reporting some level of bullying. The same pattern of results held for incivility, with not-for-profit, $F(1, 489) = 16.15$ $p < .0001$, and unionized, $F(1, 485) = 11.93, p < .001$, organizations reporting some degree of incivility.

Programmes and policies of organizations reporting bullying and incivility

Separate one-way analyses of covariance (ANCOVAs) were used to compare organizations that reported bullying and incivility with those that did not report bullying or incivility in terms of programmes and policies (Table 3.4). The structural characteristics of organizational size, unionization, for-profit vs. not-for-profit status and industry type were entered as covariates.

Results indicated that organizations that reported bullying were more likely to have training programmes for conflict resolution, $F(1, 459) = 4.36$, $p < .05$, and for managing disruptive behaviour, $F(1, 462) = 7.19, p < .01$, than did companies that did not report bullying.

Table 3.4 Programmes and policies offered by organizations in the sample according to reported presence of bullying and incivility

Programme/policy	% Sample	Bullying[a]		Incivility[a]	
		Yes	No	Yes	No
Programmes					
Sexual harassment training	54	1.53	1.53	1.59**	1.44
Diversity training	47	1.47	1.45	1.48	1.43
Violence risks/prevention training	44	0.47	0.40	0.47*	0.37
Conflict resolution training	45	0.53*	0.42	0.49*	0.39
Training in managing disruptive behaviour	35	0.45**	0.31	0.37	0.31
Policies					
Work in teams	67	0.74	0.64	0.68	0.64
Teams make assignments	82	1.85	1.81	1.84	1.79
Monthly team meetings	82	1.86	1.80	1.86*	1.76
Teams choose leaders	34	1.35	1.32	1.36	1.29
Flexible schedule	35	0.34	0.36	0.29	0.45**
Violence policy/documents	60	0.65	0.57	0.66**	0.50
Formal dispute resolution process	63	0.66	0.60	0.66**	0.54
Sexual harassment complaints procedure	63	0.68	0.60	0.69**	0.52
Pre-employment psychological testing	6	1.04	1.05	1.05	1.05

Note: N = 507. n = 121 companies reported bullying; n = 298 companies reported incivility. All programmes/policies have a range of 0–1, where 0 = no and 1 = yes, except where noted. [a]Cell entries are least squares adjusted means (covariates = organization size, unionization, industry and for-profit status).

*p < .05, **p < .01

Organizations reporting incivility were more likely to offer sexual harassment training for managers, $F(1,462) = 14.56$, $p < .0001$, workplace violence risks/prevention training, $F(1,455) = 5.72$, $p < .02$, and conflict resolution training, $F(1,457) = 4.42$, $p < .05$, than did companies that did not report incivility. Organizations having some degree of incivility also were more likely to have a violence policy/document, $F(1,462) = 15.20$, $p < .0001$, a formal dispute resolution process, $F(1,457) = 8.75$, $p < .01$, and a formal procedure for sexual harassment complaints, $F(1,461) = 16.63$, $p < .0001$, than did organizations that reported low levels of incivility. Organizations reporting incivility were also more likely to have monthly team meetings, $F(1,299) = 4.68$, $p < .05$, and were less likely to have flexible schedules for starting and quitting, $F(1,463) = 11.22$, $p < .001$.

Quality of worklife outcomes and bullying and incivility

Table 3.5 compares organizations that reported bullying and incivility to those that did not on quality of worklife indicators. Separate one-way ANCOVAs were performed with organizational size, unionization, for-profit vs. not-for-profit status and industry type as covariates.

As can be seen in the table, organizations reporting bullying also reported more adverse quality of worklife outcomes such as formal sexual harassment complaints, $F(1,283) = 22.25$, $p < .0001$, formal racial discrimination complaints, $F(1,464) = 17.41$, $p < .0001$, and formal disability discrimination complaints, $F(1,465) = 18.31$, $p < .0001$.

Organizations reporting incivility were more likely to report formal sexual harassment complaints, $F(1,283) = 6.01$, $p < .02$, a commitment to avoid layoffs, $F(1,458) = 4.96$, $p < .05$, and a high degree of close supervision, $F(1,460) = 5.17$, $p < .05$, were less likely to report that employees had a choice of how to accomplish assignments, $F(1,461) = 5.17$, $p < .05$, and reported poorer employee/management relations, $F(1,443) = 8.11$, $p < .01$.

Discussion and conclusions

Several interesting findings emerged from the present study of US organizations. Bullying and incivility were more prevalent in larger organizations, which is consistent with the European literature (Hoel, Einarsen and Cooper 2003), and in not-for-profit companies, which may agree to some extent with the European findings regarding the public sector (Hoel and Salin 2003). The issue of not-for-profit companies may be that they tend to offer services to the public, meaning that there is more opportunity for inter-personal conflict with customers or clients, and the staff may be part-time or even volunteer workers. Results also indicated that bullying

Table 3.5 Results of analyses of covariance comparing organizations reporting bullying/incivility and those not reporting bullying/incivility on quality of worklife outcomes

Quality of worklife outcomes	Range	M^a	Bullying^b Yes	Bullying^b No	Incivility^b Yes	Incivility^b No
Sexual harassment complaints	0–1	0.30	0.43**	0.19	0.32*	0.18
Racial discrimination complaints	0–1	0.14	0.23**	0.09	0.13	0.11
Age discrimination complaints	0–1	0.09	0.10	0.07	0.07	0.10
Disability discrimination complaints	0–1	0.08	0.17**	0.05	0.08	0.08
Committed to avoiding layoffs	0–1	0.33	0.34	0.32	0.37*	0.26
Choice how accomplish assignments	1–5	3.48	3.53	3.47	3.41	3.62*
Amount of supervision	1–5	2.91	2.85	2.91	2.99*	2.76
Org. strives to improve employee wellbeing	1–4	3.33	3.39	3.30	3.33	3.32
Org. offers skills useful wherever employees go	1–4	3.26	3.33	3.22	3.28	3.20
Positive employee/management relations	1–5	4.45	4.38	4.50	4.40	4.58**

Note: $N = 507$. $n = 121$ companies reported bullying; $n = 298$ companies reported incivility. Org. = organization. ^{a}Unadjusted means for entire sample ($N = 507$). ^{b}Cell entries are least squares adjusted means (covariates = organization size, unionisation, industry and for-profit status). $*p < .05$, $**p < .01$

53

and incivility were more likely to be reported in organizations that were unionized. A possible explanation is that having a union raises awareness in employees, as well as providing a mechanism for lodging complaints. Bullying and incivility were both common in the service sector, but there was no overall effect for bullying or incivility for type of industry. Future research might consider oversampling certain industries in order to have enough companies in each category for adequate statistical comparisons. These findings highlight the importance of controlling for structural factors in the workplace when examining organizational climate issues.

Organizations that reported bullying were also more likely to have adopted a variety of training programmes such as sexual harassment training, conflict resolution and training in managing disruptive behaviour. Companies that reported incivility were likely to have policies for workplace violence, a formal dispute resolution process and a formal procedure for sexual harassment complaints. It is not clear whether companies have these policies and procedures in place because of existing aggression problems in the workplace (i.e. they are being reactive), or if the training programmes and policies have created a heightened level of awareness in employees, and provide them with a means of reporting incidents. This also suggests that merely instituting a policy or programme will not necessarily ameliorate aggression problems. One must also take into account whether the programmes and policies are actually used and whether they are endorsed from the upper levels of the company down through the frontline workers.

In addition, organizations reporting incivility were more likely to have monthly team meetings. It may be the case that having frequent team meetings provides more opportunities for inter-personal conflict. This could be due to the greater inter-dependence involved in the use of teams (i.e. you must rely on others in the team to accomplish the overall task); interacting with others can be associated with increased task or emotional conflicts. The European literature suggests that the nature of the team itself is a salient issue, specifically that conflict between workers may increase as more of the workforce begin working in self-directed teams (Hoel and Salin 2003), and that enforced teamwork may provide a substrate for aggression, particularly if there is team competition for limited rewards (Hoel and Salin 2003; Zapf *et al.* 1996). In the present survey teamwork was assessed in broad terms, and future research might include a more fine-grained analysis of the teamwork dynamic.

Organizations reporting incivility and bullying were also less likely to have flexibility in terms of scheduling, did not provide a choice about how to accomplish assignments, and were characterized by close supervision. Taken as a whole this suggests micromanagement; a lack of control over the job or inability to participate in the decision-making process, which has been shown in some studies to be associated with psychological aggression (Keashly and Jagatic 2000; Vartia 1996).

Organizations reporting psychological aggression also reported that employee/management relations were poor in general, which is perhaps an overall indication of a poor psycho-social climate, and also suggestive that communication might be a concern. Both of these factors have been shown to be associated with psychological aggression in prior studies (Keashly and Jagatic 2000; Vartia 1996).

Bullying and incivility were associated with adverse quality of worklife indicators such as formal complaints of sexual harassment as well as formal complaints of racial, age and disability discrimination. Thus, it seems that bullying and incivility coexist with a number of other indicators of a hostile work environment, which could signal deeper inter-personal relations problems within the organization, or an underlying climate that either encourages or fosters such behaviours.

Additionally, companies with incivility reported that the organization was committed to avoiding layoffs, which seems counterintuitive. A possible explanation for this is that if the organization has made a statement of this commitment, there may already be some level of job insecurity or possible reorganization on the company's horizon. It could also be that a commitment to avoiding layoffs means that the internal pressures within the company are increasing, making inter-personal problems more likely, or that the company is publicly stating that they are committed to avoiding layoffs while inwardly behaving in a manner that suggests that there may be layoffs in the future. The nature of this relationship is unclear.

Limitations and future research

One limitation is that these data were provided by key informants at organizations which moderates the conclusions that can be drawn since it reflects their viewpoint only. Key informants may not be aware of more subtle forms of aggression or may be disengaged from what is actually going on in the workplace. As key informants are themselves likely to be in management positions and might therefore be reluctant to represent the organization in a bad light, it is possible that the extent of bullying and incivility was underreported. Similarly, because of their management positions, it is possible that aggressive behaviours were over-attributed to employees. It could also be the case that organizations may not acknowledge bullying and incivility as important issues, or do not have a system in place for reporting such behaviours.

Another limiting factor is that this study was cross-sectional in design. Longitudinal research is needed to investigate the antecedents and consequences of workplace bullying and incivility, particularly with regard to organizational climate.

Future surveys could benefit from input from employees, human resource professionals, and from different levels of management within the organization. Issues that were not addressed directly in the survey but that warrant further investigation include management practices, diversity, how psychological aggression might escalate into physical violence, factors that serve as moderators of psychological aggression, and how policy decisions are made within organizations.

Future research should also focus on establishing the linkages between workplace psychological aggression and work organization and climate factors in US workers, and on assessing workplace aggression as a psycho-social stressor. Further, the impact of workplace psychological aggression on worker safety, health, and wellbeing has not been addressed meaningfully in the US literature. It is important to be able to show concrete data pertaining to the cost of workplace psychological aggression to US companies. The end goal of this process is to develop processes or tools for organizational interventions for workplace bullying and to evaluate the efficacy of these interventions.

Additionally, we noticed several gaps in the knowledge base regarding psychological aggression in the US. The following are suggestions for possible ways to address these challenges:

- Coordinate research efforts amongst US and non-US researchers.

- Establish a standard nomenclature for psychological aggression in the US.

- Attain national data on the prevalence of psychological aggression in the US.

- Perform economic analysis and obtain data on cost of psychological aggression to organizations.

- Link psychological aggression to health, safety, and organizational outcome measures.

- Design intervention and evaluation studies.

- Identify 'best practices' or 'best strategies' for preventing workplace psychological aggression.

- Develop practical 'toolkits' or processes that can be used by organizations to assess psychological aggression in their workplaces as well as providing a general roadmap for how to proceed in combating the problem.

A more unified approach aimed at these issues should help advance this area of research.

References

Andersson, L.M. and Pearson, C.M. (1999). 'Tit for tat? The spiraling effect of incivility in the workplace.' *Academy of Management Review* 24, 452–71.

Bachman, R. (1994, July). *Violence and theft in the workplace. Crime Data Brief: National Crime Victimization Survey. NCJ-148199*, Washington, DC, US Department of Justice, Bureau of Justice Statistics.

Barling, J. (1996). 'The prediction, psychological experience, and consequences of workplace violence.' In VandenBos, G. and Bulatao, E.Q. (eds), *Violence on the job: Identifying risks and developing solutions*. Washington, DC, American Psychological Association.

Baron, R.A. and Neuman, J.H. (1996). 'Workplace violence and workplace aggression: Evidence on their relative frequency and potential causes', *Aggressive Behavior*, 22, 161–73.

Baron, R.A. and Neuman, J.H. (1998). 'Workplace aggression – The iceberg beneath the tip of workplace violence: Evidence on its forms, frequency, and targets.' *Public Administration Quarterly*, 21, 446–64.

Brodsky, C.M. (1976). *The Harassed Worker*. Lexington, MA: D.C. Heath and Company.

Brownell, J. (1990). 'Perceptions of effective listeners: A management study.' *Journal of Business Communication*, 27, 401–15.

Chen, P.Y. and Spector, P.E. (1992). 'Relationships of work stressors with aggression, withdrawal, theft and substance use: An exploratory study.' *Journal of Occupational and Organizational Psychology*, 65, 177–84.

Cole, L.L., Grubb, P.L., Sauter, S.L., Swanson, N.G. and Lawless, P. (1997). 'Psychosocial correlates of harassment, threats, and fear of violence in the workplace.' *Scandinavian Journal of Work, Environment and Health*, 23, 450–7.

Cortina, L.M., Magley, V.J., Williams, J.H. and Langhout, R.D. (2001). 'Incivility in the workplace: Incidence and impact.' *Journal of Occupational Health Psychology*, 6, 64–80.

Davis, J.A., Smith, T.W., and Marsden, P.V. (2002). General Social Surveys 1972–2002: Cumulative codebook (National Data Program for the Social Sciences Series, No. 17). Chicago, IL: National Opinion Research Center.

Duhart, D.T. (2001, December). *Violence in the workplace 1993–1999*. NCJ 190076. Bureau of Justice Statistics Special Report: National Crime Victimization Survey. Washington, DC, US Department of Justice, Office of Justice Programs.

Einarsen, S. (2000). 'Harassment and bullying at work: A review of the Scandinavian approach.' *Aggression and Violent Behavior*, 5, 379–401.

Einarsen, S., Hoel, H., Zapf, D. and Cooper, C.L. (2003). 'The concept of bullying at work: The European tradition.' In S. Einarsen, H. Hoel, D. Zapf and C.L. Cooper (eds), *Bullying and Emotional Abuse in the Workplace*. New York: Taylor and Francis.

Einarsen, S. and Mikkelsen, E.G. (2003). 'Individual effects of exposure to bullying at work.' In S. Einarsen, H. Hoel, D. Zapf and C.L. Cooper (eds), *Bullying and Emotional Abuse in the Workplace*. New York: Taylor and Francis.

Einarsen, S., Raknes, B.I. and Matthiesen, S.B. (1994). 'Bullying and harassment at work and their relationships to work environment quality: An exploratory study.' *European Work and Organizational Psychologist*, 4, 381–401.

Einarsen, S. and Skogstad, A. (1996). 'Prevalence and risk groups of bullying and harassment at work.' *European Journal of Work and Organizational Psychology*, 5, 185–202.

Grandey, A.A., Tam, A.P. and Brauburger, A.L. (2002). 'Affective states and traits in the workplace: Diary and survey data from young workers.' *Motivation and Emotion*, 26, 31–55.

Hoel, H., Einarsen, S. and Cooper, C.L. (2003). 'Organizational effects of bullying.' In S. Einarsen, H. Hoel, D. Zapf and C.L. Cooper (eds), *Bullying and Emotional Abuse in the Workplace*. New York: Taylor and Francis.

Hoel, H., Rayner, C. and Cooper, C.L. (1999). 'Workplace bullying.' In C.L. Cooper and I.T. Robertson (eds), *International Review of Industrial and Organizational Psychology* (Vol. 14, pp. 195–230). New York: John Wiley and Sons, Ltd.

Hoel, H. and Salin, D. (2003). 'Organizational antecedents of workplace bullying.' In S. Einarsen, H. Hoel, D. Zapf and C.L. Cooper (eds), *Bullying and Emotional Abuse in the Workplace*. New York: Taylor and Francis.

Jenkins, E.L. (1996). 'Workplace homicide: Industries and occupations at high risk.' In R. Harrison (ed.), *Violence in the Workplace: Occupational State of the Art Reviews*. Philadelphia, PA: Hanley and Belfus, Inc.

Jenkins, E.L., Layne, L.A. and Kisner, S.M. (1992). 'Homicide in the workplace: The US experience 1980–1988.' *Am. Assoc. Occup. Health Nurses J.*, 40, 215–18.

Kalleberg, A.L., Knoke, D., Marsden, P.V. and Spaeth, J.L. (1994). *Organizations in America: Analyzing their structures and human resources practices*. Thousand Oaks, CA: Sage.

Keashly. L., Hunter, S. and Harvey, S. (1997). 'Abusive interaction and role state stressors: Relative impact on student residence assistant stress and work attitudes.' *Work and Stress*, 11, 175–85.

Keashly, L. and Jagatic, K. (2000). 'The nature, extent and impact of emotional abuse in the workplace: Results of a state-wide survey.' Paper presented at the meeting of the Academy of Management, Toronto.

Keashly, L. and Jagatic, K. (2003). 'By any other name: American perspectives on workplace bullying.' In S. Einarsen, H. Hoel, D. Zapf and C.L. Cooper (eds), *Bullying and Emotional Abuse in the Workplace*. New York: Taylor and Francis.

Keashly, L., Trott, V. and MacLean, L.M. (1994). 'Abusive behavior in the workplace: A preliminary investigation.' *Violence and Victims*, 9, 341–57.

National Institute for Occupational Safety and Health (1992). *Homicide in US workplaces: A strategy for prevention and research*. US Department of Health and Human Services, Public Health Service, Centers for Disease Control and Prevention, NIOSH, Publication No. 92–103.

National Institute for Occupational Safety and Health (1993). *Fatal injuries to workers in the United States 1980–1989: A decade of surveillance, national profile*. US

Department of Health and Human Services, Public Health Service, Centers for Disease Control and Prevention, NIOSH, Publication No. 93–108.

National Institute for Occupational Safety and Health (1995). *NIOSH Alert: Preventing homicide in the workplace.* US Department of Health and Human Services, Public Health Service, Centers for Disease Control and Prevention, NIOSH, Publication No. 93–109.

Neuman, J.H. and Baron, R.A. (1997). 'Aggression in the workplace.' In R.A. Giacalone and J. Greenberg (eds), *Antisocial Behavior in Organizations.* Thousand Oaks, CA: Sage.

Neuman, J.H. and Baron, R.A. (1998). 'Workplace violence and workplace aggression: Evidence concerning specific forms, potential causes, and preferred targets.' *Journal of Management*, 24, 391–419.

Neuman, J.H. and Baron, R.A. (2003) 'Social antecendents of bullying: A social interactionist perspective.' In S. Einarsen, H. Hoel, D. Zapf and C. Cooper (eds) *Bullying and Emotional Abuse in the Workplace: International perspectives in research and practice.* London: Taylor & Francis.

Northwestern National Life Insurance Company. (1993). *Fear and violence in the workplace.* Minneapolis, MN: Northwestern National Life.

Pryor, J.B. (1987). 'Sexual harassment proclivities in men.' *Sex Roles* 17, 269–290.

Richman, J.A., Rospenda, K.M., Nawyn, S.J., Flaherty, J.A., Fendrich, M., Drum, M.L., and Johnson, T.P. (1999). 'Sexual harassment and generalized workplace abuse among university employees: Prevalence and mental health correlates.' *American Journal of Public Health*, 89(3), 358–363.

Robinson, S. L., and Greenberg, J. (1998). 'Employees behaving badly: Dimension, determinants and dilemmas in the study of workplace deviance.' In C.L. Cooper and D.M. Rousseau (eds.), *Trends in Organizational Behavior* (Vol. 5, pp. 1–30). New York: John Wiley and Sons, Ltd.

Rogers, K.A. and Kelloway, E.K. (1997). 'Violence at work: Personal and organizational outcomes.' *Journal of Occupational Health Psychology*, 2, 63–71.

Snyder, L., Chen, P., Grubb, P., Roberts, R., Sauter, S. and Swanson, N. (2004). 'Workplace aggression and violence against individuals and organizations: Causes, consequences, and interventions.' In P. Perrewe and D. Ganster (eds). *Research in Occupational Stress and Well Being* (Vol. 4). St. Louis, MO: Elsevier.

Tepper, B.J. (2000). 'Consequences of abusive supervision.' *Academy of Management Journal*, 43, 178–190.

Vartia, M., (1996). The sources of bullying: Psychological work environment and organizational climate, *European Journal of Work and Organizational Psychology*, 52, 203–214.

Zapf, D., Dormann, C. and Frese, M. (1996). 'Longitudinal studies in organizational stress research: A review of the literature with reference to methodological issues.' *Journal of Occupational Health Psychology*, 1, 145–169.

Zapf, D., Einarsen, S., Hoel, H. and Vartia, M. (2003). 'Individual effects of exposure to bullying at work.' In S. Einarsen, H. Hoel, D. Zapf, and C.L. Cooper (eds), *Bullying and Emotional Abuse in the Workplace.* New York: Taylor and Francis.

Chapter 4

Reforming abusive organizations

Charlotte Rayner

Introduction

This chapter seeks to tackle abuse at the organizational level with a focus on action to reform organizations. This chapter will take the position that an organization can be abusive if it does not take effective steps to protect its staff from such threats. Where the threat is internal, there are two forms of abuse. The first is inter-personal abuse including bullying. This will be called 'Negative Inter-personal Behaviour' (NiB). The second is organizational abuse where systems and processes directly fail to support, undermine or otherwise cause harm to employees. This will be termed 'Negative Organizational Behaviour' (NoB).

The first part of this chapter will focus on reform that tackles NiB. It will lay the foundation for a variety of processes such as complaints and disciplinary codes that can be used for NiB but also for other aspects of reform. The second part of the chapter will identify how the organization itself might be abusive.

Two key points underpin both NiB and NoB events. The first is that they are repeated experiences. Rarely are we talking about a single event, but rather a sequence of (often small) events that persist over time. One needs to look at these events *in total* rather than individually to understand the pattern that the employee perceives and to which they are reacting. Second, is that it is usually a situation of escalating conflict. Sequences of small events and weak (or no) remedial actions (Rayner 1998) serve to fuel a spiral of conflict (e.g. Einarsen 2001; Dupre and Barling 2004). In some instances it is quite possible that the original 'target' appears to be part of the process and part of 'the problem' as they continually try to get their concerns addressed. In other instances, the conflict 'spiral' is simply broken as the target decides to leave the organization.

Combating negative interpersonal behaviours

Bullying and one-off events that are perceived by staff to be negative inter-personal interactions are pervasive in all countries where studies have been conducted (e.g. Einarsen 2000; Rayner and Keashly 2004; McCarthy, Rylance, Bennett and Zimmerman 2001). The behaviours can take many forms and serve to undermine or attack the self-confidence and self-worth of employees. Whether or not someone labels themselves as 'bullied' (or an equivalent term), those who experience negative behaviour are much more likely to have worse health than those who do not report these experiences (Hoel, Faragher and Cooper 2004).

Awareness of the negative effects of bullying-related actions in western societies has been growing through the 1990s. In 2000, the European Agency for Safety and Health at Work held a forum for Best Practice and published a series of case studies (OSHA 2000) for preventing psycho-social stress at work. They found the following process common to the submissions for Best Practice:

1 Risk analysis
2 Clear planning and stepwise approach to goals, tasks and responsibilities
3 Combining work-directed and worker-directed approaches for focus
4 Context-specific solutions taking into account on-the-job experience
5 Interventions that are evidence-based and staff who are competent
6 Social dialogue throughout the organization
7 Sustainable improvements through management support at all levels

Adapted from: http://agency.osha.eu.int/publicatiuons/reports/104 en/index_1.htm

The report demonstrates the real need for focus and assigning resources to interventions. Half-hearted attempts or quick fixes will not achieve results, and the report evidences the thoughtfulness and care that needs to be taken if an organization is to succeed. The message is to take it seriously from the start. But, drawing on examples from many different countries, the report also demonstrates that success is possible.

Let us start by using risk analysis to look at the potential areas of organizational intervention in bullying and other inter-personal types of abuse. Over a number years I have developed a schema that many organizations have found useful for thinking about their actions, The Event Hierarchy. This has its roots in health and safety thinking, and borrows from a well-established accident (or safety) pyramid originally conceived by Heinrich (1931) and still in use (e.g. Fulwiler 2000). Heinrich reported that for every fatality there were 29 minor injuries and 300 unsafe acts, and suggested tackling fatalities through reducing the number of unsafe acts as a bottom-up approach. Adapting this method into bullying at work as an example, The Event Hierarchy provides a way of conceptualizing actions to reform the situation.

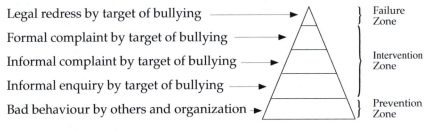

Legal redress by target of bullying — Failure Zone

Formal complaint by target of bullying —

Informal complaint by target of bullying — Intervention Zone

Informal enquiry by target of bullying —

Bad behaviour by others and organization — Prevention Zone

Figure 4.1 The Event Hierarchy

The Event Hierarchy has litigation as equivalent of 'fatality' in health and safety terms and is the ultimate failure. Interventions are at stages prior to this where individuals 'voice' through formal and informal complaints as well as what has been termed 'informal enquiries' where they ask others about the behaviour (this is likely to be as part of their sense-making process). Each time employees engage in some form of 'voice' through enquiry or compliant, the organization has a chance to deal with the issue through intervention.

At the bottom of the Event Hierarchy is the root of the problem, the 'bad behaviour' surfaced in NiB and NoB. In this area of 'bad behaviour', reformers are working in a prevention mode to minimise the behaviour itself rather than intervene which exemplifies action taken after negative events have occurred.

Policies

Interventions depend on employees 'voicing' their concerns. Organizations which are concerned about negative inter-personal behaviour (bullying, harassment or discrimination of any kind, for example) need to have a policy. A policy begins with stipulating what behaviour it concerns, and here organizations can opt for taking a 'do' or a 'don't' approach. The 'don't' approach would involve stating what behaviour is not acceptable using exemplars. With this option the policies will be 'anti-bullying' or 'anti-discrimination', etc. The problem with this approach is that as new aspects of 'discrimination' appear (such as age and religion in the European States for example), so the policy will need to be re-written. The other option is to take a positive 'do' approach and state what behaviour is sought, and use exemplars of that which fall outside this. These policies might be termed 'Dignity and Respect' policies. There are several advantages to this second approach. First, the policies do not have to be re-written as new 'Don'ts' appear in legislation and other aspects of the external environment. Second, they give rights and responsibilities to everyone thus making ownership and the importance of the policy easier to 'sell'. For example we all have the right to be treated with dignity and respect, and equally we all have the responsibility to treat others as such. Of special importance in western societies is the need to engage white men for whom discrimination-biased policies rarely hold any direct benefit. Dignity policies do this.

A well-written policy will state the focus of the policy and have a statement of commitment to do something about it (normally that this constitutes a dismissal offence). Clearly such statements need to garner the support of the highest levels of management (Board Executives), otherwise implementation will fail. Those wanting to eradicate NiB will not succeed unless they have top-level backing, so it is worth establishing such support as the first step, however long it takes.

Finally (although probably the major section of the policy) are the processes in place for someone who thinks they have a concern about how they are treated. This section of the policy and procedure effectively channels employees' 'voice' so that they know where, when, and who to contact if they think they may have a problem. The policy will need to state the roles and responsibilities of the various parties involved such as mediators, investigators and decision panels. It is crucial that there is more than one avenue for complaint. This is necessary because the person who is bullying or harassing might be the person who is identified in the policy as the person to complain to – a UK survey found 83 per cent of bullies were the boss (UNISON 1997). Often, Personnel or Human Resource Management departments are defined as 'the other' route as well as line management. However, one needs to be careful that Personnel or HR themselves have 'another route' too because these departments are not exempt from such behaviour (Thomas 2004). All procedures need timeframes for the various parts of the process and clarity regarding information supplied to and by whom, as well as representation rights and staff support for both the accused and the complainant. More detailed advice is available in Richards and Daley (2003).

Complaints process

How can organizations avoid being at the top of The Event Hierarchy? One answer is to solve the problems early on before they 'escalate' (Einarsen 2000). Several studies have been conducted with badly affected targets of bullying (e.g. Zapf and Gross 2001; Neidl 1996) where respondents were asked what they did about the bullying using the EVLN framework. The EVLN framework (e.g. Withey and Cooper 1989) has four actions; Exit (leave the organization), Voice (say something to someone), Loyalty (just do your job well) and Neglect (neglect your job). These qualitative studies on targets have been successful in applying the framework to targets (which is not always the case; see Luchak 2003 for a review) and have found that all interviewees voiced their concerns at work. Large-scale questionnaire-based studies have found that many people who have been psychologically abused at work through NiB often leave (Exit), with rates of about 25 per cent in both the UK (Rayner 1998) and Australia (McCarthy, Sheehan and Kearns 1996). Furthermore, witnesses also leave the organization, which creates an even higher cost to the organization (Rayner and Keashly 2004).

If we think that people first 'voice' and later 'exit', then it is either the case that the organization is not sensitive enough to pick up and react to the 'voice' or that the organization quietly sits back and lets these people quit their jobs. The latter is unlikely as the costs of replacing staff are tremendous. It would appear that often organizations are ineffective in taking advantage of early opportunities to resolve the situations of individuals and groups that are experiencing NiB, as so many people leave. Reforming the organization depends not only on making sure that employees have the opportunity to 'voice' (such as telling them to whom they should go) but making sure that the employee concerns are listened to, taken seriously and acted upon. That is, the system outlined in the policy needs to work.

Why don't organizations react at the early stages? In many UK organizations, staff in Human Resource Management departments or Personnel will only take action on official complaints. That is, they wait until the penultimate stage of The Event Hierarchy before they act. To some extent one can understand this as they might see themselves as needing to protect the complainant (who has not made their complaint official) and in a dialogue with the 'accused' would feel unable to divulge the case against them. They may also see it as unfair to the accused if they need to respond to questions about a situation about which there is no official complaint.

I would suggest this is a misguided approach for several reasons. The need for earlier intervention is that this approach is simply too late from a risk point of view. The situation will most likely have already escalated, and the opportunity for an amicable resolution where people simply go back to their jobs is unlikely. Hence both the organization and the individuals lose. The risk of 'getting it wrong' at this late stage brings one closer to the worst-case scenario of a litigious situation – there is no 'wiggle-room' for error. It would appear many employees are unwilling to go as far as an official complaint for fear of reprisals (for example, being labelled a troublemaker and having reduced opportunities for promotion, etc.) or to avoid the stress that such a process would necessarily involve. While we have no official data for this, the author has accessed a confidential project where it was estimated that only one in 30 cases of bullying was taken forward from an informal to a formal situation. It was unclear what the other 29 people did, but presumably many staff leave the organization.

A more positive situation would be for HR and Personnel (or any other manager) to feel able to investigate unofficial complaints, which are at a stage lower down in The Event Hierarchy. Personnel staff would need to uncouple themselves from a litigious approach, and not 'investigate' the (unofficial) complaint as they would an official one. In a recent interview, Isabel Doverty, an HR Director of Credit Suisse First Boston said, 'There is an inherent problem with the adversarial nature of most grievance procedures' (Roberts 2004: 30), suggesting that mediation 'before the relationship breaks down' (ibid) is much more appropriate.

However, such a role as formal or informal mediator would entail the HR or Personnel Department employing considerably wider skills and approaches themselves. HR staff would need to take a more generalized approach as if they were investigating a rumour that might damage the organization. They would need some key components to be able to do this effectively. First, they would require sufficient people-networks in place so that they could have access to data from others working with 'the accused'. Second, the social skills to be able to discuss the issue indirectly. They might, for example, suggest they are exploring 'management style' within a department, or improving staff morale – or other topics directly linked to bullying at work. Such entrées, initially using issues less threatening than bullying, allow neutral points of commonality to be established, such as the need for fair treatment and how hard it is sometimes to differentiate between being positively assertive and destructively aggressive. Initiating such discourse and, in as many ways as possible, opening up the area for discussion prompts self-reflection by all parties, including the potential bully/harasser and those who work closely with them, thus achieving the social dialogue encouraged in the Best Practice from OSHA (2000).

In this respect the reader will have realized that the focus for intervention being asserted here is that which conforms to the risk approach adopted by Heinrich so many years ago and echoed in the OSHA Best Practice. The process of dealing with reports of bullying at the early stages is not only more efficient for the organization (including not losing staff and avoiding staff going through a distressing escalation of conflict), but it can be easier as misunderstandings in communication can be dealt with if they are just that. Ideally such interventions are so close to the bottom of The Event Hierarchy that they might be experienced as almost preventative. Mediation in a formal capacity might (ideally) be triggered by informal enquiries or informal complaints. Quite possibly the 'bully' does not appreciate how their behaviour is interpreted, and early intervention might mean it is a question of 'trimming the sails' rather than the later scenario which might be of a disciplinary nature. Less likely (but possible), the employee might need to recalibrate their interpretation of signals.

A Chartered Institute of Personnel and Development report (the HR professional body in the UK) found that organizations which trained their managers in mediating skills had less than half the number of disciplinary complaints than those who did not (Roberts 2004). However, the study found that only 26 per cent of organizations undertook mediation skills training. This is a useful potential for further development towards achieving reform. However, anecdotal data suggests that mediation does need to be used at early stages in The Event Hierarchy before conflict has escalated, as it not effective after this.

Having stated that dealing with earlier enquiries can be easier, such a situation is highly problematic when there is a history and a tacit acceptance of bullying within the organization as a whole. In such situations, the process of 'reform' needs to be far-reaching. In addition, policies and clear statements from the top are meaningful, but unless the subcultures are dealt with, bullying will continue.

What therefore supports such subcultures? At this point the emphasis shifts from using The Event Hierarchy not only as a concept for understanding interventions, but also as a mechanism for influencing the pervasiveness of the 'bad behaviour' at the base of the Hierarchy. If disciplinary processes are not seen as fair in the outcomes for the parties, then a subculture of acceptance will be supported, i.e. one can be found to be bullying but there are no sanctions worth worrying about. If the process of formal investigation is not seen to be fair for all parties, activity to implement policies will be undermined and a signal transmitted that the policy itself cannot be trusted. This process of gaining trust, that cases of bullying will be taken seriously and dealt with effectively, is one where employees use the data around them. An early finding from UK surveys was that staff felt 'bullies could get away with it' and 'staff are too scared to report it' (UNISON 1997). Undoubtedly this is not always the case, but it was striking that over 90 per cent of respondents thought these two statements reflected the reasons for bullying to exist. Personnel may be hampered in their efforts by an agreement of non-disclosure on the results of internal investigations of cases of bullying. How does anyone know that negative consequences come to the 'bullies'? Not only is it important that bullies cannot get away with it, but it is crucial that employees know this. Reform in organizations will be much faster if disclosure is used.

At a fundamental level, negative inter-personal behaviour is a disturbing experience that any employee would wish to avoid. If the organization fails to act on reports, the situation for an employee becomes very difficult and it is not surprising that so many staff leave. Achieving reform means having empowered people who will act on reports of NiB every time, all the time. This may require awareness-raising about what NiB is. It may require training on how managers can deal with situations they are told about. Further, it may require training for managers to be proactive in developing a sense of when interactions between people are not optimal, and be empowered to act quickly. Such reform will cost money, and may have implications for placing 'people skills' higher up the agenda for selection panels. However, balanced with the costs of replacing lost staff, investigations and employees constantly 'playing safe' in their roles, the cost of training is likely to be offset many times.

Confronting and dealing with negative inter-personal behaviour when it is endemic in organizations requires courage on the part of senior staff, HR and other key personnel. However, as many developed countries are reporting skills shortages, retaining staff will be of competitive importance. Ensuring that negative inter-personal behaviour is dealt with will become a threshold competence for any employer.

Negative organizational behaviour

Research in this area is considerably less developed than in NiB (above), although it has potential linkages to a wide range of employment-relations literature, as we shall see. Two key studies can be of assistance to understanding the nature of negative organizational behaviour in the 'bullying' context. The qualitative work of Karen Harlos and Craig Pinder in Canada, and Andreas Liefooghe working with Kate MacKenzie Davey in the UK hold surprising parallels in their findings.

Harlos and Pinder, interested in injustice (1999), asked employees where they saw injustice at work. Their study revealed a considerable number of negative inter-personal behaviours, as one would expect. However, several aspects of perceived injustice were of a nature that the true sources of problems were unlikely to reside within individuals, but more in the systems and processes that were being used in workplaces. A classic example, and mentioned by Harlos and Pinder's interviewees, was that of poor appraisal systems. Appraisal systems should be an opportunity for an exchange of feedback between managers and their direct reports with the purpose of constructing a plan to include training needs and other support. Some organizations also attach performance-related pay discussions to appraisals. For the employee it is an opportunity to gain generalized feedback and systematically review their role and career, for which there is rarely another forum. Quite often employees may have positive expectations of such events (Porter and Lawler 1968; Rousseau 1995) and this may partly explain the reason for poor appraisal systems to rank high among Harlos *et al*'s negative organizational behaviours. Examples would include whole systems that failed to link into training and development opportunities, judgements passed down by appraisers that were not based on clear evidence and seen as unfair by appraisees, and a lack of opportunity to appeal regarding problematic issues (Harlos and Pinder 1999).

Liefooghe and MacKenzie Davey had a similar approach and findings. They illustrated, with good examples, behaviours that were apparently understood by focus-group members as being that of managers who were themselves under pressure (2003). Their study in call centres (2001) found 'work practice bullying' which centred on the control information picked up via the operators' consoles. Feedback for improvement was automatically public to the whole group, which the operators found humiliating.

Call-handling time was a fundamental statistic used for performance measurement. Staff reported wanting to take longer on calls in order to solve customer queries, but were unable to do so as the performance targets ('the statistics' p. 381) stipulated a certain maximum time. Failure to reach call-time targets resulted in denial of access to overtime, which, for these workers, had a fundamental impact on their employment. Employees described situations where the managers chose to view problems with performance as belonging to the workers rather than 'the system'. Employees did not 'blame' their supervisors, but rather felt 'bullied by the system'. In the conceptual context of this chapter it can be seen that the resultant situation evidenced an ineffective loop where the staff saw the problem as systemic (NoB) while the managers treated it as inter-personal (NiB). Liefooghe and Mackenzie Davey suggest 'presenting bullying as a purely inter-personal issue may prevent organizations from examining and reflecting on wider practices and their impact on wellbeing' (2001: 390), with which this author would concur.

Such examples provide a different perspective on negative behaviour at work, and one that might be more challenging than NiB (on which most people can agree). These types of 'organizational' behaviour link directly into collective issues of industrial relations and employment conditions that have received considerable attention in the past and, one might argue, have been lost in more recent years of performance-focused climates.

In addition to specific forms of organizational abuse (as illustrated above), one cannot consider negative organizational behaviour without mentioning systems that fail to cope with employee complaints, or act in a way to allow forms of abuse to continue or appear to be supported. Fundamental for those seeking to persuade others to reform is the message that *inaction is not a neutral position*. Employees judge inaction (and, one suspects, insufficient action) as supporting (through colluding) abuse, and unfortunately inaction is pervasive (UNISON 1997, 2000). This chapter has outlined approaches that can be taken to deal with negative inter-personal abuse, and if these do not work effectively, it is likely they will be termed abusive at the organizational level (Rayner, Hoel and Cooper 2002). Thus, systems that are set up, but fail, to deal with NiB, sadly (but ironically) become NoB. Thus, it is the case that complaint systems really must work. If they are not present, employees will judge the organization as collusive with negative behaviour (of any sort), and if they are present but ineffective, they risk becoming part of the abuse as NoB.

Dealing with negative organisational behaviour

How then, does one deal with negative organization behaviours? NoBs are systems that are directly abusive (such as disallowing legitimate access to overtime) or decent systems that have failed (such as a complaints process that does not work). Clearly the two different types require different treatments. The latter will be taken first as it is more straightforward.

A decent system that has not been implemented effectively needs to be examined to find out where the failures are. A systems approach is usually appropriate, working through the information and process flows. Colquitt *et al.* (2001) undertook a review of organizational justice and found that problems could be traced back to three main conceptual areas of interactive, procedural and distributive justice.

People experience interactional injustice when the organization fails to seek input or listen to that which is provided (Fontenot Premeaux and Bedian 2003). This would be exemplified by communication failure such as Harlos and Pinder (1999) reported in their malfunctioning system of apparently non-listening appraisers. A clear monitoring of the system would locate a problem, and this might be straightforward to solve, for example through training those managers to listen better. However, it might expose a flawed component. For example, the apparent 'non-listening' of managers might mask a lack of resources to meet any training at all. Lying underneath this might be the managers' feeling unable to challenge the policies of those further up the hierarchy for training resources to be able to implement the appraisal scheme effectively (which would evidence a lack of 'procedural justice' according to Colquitt *et al.* 2001). In their turn the managers may have asked for resources, but not been able to secure any. Thus, the picture appears grim to Harlos and Pinder's recipients (who may only see the results or 'distributive justice' from a poor system), but the problems might be complex in their formation. Reforming these organizations requires a standard process of problem solving with a level of honesty regarding weak links that will push through both problem exposure and work towards the solution.

Thus, where NoBs are the result of a decent system that has failed, the causes are rarely simple, but layer on layer of 'reasons'. It is likely that reform will have been attempted before, but failed as the complexity emerged. In these circumstances, there is no magic answer except to keep going through the layers of processes. Tom Peters (1989) would suggest these circumstances require a 'megalomaniac with a mission' with high levels of tenacity, persuasion and energy.

Very often, unless these NoBs are solved quite quickly, they are exposed as being like their poor-systems counterparts. At this point it is important for us to revisit the OSHA guidelines on page 61 that may become untenable in the normal political context within organizations (Buchanan and Badham 1999). One would need to convince others that there was a problem (step one – risk analysis), and if managers were sceptical it would be important that there was a trade union or other staff representative body willing to do this, otherwise the issue is simply left unresolved.

Reforming poor or abusive systems, similarly, rests on a convincing risk appraisal, which might be done formally or informally (Spurgeon, 2003), and we shall return to why organizations should bother about these behaviours. However, as in the example above, it is quite possible that this first hurdle is not completed. Indeed it is when considering NoB that it becomes clear that all of the OSHA (ibid) facets need to be in place for successful reform. That is a balance between worker and work priorities, flexibility regarding solutions (context specificity), competent (thus trained) staff and a broad social dialogue that has support at all hierarchical levels. This presents us with clear 'shopping list' to be able to implement reform, but one that may stretch many organizations.

Simply making the case for the reform of negative organizational behaviours is likely to be expensive. Where exploitative practices are present (such as making performance bonuses or overtime inaccessible) there will be a direct cost for making the change. Further, the process of change is likely to be very costly as these practices will be argued over and use considerable management time (e.g. 'I went through this system, so why shouldn't they?'). But through failures to recruit, exit interviews and gathering other 'voice' data (such as through appraisal systems), the changing agenda for the organization can be substantiated (Vartia, Korppoo, Fallenius and Mattila 2003). However, as recruitment and retention rates for staff improve, the reforms will undoubtedly pay for themselves.

Why should organizations bother now? For the developed economies, skills shortages are endemic in their organizations (Robinson 2004). I would suggest that it is no coincidence that inter-personal and other types of abuse are on our agenda at this time – all organizations need to keep their staff. Abuse that causes workers to leave or affects reputation to make recruitment difficult are under the microscope for very good reason. As we understand the dynamics of 'knowledge' economies, so retention of staff (who possess the knowledge) becomes paramount.

For many employers the need to stem outflows of staff forces an investigation of what underpins employees' decision to leave, and motivates them to take action. The studies of Liefooghe, MacKenzie Davey and Harlos and Pinder provide useful insights. An optimistic view would be that the boundaries of that which might be 'negotiable' in employment practices may be shifting as the skills shortages bite and attracting and retaining staff becomes a competitive imperative. Thus, while there is a need for us to examine forms of abuse, we should expect that our boundary for what is termed 'abuse' is likely to be a shifting parameter.

References

Buchanan, D. and Badham, R. (1999) *Power, Politics and Organizational Change: Winning the Turf Game*, London: Sage Publications.

Colquitt, J.A., Conlon, D.E., Wesson, M.J., Porter, C.O.L.H. and Yee Ng, K. (2001) 'Justice at the Millennium: A meta-analytic review of 25 years of organizational justice research', *Journal of Applied Psychology*, Vol. 86 No. 3 pp. 425–445.

Dupre, K.E. and Barling, J. (2004) *The Escalation of Workplace Aggression*. Paper presented at the annual Meeting of the Academy of Management, New Orleans, August 2004.

Einarsen, S. (2000) 'Harassment and bullying at work: A review of the Scandinavian approach', *Aggression and Violent Behavior*, Vol. 4 pp. 371–401.

Fontenot Premeaux, S. and Bedian, A.G. (2003) 'Breaking the silence: The moderating effects of self-monitoring in predicting speaking up in the workplace', *Journal of Management Studies*, Vol. 40 No. 6 pp. 1537–62.

Fulwiler, R.D. (2000) 'Behaviour-based safety and the missing links', *Occupational Hazards*, Vol. 62 No. 1 pp. 53–6.

Harlos, K. and Pinder, C.C. (1999) 'Patterns of Organizational injustice: A taxonomy of what employees regard as unjust' *Qualitative Organizational Research*, Vol. 2 pp. 97–125.

Heinrich, H.W. (1931) *Industrial Accident and Prevention: A Scientific Approach*, London: McGraw Hill.

Hoel, H., Faragher, B. and Cooper, C.L. (2004) 'Bullying is detrimental to health, but all bullying behaviours are not necessarily equally damaging', *British Journal of Guidance and Counselling*, Vol. 32 No. 3 pp. 367–387.

Liefooghe, A.P.D. and Mackenzie Davey, K. (2001) 'Accounts of workplace bullying: The role of the organization' *European Journal of Work and Organizational Psychology*, Vol. 10 No. 4 pp. 375–393.

Liefooghe, A.P.D. and Mackenzie Davey, K. (2003) 'Explaining bullying at work: Why should we listen to employee accounts?' In S. Einarsen, H. Hoel, D. Zapf and C.L. Cooper (eds) *Bullying and Emotional Abuse in the Workplace: International perspectives in research and practice*, London: Taylor & Francis.

Luchak, A.A. (2003) 'What kind of a voice do loyal employees use?' *British Journal of Industrial Relations*, Vol. 44, No. 1 pp. 115–134.

McCarthy, P., Rylance, J., Bennett, R. and Zimmerman, H. (2001) *Bullying: From Backyard to Boardroom*, 2nd edition, Sydney: The Federation Press.

OSHA (2000) *European Agency for Safety and Health Reports Issue 104* http://agency.osha.eu.int/publications/reports/104/en/index_1.htm (accessed 12 July 2005).

Peters, T. (1989) *Thriving on Chaos*, London: Macmillan.

Porter, L.W. and Lawler, E.E. (1968) *Managerial Attitudes and Performance*, Homewood, IL: Irwin.

Rayner, C. (1998) 'Workplace bullying: Do something!', *Journal of Occupational Health and Safety – Australia and New Zealand*, Vol. 14 No. 6 pp. 581–5.

Rayner, C., Hoel, H. and Cooper, C.L. (2002) *Workplace Bullying: What we know, who is to blame and what can we do?* London: Taylor & Francis.

Rayner, C. and Keashly, L. (2004) 'Bullying at work: A perspective from Britain and North America'. In S. Fox and P.E. Spector (eds) *Counterproductive work behavior: Investigations of actors and targets*, Washington, DC: American Psychological Association Publishers.

Roberts, Z. (2004) 'Alternative dispute resolution: A thoroughly modern melee', *People Management*, 30 September pp. 29–32.

Robinson, P. (2004) *Going for Growth*, London: Institute of Public Policy Research.

Rousseau, D. (1995) *Psychological Contracts in Organizations*, Thousand Oaks, CA: Sage.

Thomas, D. (2004) 'HR the victim as bullying takes hold in UK businesses', *Personnel Today*, 28th September p. 1.

Sprugeon, A. (2003) 'Bullying from a risk management perspective'. In S. Einarsen, H. Hoel, D. Zapf and C.L. Cooper (eds) *Bullying and Emotional Abuse in the Workplace: International perspectives in research and practice*, London: Taylor & Francis.

UNISON (1997) *UNISON members' experience of bullying at work*, London: UNISON.

UNISON (2000) *Police staff bullying report*, London: UNISON.

Vartia, M., Korppoo, L., Fallenius, S. and Mattila, M. (2003) 'Workplace bullying: The role of occupational health services.' In S. Einarsen, H. Hoel, D. Zapf and C.L. Cooper (eds) *Bullying and Emotional Abuse in the Workplace: International perspectives in research and practice*, London, Taylor & Francis.

Withy, M. and Cooper, W. (1989) 'Predicting exit, voice, loyalty and neglect', *Administrative Science Quarterly*, Vol. 34 pp. 521–539.

Zapf, D. and Gross, C. (2001) 'Conflict escalation and coping with workplace bullying: A replication and extension', *European Journal of Work and Organizational Psychology*, Vol. 10 No. 4 pp. 497–522.

Section 2

Identifying and responding to at-risk groups

Chapter 5

Staff violence against those in their care

Charmaine Hockley

Introduction

Staff violence against those in their care is one of the last of the taboo areas revealed in workplace violence discourse. It is paradoxical that those whose overriding responsibility is to provide care and promote an environment in which the human rights, values, customs and spiritual beliefs of those in their care should be respected, should at the same time be also potentially capable of violent actions against those they are committed to care for. Furthermore, those who are targeted have the potential to have traumatic experiences similar to victims of violent crime in other contexts.

Many of these perpetrators and their acts go unnoticed and unreported while others attract attention when eventually exposed with the reporting of their unprofessional conduct. It is this small element that attracts the most media attention because of the heinous crimes they commit and that their targets are generally the most vulnerable in our society – the elderly or mentally ill. However, these types of violence are only the tip of the iceberg compared to the day-to-day forms of antisocial workplace behaviour, such as verbal abuse, maltreatment and neglect, that staff commit towards those in their care (Speaks 1996; Hockley 2003a, 2003b).

This chapter examines the phenomenon of violence between staff and those in their care from the ethical and legal perspectives expected of a health professional. Other core issues covered are the typology of workplace violence in healthcare settings, staff-initiated violence, the victim's and perpetrator's profile, causes and methods, and finally strategies to manage this category of violence.

Because of the wide range of employees within the healthcare industry, for ease and flow of reading the term 'healthcare worker' will be used generically to refer to all those who provide 'direct care' to patients, unless discussing a specific group such as nurses and medical practitioners. The phrase 'those in their care' will be interchanged with the terms 'consumers', 'patients' or 'residents' depending upon the healthcare setting. This chapter will focus on violence caused by those who, because of the nature of their work, have the greatest opportunity to commit these acts – formal carers in aged care settings, nurses and medical practitioners.

Defining staff-initiated violence

The law generally recognizes three types of harm – physical, emotional, and economic (Wallace 2001) – and if legal action is taken against the perpetrator then the following definition of staff-initiated violence is worth considering:

> Staff-initiated violence is the outcome of any act that causes harm to a person in their care. Along a continuum, these acts can range from non-physical (verbal abuse) to physical (manslaughter and homicide). Violence is not so much the act itself; it is the outcome of a harmful experience. Harmful experiences may include physical, psychological or economic harm and can affect those who have a relationship with the targeted person (e.g. family members) (adapted from Hockley 2002).

Ethical and legal issues

Discussing staff-initiated violence challenges many of the traditional views of healthcare workers as being trustworthy and caring. The two main ethical and legal principles that apply to healthcare workers are that they (1) should do no harm and (2) have a duty of providing care to persons in their care. Acts of violence pervade human society but there is an expectation that when individuals enter a health setting they are going to be cared for in a professional and safe manner. It is ignoring these two principles that makes unprofessional conduct towards patients so disturbing and dangerous.

Healthcare workers, wherever they may be employed, and in whatever capacity, have the potential to act in an unethical or illegal capacity towards those in their care. This behaviour is not new and various governments and professional organizations such as the International Council of Nurses (ICN) (2000a), American Nurses Association (ANA) (2001), and Australian Nurses Council (ANC) (2002) have recognized this fact and developed federal and state legislation as well as professional codes of conduct to address these behaviours. The ICN (2000b) in their policy on violence against nurses acknowledges that nurses can be perpetrators as follows: '[R]egrettably, a small number of nurses have also been known to be perpetrators of violence, patient or colleague abuse in violation of nursing's code of conduct' (p. 1).

Health professionals generally have a code of ethics and professional conduct that informs them of the parameters in which they work. In nursing, for example, the ICN Code of Ethics is one such code. Included in this code is: 'the nurse takes appropriate action to safeguard individuals when their care is endangered by a co-worker or any other person' (ICN 2000a: 3).

The legal requirements for healthcare workers may vary but they must consider the consequences of their actions to ensure that they have not breached their legal obligations towards those in their care. For example, occupational health and safety legislation and the laws that relate to negligence, discrimination, assault and homicide (Wallace 2001).

Typology of workplace violence

In recent years there have been typologies developed (Bowie 2002a; Bowie 2002b; Mayhew and Chappell 2001; Bowie, Fisher and Cooper 2005; Hockley 2005) to categorize workplace violence. To appreciate where staff-initiated violence fits into these typologies Table 5.1 lists eight basic categories. These categories have been adapted from the previously mentioned authors' typologies.

Staff-initiated violence in context

While many factors contribute to this form of violence, two will be emphasized here. The first is that there are inherent perceptions about healthcare workers that do not necessarily apply to other workers in society; these are that they are caring and trustworthy. For the past ten years or so, national communities have overwhelmingly voted nurses as one of the trustworthiest of professions.

The second factor is that the patient's rights appear to be more clearly defined than for other categories of violence that occur in the workplace.

Table 5.1   Typology of workplace violence within the healthcare area

- Internal violence – In this form of violence, the perpetrators are employees within the same organization, e.g. employer/employee.
- Client-initiated violence – When patients/clients and their families act violently towards staff.
- Organisational violence – This type of violence refers to the harm that may occur to staff *per se* when an organization is experiencing economic pressures resulting in restructuring, redundancy, redeployment or resignations.
- External violence – This form of violence occurs when perpetrators enter the workplace with criminal intent, such as armed robbery for drugs or gang reprisals in emergency departments.
- Third-party violence – This type of violence refers to the witnesses of violence, either directly or indirectly, by other staff or the targeted persons family.
- Staff-initiated violence – This form of violence occurs when staff act violently towards those in their professional care.
- Traumatic work-related events violence – Repetitive exposure to traumatic events can cause staff in turn to become victims of trauma (Michael 2003). This form of violence may occur once (e.g. a terrorist attack; school yard or work massacres) or at special events (e.g. football final season, such as in Europe and USA) or during wars or working in specialized volatile areas, such as highly dependent care units or natural disasters such as the tsunami disaster in Asia.
- Client-to-client violence – Where a resident/patient attacks another resident/patient.

There could be several reasons why this is so. For example, it may be that patients and their families are more likely to report unprofessional conduct such as abuse and negligence and take legal action than employees who are abused, or it could be that the reported cases of violence against patients are more physical in nature, some even leading to their death. It could also be that those working in the healthcare industry are more willing to report violent acts towards patients than they are about their colleagues or themselves.

Victim's profile

When a person requires healthcare they can become a target of violence at any time – as a patient in hospital, visiting a general practitioner or visiting a clinic. The targeted person could be mentally ill, a homeless adolescent, a resident in an aged-care facility, or a woman in childbirth. They could be any representative of the identified minority groups such as indigenous people, migrants, the aged, women, or have a disability. The targeted person can be of any age. In an attempt to protect vulnerable groups, federal and state laws to cover the lifespan from conception (e.g. laws to protect the unborn child, including IVF) to after death (e.g. laws to protect the dead, including autopsies) were introduced into the workplace.

Staff violence in the healthcare system can occur across the age spectrum – from conception to death and postmortem – as well as in different settings and locations wherever health professionals work – from laboratories to mortuaries. Staff violence towards those in their care can range from disrespect at a cellular level to necrophilia.

With the above in mind, it becomes obvious that the range of targets discussed in this chapter goes way beyond what is 'normally' considered in workplace violence discourse. Therefore, in the context of this chapter the main focus will be on the various acts of violence occurring to those most at risk – the aged and mentally ill – by staff who provide direct care, such as carers in aged-care settings, nurses and medical practitioners.

The literature shows that most of the research on staff-initiated violence is towards the elderly and therefore has different characteristics compared to other forms of workplace violence. For example, unlike other studies into workplace violence the victims in this context are generally elderly women, in ill health, residing in an aged-care facility. Conlin Shaw (nd: 2) reported that those at high risk are women, are generally mentally impaired (dementia), have suffered a 'stroke' (CVA) or been diagnosed with Parkinson's disease. They are aged 75 years or older and highly dependent on others (Conlin Shaw nd: 2).

Hockley's (1999 cited in 2003a, 2003b) studies show that although there is the potential for patients of any age and health status to be victims of this form of violence it is the elderly and the mentally ill who are particularly at risk. Their inability to report this behaviour may be one of the reasons why these groups of people are targeted, or it may be because of their mental state, or that they are vulnerable, or because they do not have people to advocate on their behalf (Hockley 2003a).

Perpetrator's profile

There is the potential for any healthcare worker to become a perpetrator – from untrained carers to university-prepared staff (Speaks 1996; Hockley 2003a). Conlin Shaw (1998) identified certain characteristics in caregiver abusers which could equally apply to health professionals. She categorized caregiver abusers into three types – sadistic, reactive and negligent. One of the key factors identified by Conlin Shaw (in Bowie 2002b: 4) to recognize if care workers were sadistic or reactive abusers was their ability to develop psychological immunity. This derived 'from the impact of abuse by residents that allow staff to resist to responding to abuse in ways detrimental to the residents or themselves. It is a self-protecting mind-set that permits them to continue to work ... staff members who develop and sustain immunity tend to feel good about the outcomes of their work ...' (Conlin Shaw 1998 in Bowie 2002b: 4).

According to Conlin Shaw, sadistic abusers methodically and repeatedly abuse residents, are not remorseful, are incapable of developing this immunity and often deny or blame others for their abusive behaviours. In comparison, reactive abusers are 'unable to control their impulses, lose their immunity suddenly and without thinking. They react negatively towards the resident with impulsive, almost instinctive reactions, often related to invasion of their personal body space' (Conlin Shaw 1998: 8–9).

Some of the factors that may influence the development, maintenance or loss of psychological immunity are identified in Table 5.2 below.

Table 5.2 Factors influencing psychological immunity

- Life experiences
- Work satisfaction
- Financial stress
- Physical and emotional fatigue
- Substance abuse
- Domestic problems

Source: Conlin Shaw (nd: 3)

Care workers who are stressed and overburdened with work because of organizational factors such as inadequate staffing, exhausted staff or poor work environment may intentionally neglect those in their care. These factors may cause neglect because care workers take short cuts to get work done and are unwilling to deal with difficult residents (Speaks 1996; Conlin Shaw 1998).

Nurses in Hockley's (1999 cited in 2003a: 67) study identified how nurses deal with difficult patients as follows:

There are patients who are victimised because the nurses find them so difficult... Patients who smell [because of their] fungating wounds. On one level, nurses may pity them and on another, they avoid them. I think victimisation in terms of nurses to patient, is usually avoidance.

Table 5.3 presents the characteristics of abusive caregivers as identified by Conlin Shaw.

Table 5.3 Abusive caregivers' characteristics

- Abuse often present before illness.
- Least socially integrated adult in family.
- Arrests, hospitalizations for mental illness, violent behaviour or limited health problems.
- Alcoholism and/or drug abuse.
- Poor emotional reserve and coping skills (Pillemer and Finklehor 1989).
- Most significant factor for physical abuse was alcohol use by caregiver and abuse by victim (Homer and Gilleard 1990).
- Unrealistic, hypercritical, demanding, and rigid.

Source: Conlin Shaw (nd: 2)

Conlin Shaw (1998) perceives neglect as a separate issue compared to the other two types of abuse – sadistic and reactive. Table 5.4 outlines specific characteristics of neglect.

Table 5.4 Characteristics of neglect

- Life-threatening and difficult to detect.
- Is the main type of mistreatment (*Source*: 55 per cent in Movasas and Movasas 1990).
- There are multi-causes such as education, ability, cognitive decline, depression and anxiety.
- Caregiver stress is a major factor in passive neglect.

Source: Conlin Shaw (nd: 3)

Conceptualizing perpetrators and the meaning of the language used to describe and discuss them is an integral part of the phenomenon. For example, describing a perpetrator can range from general statements – 'constant critic' – to metaphorical – 'two-headed snake' (Namie and Namie 2003) – to emotionally loaded terms such as 'killers', 'murderer', or 'angels of death' (Hampson 2003).

There is also another category of perpetrator – management – who may cause harm to those in their 'indirect care' by having a culture and processes that are in contravention of the patient's human rights. For example, the organizational culture may be discriminatory in accessing healthcare, or may have policies that violate the rights of the patient or may have practices that could be perceived as torture, such as some medical procedures, unethical research practices (The Health Rights 2004) and professional opportunism (Smith 2002). They may be organizations who recruit inappropriate staff, or do not maintain standards (Kendrick and Taylor 2000) or have a culture that does not support staff who are experiencing stressors in their personal or professional life, which in turn may lead to them being violent (Hockley 2003a). Conlin Shaw (in Bowie 2002b: 4) 'lays much of the blame for abuse and neglect by staff on the financially driven medical model with productivity and efficiency as its primary goals rather than caring and human relationships.'

Types of staff-initiated violence

One of the most difficult aspects of defining workplace violence is to change the perception of most people to recognize that violence has non-physical qualities as well as physical aspects. Moreover, when discussing the non-physical qualities of violence, the acts are often perceived as 'invisible' because it is more difficult to prove that they occurred compared to physical violence.

Non-physical types

Many of the non-physical types of violence experienced by those requiring care are similar to those that are experienced in other contexts, such as acts of neglect, abuse of power, humiliation and intimidation. Hockley (2003a) found that the more high risk the area was for patients to be abused and the more disempowered they were, the more overt the acts became. That is, the greater the power disparity, such as in aged-care and mental health, the greater the potential for abuse (Hockley 2003a). For example, in Hockley's (2003a) study a participant discussed how one nurse treated mentally ill patients. The nurse reported that a nurse 'intimidated the patients, because they were chronic long term patients ... just made all these remarks about them [patients] to make them perform, to make them perform in the way that he thought it was funny' (Hockley 2003a: 66).

Speaks' (1996) study, researched while working undercover as a nurse's aide in a private nursing home, highlighted the various forms of neglect he saw. He noted that 'some of the call bells did not work, with some even having exposed wiring. Some of the residents' urine smelled of ammonia and their stools were very dark ... indicating possible dehydration' (Speaks 1996: 39). Other areas of abuse reported by Speaks included residents with severe decubitus ulcers (pressure area sores), wound dressings unchanged for days and wounds left exposed for long periods of time (Speaks 1996: 39–41). Other cases reported about nurses causing harm to their patients include 'two senior nurses at a ... nursing home, who order baths of diluted kerosene for more than 50 residents' (Cauchi 2002: 1).

However, there are also incidents of nurses acting unprofessionally in low-risk areas, such as in acute general hospitals, where patients were targeted by nurses by withholding analgesics, or allowing patients' meals to go cold, or by leaving incontinent patients wet or soiled for long periods of time (Hockley 2003a).

It is noteworthy that when a person is targeted the perpetrator may use a range of non-physical and physical forms of violence. Furthermore, the perpetrator may escalate their violence, beginning with non-physical types of neglect and gradually extending this neglect to a physical form leading to the death of the patient (Speaks 1996).

Physical types of violence

The physical aspects of violence are similar to those which occur in other contexts ranging from physical abuse to homicide. However, what often makes this form of violence different from that which occurs in society are the perpetrators. In a survey of 34 serial murders in the USA, six were nurses (Hickey 1991). Hampson (2003: 1) talks about nurses as the 'least likely of criminals committing the most heinous of crimes'. He continues, 'nurses who, instead of leading patients to health, usher them to the grave. However, over the past three decades, serial killer nurses have become increasingly common – or perhaps just increasingly obvious' (Hampson 2003: 1).

Two very highly publicized cases of physical violence were from the USA and the UK. The USA case study involved a registered nurse charged with murdering a patient. He was reported to have told police that 'he used drugs to kill up to 40 other seriously ill patients in nine hospitals since 1987. He said he wanted to put them out of misery' (Hampson 2003: 1). The second case study involves a British physician, Dr Shipman, who was convicted in 2000 of killing 15 patients but a 'government inquiry that examined nearly 500 deaths concluded that he had killed at least 215' (Hampson 2003: 1).

An Australian doctor abused patient trust by having unprotected sex, despite the known risk of transmission of HIV. He received a four-year jail sentence (R. v *Dirckze* County Court Victoria, 13 August 1999, Anderson, J. in Smith 2002).

Although the focus above has been on healthcare workers, nurses and medical officers, this does not imply that other health professionals are not accused of physical violence, such as the radiographer who used an ultrasound procedure for his own sexual gratification (R. v *Mobilio* [1991] 1 VR 339, Victorian Criminal Court of Appeal in Smith 2002).

Causes and methods

What causes staff to target those in their care may be similar to other contexts but the methods they use make these violent acts very different to other forms of workplace violence.

Causes

At times, the perpetrators are victims themselves and then in turn become perpetrators reacting to a given situation (Engel 2004). A first-year registered nurse in Hockley's (2003a: 70) study stated, 'I think nurses are not really violent people but I think that nurses are (pause) something that happens which make nurses change.' Along similar lines, Engel (2004) reported that although staff members may not start out by being abusive, nor do they mean to be, there is a build-up of tension that causes them to be abusive towards patients. At times, both caregivers and patients are caught in the middle, with staff becoming frantic with so many demands made on them by patients and supervisors that at times they feel exploited (Engel 2004). Another factor that allows healthcare workers to behave in this manner is because of their position of power, by taking advantage of the situation and breaking the trusting relationship.

The causes of some of the more serious forms of physical violence that have resulted in the deaths of patients range from financial gain (Smith 2002) to psychological instabilities. For example, a UK general practitioner admitted at his trial that of the 400 patients he might have assisted in 'easing their passing', he was mentioned in 132 of their wills (Kinnell 2000). One nurse convicted of six counts of murder in 1999 was sick of complaining patients (Hampson 2003), while another nurse in 1984 apparently enjoyed watching babies going into cardiac arrest (Hampson 2003). Some health professionals killed for 'organs' (Kinnell 2000) and for some it was 'because they can' (Hampson 2003). Some health professionals who kill are motivated by 'Munchausen syndrome by proxy', a psychological disorder attributed to those who create medical emergencies in those under their care in order to draw attention to themselves (Hampson 2003).

Some of the serial killers have claimed a variety of medical conditions, such as the case of Cullen, an American nurse whose defence argued he suffered from a disassociative disorder, had previously attempted to commit suicide and had undergone treatment for depression (Coscarelli 2003). Another suggestion is that the incidence of serial homicide among doctors may indicate 'a pathological interest in the power of life and death' (Stark 2001). Stark suggests that although all paths of life have individuals with the potential to murder, the key additional difference with health professionals is that they have the opportunity as well.

Methods

The methods that doctors and nurses have used have mainly involved drugs such as curare (Kinnell 2000), lignocaine (lidocaine) (Wilson and Seaman 1992), *Oxycotin* (reported in *New York Times* 2002), sodium pentothal (cited in Kinnell 2000), digoxin and insulin (Coscarelli 2003), and muscle relaxant (Coscarelli 2003).

Wilson and Seaman (1992) report on a nurse in the USA who was sentenced to the gas chamber in 1984 for murdering 12 patients with lignocaine (lidocaine). One US doctor convicted of manslaughter in the deaths of four patients who overdosed on the painkiller *Oxycotin* testified that the patients lied to him about their symptoms and would not have died if they had taken the drug as prescribed (*New York Times* 2002).

Medical practitioners and nurses care for patients who are often very sick, very old or very young, and have access to drugs powerful enough to kill unobtrusively through an intravenous tube (Hampson 2003: 2). It is easier to target certain victims by the circumstances of location (in bed and out of sight of nursing stations), time and lack of supervision (evening and night shifts), and ease of administration (intravenous therapy) (Stark *et al.* 1997). For example, a registered nurse while working on night duty in an aged-care facility secluded a resident in his room for a number of hours during the night ... (Nurses Board of South Australia (NBSA) 2004:36).

These examples are not unique to the USA, UK or Australia. A Norwegian doctor is reported to have possibly killed as many as 138 of his patients using curare over a five-year period in the late 1970s (Kinnell 2000). A recent Swedish study (Strand, Benzein and Saveman 2004: 506) reported that '35 per cent of 122 respondents admitted they had been implicated in or witnessed a violent incident towards an adult person with intellectual disabilities and 14 per cent of the staff members admitted they themselves had been perpetrators'. The same authors reported that 'physical violence was most frequently reported. Most of the aggression occurred in helping situations when persons with intellectual disabilities did not cooperate or when both actors reacted with violence' (Strand *et al.* 2004: 506).

The extent of the problem

Although the extent of the problem may be difficult to define, it is possible to demonstrate that this violence occurs through various legal reports (Wallace 2001; Di Martino 2002), research (Ramsey-Klawsnik 1995; Hockley 2003a) and professional regulatory bodies (NBSA 2004). For example, the NBSA reported that 'complaints about nurses, including violence against patients, average 100 each year' (Kemp 2004: 15). These complaints included nurses who were 'reprimanded and fined for hitting a patient 12 to 15 times on the head and another nurse being reprimanded for removing a patient's call bell' (Kemp 2004: 15).

One USA State study reports that 'mistreatment of adults, including abuse, neglect and exploitation, affects more than 1.8 million older Americans' (Pavlik *et al*. 2001). Although perpetrators by profession or employment were not identified in this study, the authors reported that 'women are 40% to 300% more likely than men to be reported for abuse/ neglect by others, depending on the age group ... as people age and become frailer, their risk of experiencing abuse, neglect or exploitation increases' (Pavlik *et al*. 2001: 47–8).

Much mistreatment of the elderly is of a non-physical nature, making it very difficult to gather data on the extent of the problem compared to the physical nature of violence, in particular homicide cases.

In the USA, extreme incidents of violence – homicide – were almost unheard of before 1970, when four cases were reported (Hampson 2003). In the 1980s 12 homicides and in the 1990s 14 homicides were reported. However, in the first three years of the 21st century acts of homicide have increased alarmingly to such a degree that five cases have been reported already (Hampson 2003). The media has covered many of these cases and in some instances it may be the first time the public has been made aware that this type of violence does occur.

Addressing the problem

Most countries with occupational health and safety (OHS) legislation include in their jurisdiction a general provision requiring employers to have a 'duty of care' by taking reasonable precautions to protect the health and safety of their employees. This provision includes protecting employees from the risk of workplace violence and extends to those in their care such as patients.

National agencies, such as the US National Institute for Occupational Safety and Health (NIOSH), the Canadian Centre for Occupational Health and Safety, the European Agency for Safety and Health at Work, and the UK Health and Safety Executive (HSE), have been created with a range of roles from publicity to education and training, as well as enforcement of the various Acts relating to OHS.

Although there are provisions in place to deal with physical violence and harassment based on equal opportunity principles of race and sex, for example, there is a growing need to emphasize particular problems posed

by psychological violence in the workplace (Hoel 2004). Some countries such as Belgium and France are introducing new special legislation to deal with this problem, and countries such as Ireland and the UK are dealing with this issue through existing legislation (Di Martino *et al.* in Hoel 2004).

Although specific legislation may not include workplace bullying and non-physical violence *per se,* there has been a plethora of strategies proposed to address this issue (for example, WHO 2003). Some researchers and practitioners, for example, concentrate on education, training and research (Hockley 2003b), or on organizational responses (Sheehan 2002). Others see advantages in human resource processes (Hosie, Forster and Sevastos 2002), occupational health and safety perspectives (Mayhew and Chappell 2001) or in developing a global database of convicted health professionals (Oliver 2000). However, a perspective that could be particularly promising in addressing staff-initiated violence against those in their care is the legal perspective. Professional negligence or malpractice 'is perhaps the area of greatest legal importance for health care workers as it provides the most common reason for legal action against them' (Wallace 2001: 185).

It is important to note here that taking legal action to address staff-initiated violence against those in their care has both advantages and disadvantages. An advantage is that it is one way of making the individual and the organization accountable for their actions because of the strong legal framework in place. One of the disadvantages with this approach is the difficulty of obtaining the necessary evidence in abuse cases in aged-care and mental health facilities because the age of the victims, their medical and mental condition may compromise their ability to describe and testify about their treatment.

In the context of this chapter, it is not possible to cover every legal action an individual or organization could take in situations of violence initiated by staff towards patients in part because each country would have its own unique legal system. Therefore, the following is a general discussion restricted to legally regulated systems, and although the following four step model, adapted from Smith (2002), may appear straightforward many of these systems and regulatory responses overlap.

Step 1: Conciliation

Many countries have a statutory health complaint agency whose function it is to respond to and investigate patient complaints. At times, through conciliation complaints may be resolved with an apology or the payment of a sum of money to the complainant. However, if conciliation fails, the agency may refer the complaint to the registration body for disciplinary action (Smith 2002) as outlined below.

	Systems	Sanctions
Step 4	Criminal action	Custodial action Fines/Non-custodial
Step 3	Disciplinary action	Licensing restrictions/de-registered
Step 2	Civil action	Compensation (e.g. financial or emotional)
Step 1	Conciliation	Apology/explanation/payment/refer to registering body

Figure 5.1 Four-step regulatory systems and sanctions for staff-initiated violence against those in their care (adapted from Smith 2002)

Steps 2, 3 and 4: civil, disciplinary and criminal action

These three terms distinguish the different aspects of legal relations between groups and individuals in society, and with society itself represented by the state. To see how these actions could be used in a professional situation, consider the hypothetical case of a nurse who is attacked by a patient and the nurse retaliates, causing the patient life-threatening and long-term injuries. The following legal actions are possible from the nurse's perspective.

Civil action

To take action in the legal sense is to seek to enforce resolution of a right, to seek redress for a wrong, to punish or to deter. A civil action occurs

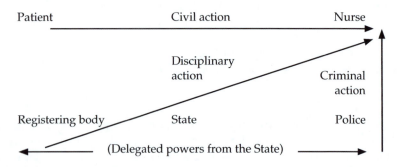

Figure 5.2 A map of the legal possibilities in a hypothetical situation
Note: A criminal action, if launched, would take precedence over the civil action. The disciplinary action could depend upon the outcome of the criminal action.

when one person seeks redress or compensation for wrongs committed by another party, such as in medical malpractice. Smith (2002: 8) reports 'consumers of professional services who have suffered loss as a result of unprofessional conduct may commence civil proceedings for damages in negligence, trespass or breach of contract.' If successful, civil proceedings provide 'a financial sum to successful claimants, which aims to place them in the same position they would have been in, had the wrongful act not taken place. Normally, an award of damages aims at compensation rather than punishment' (Collis 1996 in Smith 2002).

Disciplinary action

In society many professions, such as medicine and nursing, have regulatory or statutory bodies that exercise powers delegated under legislation such as, in Australia, the Medical Practitioners Act 1983 (SA), s5 and the Nurses Act 1984 (SA), s3. In the United Kingdom there are, for example, the Medical Practitioners Act, 1927, the Medical (Professional Performance) Act 1995 (c.51), and the Nursing and Midwifery Council (NMC), an organization set up by Parliament to ensure nurses, midwives and health visitors provide appropriate standards of care to their patients and clients. In Canada there are similar Acts and regulations such as the Nurses (Registration) Act [RSBC 1996] Chapter 335, and the Canadian Medical Act, RSC 1952. In the United States of America there are, for example, the California Nurses Practice Act (NPA), which empowers the Board of Registered Nursing to set out the scope of practice and responsibilities for registered nurses, and the Office of Professional Medical Conduct (OPMC), New York State Department of Health. These various regulatory and statutory bodies maintain professional and ethical standards through a range of disciplinary powers and sanctions. For both nurses and medical practitioners the law provides that 'unprofessional misconduct' includes improper or unethical conduct, incompetence or negligence in relation to practice, as well as a code of conduct and professional standards endorsed by their respective boards (Wallace 2001). For example, the Office of Professional Medical Conduct (OPMC), New York State Department of Health, which is responsible for investigating complaints about physicians, physician assistants and specialist assistants, can under relevant New York Statute laws such as the Public Health Law, Section 230, prescribe penalties for professional misconduct, such as a physician 'wilfully harassing, abusing, or intimidating a patient either physically or verbally' (OPMC 2004:6).

Criminal action

A criminal action, in contrast, could arise when the behaviour of a person in society is considered of such a serious nature that the State uses its powers to punish or deter that behaviour, such as in cases of homicide, for example, the cases regarding Dr Shipman from the UK and the pending case involving Charles Cullen, a nurse in the USA.

Organizational response

The question that arises is what should an organization do in incidents of physical and non-physical violence. The actions available to the patient are not always acceptable to the organization and/or the employees. Except in known cases of homicide reported to the coroner, or criminal acts where police are notified, staff may be unwilling to report incidents of abuse outside the organization in case they are labelled whistleblowers and put their employment at risk (De Maria 1999). In addition, the organization may be reluctant to report cases of staff-initiated violence because it has an inherent aversion to litigation and publicity (Hampson 2003: 2).

One of the reasons that legal options have not been fully considered may be because 'some hospitals don't want the public to know they had someone like this [who is being investigated for killing patients], so they sort of shove the problem aside with a dismissal ... but then the nurse gets a job somewhere else' (Ramsland in Hampson 2003: 2). For example, following an employment interview, one nurse's credentials checked out even though he was under investigation in the deaths of patients from his previous employer (Hampson 2003: 2). Such omissions show deficiencies in personnel procedures which may lead later to legal action of 'negligent hiring' and potential 'vicarious liability'.

The outcome of the reluctance to report to respective authorities allows health professionals to avoid accountability and public and professional notoriety. Furthermore, if the perpetrators are not stopped they may be unwittingly employed by other healthcare agencies. There is the potential for many more patients to be harmed while the health professional's history of unprofessional conduct goes undetected. Legislative developments regarding dismissal, references and licensing requirements have made it more difficult for organizations quietly to dismiss staff with questionable professional practices. However, the staff member may choose to leave before legal action commences, which in turn allows the organization to provide a reference for the exiting employee. This may be unethical but not illegal.

The organizational challenge is to recognize and respond to deficiencies in human resource processes such as recruitment, dismissal practices and staff development, as well as professional monitoring.

Conclusion

When an individual enters a healthcare facility they have the right to expect that they are entering a safe environment free from violence. One of the major issues of being an abused patient is that the abuse comes from staff employed to care for them. Staff violence against those in their care is an important professional issue that is under-recognized and poorly reported. The impact of this behaviour has far-reaching effects for the individual, the workplace, the community and the government.

Fortunately, it is accepted by the public that most health professionals are non-violent and caring. Unfortunately, there is a small element within the healthcare industry that exhibits violent acts towards those they care for. Furthermore, many of these acts are so horrendous, not only because of their effects, but also because they target some of the most vulnerable people in our society and because the perpetrator is often a repeat offender.

Many factors, such as the organizational culture of the workplace and inappropriately trained staff, obstruct full reporting of unprofessional conduct. Until some of these factors are addressed, such as changing the culture through education and training, and improving human resource procedures, this form of violence will continue.

Victims pay a high price for being targeted – emotionally, physically, psychologically, spiritually, socially and financially. One approach to redressing what has happened to the victims is through the legal system. Exposing even the most marginal of cases may go some way towards bringing a halt to the phenomenon of staff-initiated violence against those in their care.

References

American Nurse's Association (ANA) (2001) *Code of ethics for nurses with interpretive statements*, Washington, DC: American Nurses Publishing.

Australian Nursing Council (ANC) (2002) *Code of Ethics for Nurses in Australia*, ACT Australia, Australian Nursing Council. Now Australian Nursing and Midwifery Council (ANMC) since 2004.

Bowie, V. (2002a) 'Defining violence at work: a new typology', in M. Gill, B. Fisher, and V. Bowie (eds) *Violence at work: Causes, patterns and prevention*, Devon: Willan.

Bowie, V. (2002b) 'Workplace violence.' Speech. WorkCover, New South Wales. November. Brooks/Cole.

Bowie, V., Fisher, B.S. and Cooper. C.L. (2005) 'Introduction: new issues, trends and strategies in workplace violence'. This volume.

California Nursing Practice Act (NPA) (2004) http://www.rn.ca.gov/npa/npa.htm (Date accessed 12/12/04).

Canadian Centre for Occupational Health and Safety (2004) *Violence in the Workplace Prevention Guide.* http:/www.ccohs.ca/products/publications/violence.html (date accessed 13 July 2005).

Canadian Medical Act, RSC 1952. Section 25. http://www.cpsnb.org/english/MedicalAct/med-act-25.html (date accessed 12/12/04).

Cauchi, S. (2002) 'Kerosene bath nurses banned', *The Age.* http: //www.newsstore.theage.com.au/apps/newsSearch.ac?/index.html (date accessed 13 July 2005).

Conlin Shaw, M. (1998) 'Nursing Home Resident Abuse by Staff', *Journal of Elder Abuse and Neglect,* 9(4), pp. 1–21.

Conlin Shaw, M. (nd) Abuse and Neglect of Older Persons. http: //medinfo.ufl.edu/pa/faculty/nancy/abuse.htm (date accessed 6/8/04).

Coscarelli, K. (2003) 'Apparent admission doesn't seal Cullen case', *Star-Ledger* 21 December. Hospital deaths. p. 14 http://wawa.starledge.com

De Maria, W. (1999) *Deadly Disclosure.* Kent Town, South Australia: Wakefield Press.

Di Martino, V. (2002) 'Workplace violence in the health sector. Country Case Studies. Brazil, Bulgaria, Lebanon, Portugal, South Africa and an additional Australian study. Synthesis report of the International Labour Organisation, International Council of Nurses, World Health Organisation and Public Services', Geneva, Switzerland: International Labour Office.

Engel, F. (2004) *Taming the Beast: Getting Violence Out of the Workplace,* 2nd edition, Montreal, Canada: Ashwell.

European Agency for Safety and Health at Work. http://agency.osha.eu (date accessed 13/12/04).

Hampson, R. (2003) 'Angels of Mercy: The dark side' *USA Today,* 16/12/2003. http://www.usatoday.com (date accessed 27/1/2004).

Health and Safety Executive (HSE) (2004) *Violence at Work.* www.hse.gov.uk (date accessed 12/12/04).

Hickey, E.W. (1991) *Serial Murderers and their Victims.* Belmont, CA: Wadsworth Publishing, CA:

Hockley, C. (1999) 'Organisational Violence: An ethnomethodological perspective of nurses' experiences', PhD thesis. Faculty of Nursing, University of South Australia.

Hockley, C. (2002) 'The silent third-party victims of workplace bullying: Family members', Adelaide International Workplace Bullying Conference – Skills for survival, solutions and strategies, 20–22 February 2002, Adelaide, South Australia.

Hockley, C. (2003a) *Silent Hell: workplace violence and bullying,* Norwood, South Australia: Peacock.

Hockley, C. (2003b) 'The impact of workplace violence on third-party victims: A mental health perspective', AeJAMH (The Australian e-Journal for the Advancement of Mental Health) Vol. 2 Issue 2 (July 2003) http://auseinet.flinders.edu.au/journal/vol2iss2/index.php

Hockley, C. (2005) 'Violence in Nursing: The Expectations and the Reality', in C. Huston (ed.) *Professional Issues in Nursing: Challenges and Opportunities*, Philadelphia: Lippincott, Williams and Wilkins.

Hoel, H. (2004) 'Violence and harassment in European workplaces: trends and political responses.' Paper presented at The Fourth International Conference on Bullying and Harassment in the workplace, Bergen, Norway, June 28–29, S. Einarsen and M.B. Nielsen (eds), pp. 8–11.

Hosie, P., Forster, N. and Sevastos, P. (2002) 'Job-related affective wellbeing and intrinsic job satisfaction related to managers' performance', in L. Morrow, I. Verins and E. Willis (eds) *Mental Health and Work: Issues and Perspectives*, South Australia: Auseinet and Flinders University.

International Council of Nurses (2000a) *The ICN Code of Ethics for Nurses*. Geneva, Switzerland: ICN. http://www.icn.ch (date accessed 7/2/04).

International Council of Nurses (2000b) *Position Statement. Abuse or violence against nursing personnel*, Geneva, Switzerland: ICN.
http://www.icn.ch/psviolence00.htm (date accessed 29/1/04).

Kemp, M. (2004) 'Nursing complaints reach 100', *The Advertiser*, 22 May, p. 15.

Kendrick, A. and Taylor, J. (2000) 'Hidden on the ward: the abuse of children in hospitals,' *Journal of Advanced Nursing*, 31(3): pp. 565–73.

Kinnell, H.G. (2000) 'Serial homicide by doctors: Shipman in perspective', *British Medical Journal*, 321, pp. 1594–7.

Mayhew, C. and Chappell, D. (2001) '"Internal" Violence (Or Bullying) and the Health Workforce. Taskforce on the prevention and management of violence in the health workplace'. Discussion Paper No.1. School of Industrial Relations and Organisation Behaviour and Industrial Relations Research Centre. Working papers series. December, p. 141.

Medical (Professional Performance) Act 1995 (c.51) (1995) http://www.hmso.gov. uk/acts/acts1995.htm (date accessed 13 July 2005).

Medical Practitioners Act 1927. http://www.irishstatutebook.i.e. (date accessed 12/12/04).

Michael, R. (2003) 'Trauma in the workplace', *Nursing Review*. April, p. 17.

Namie, G. and Namie, R. (2003) *The Bully at Work*, Naperville, Illinois: Sourcebooks.

New York Times (2002) 'Doctor is sentenced for Oxycotin Deaths', *New York Times*, 23rd March. http://www.nytimes.com/2002/03/23/health/23OXYC.html (date accessed 12/77/04).

Nurses (Registered) Act [RSBC 1996] Chapter 334. http://www.qp.gov.bc.ca/ statreg/stat/tlc/edition1/tlc96335.htm (date accessed 13 July 2005).

Nurses Board of South Australia (2004) Bulletin 17. Adelaide, South Australia.

Nursing and Midwifery Council (NMC) http://www.nursingnetuk.com/ registration/NMC.html (date accessed 12/12/04).

Office of Professional Medical Conduct (OPMC), New York State Department of Health. Section 6530 (Education and Law) – Definitions of Professional Misconduct. http://www.health.state.ny.us/nysdoh/opmc/laws/6530.htm (date accessed 12/12/04).

Oliver, M. (2000) 'Serial homicide by doctors: Swango in perspective!' http://bmj. bmjjournals.com (date accessed 12/7/04).

Pavlik, V.N., Hyman, D.J., Festa, N.A. and Dyer, C.B. (2001) 'Quantifying the problem of abuse and neglect in adults – Analysis of a statewide database'. *Journal of American Geriatrics Society*, 49, 45–8.

Ramsey-Klawsnik, H. (1995) 'Investigating suspected elder abuse', *Journal of Elder Abuse and Neglect*, 7(1): pp. 41–67.

Sheehan, M. (2002) 'Workplace bullying. Organisational responses', Adelaide International Workplace Bullying Conference – Skills for survival, solutions and strategies, 20–22 February 2002, Adelaide, South Australia.

Smith, R.G. (2002) 'Regulating dishonest conduct in the professions.' Paper presented to the Current Issues in Regulation: Enforcement and Compliance Conference convened by the Australian Institute of Criminology in conjunction with the Regulatory Institutions Network, RSSS, Australian National University and the Division of Business and Enterprise, University of South Australia, Melbourne, 2–3rd September 2002.

Speaks, G.E. (1996) 'Documenting inadequate care in the nursing home: The story of an undercover agent', *Journal of Elder Abuse and Neglect*, 8(3), pp. 37–45.

Stark, C., Paterson, B., Henderson, T., Kidd, B. and Goodwin, M. (1997) 'Counting the dead'. *Nursing Times*, 93(46) pp. 34–37.

Stark, C. (2001) 'Opportunity may be more important than profession', bmj.com Rapid Responses for Kinnell, 321 (7276) 1594-1597 http://bmj.bmjjournals.com (date accessed 12/7/04).

Strand, M., Benzein, E. and Saveman, B. (2004) 'Violence in the care of adult persons with intellectual disabilities'. *Journal of Clinical Nursing*, 13, pp. 506–14.

The Health Rights (2004) 'The link between health and human rights', *Physicians for Human Rights*. http://www.phrusa.org/healthrights/link.html (date accessed 27/3/04).

Wallace, M. (2001) *Healthcare and the Law*, 3rd edition, NSW: Lawbook.

Wilson, C. and Seaman, D. (1992) *The Serial Killers*, London: Virgin.

World Health Organization (WHO) (2003) Department of injuries and violence prevention Annual Report 2002, Geneva, Switzerland: WHO.

Chapter 6

Domestic violence and the workplace: do we know too much of nothing?

Bonnie S. Fisher and Corinne Peek-Asa

Issues surrounding domestic violence and the workplace are usually considered as independent phenomena. Our personal and work lives, however, are increasingly intermixed; factors affecting one aspect of our lives invariably will affect another. An all-too-common lead story found in our news media – 'current spouse commits heinous acts against his loved one at work' – has helped to garner widespread public concern in the United States that domestic violence and the workplace do inter-mingle, sometimes with a deadly outcome (for cross-national perspective, see Di Martino 2005).

Several studies have documented that domestic violence victims are in fact at risk in a variety of circumstances and places, including the work environment (Duhart 2001; Warchol 1998). Equally alarmingly, research has shown that those victims who are actively trying to leave violent relationships are at an increased risk of being attacked or stalked by the perpetrator (Campbell, *et al.* 2003; Tjaden and Thoennes 1998). The workplace offers a predictable setting for the estranged partner to encounter the victim because the victim's work site and schedule are known to the perpetrator and, in many cases, the work site is accessible to the public regardless of the occupation, employer or location.

Many acts of domestic violence are committed outside the boundaries of the workplace. Even so, their negative effects permeate into the labour market. Over and above the toll that the immediate bruises and broken teeth or bones have on job tardiness and attendance and health costs, studies have shown that domestic violence victims experience low morale and diminished productivity while on the job and are more likely to have experienced unemployment compared to non-victims (Farmer and Tiefenthaler, 2003; Lloyd 1997; Lloyd and Tatuc 1999). Collectively, these adverse effects can lead to deleterious consequences for other employees and ultimately undercut work productivity, quality and annual profit.

Given the growing number of persons who are working worldwide, employers, managers, supervisors, human resources departments, unions and co-workers need to recognize that violent personal relationships, in particular those involving intimate partners, are one of many potential external and internal threats that pose a serious workplace hazard. Workplace security plans often address external threats from robbers, terrorists, disgruntled past employees or clients. Less frequently, however, do they consider the potential for inter-personal violent offenders to enter the workplace. Workplace security plans often fail to account for the various means by which access is possible, including telephone, fax and e-mail in addition to a personal appearance. Even more infrequently, workplace security plans fail to recognize that it can be the employee who is the perpetrator of the inter-personal violence.

A unique feature of the work environment is that it is subject to statutory and contractual controls and court decisions that are not applicable to non-work settings. For example, employers are required to protect workers from hazards under the OSHA General Duty Clause. Many other more specific requirements and guidelines related to specific hazards exist. As a result, there are opportunities for education, prevention and intervention that can have important benefits both within and outside the workplace.

This chapter critically examines the current body of research and recommendations about workplace domestic violence in the United States. The first section presents an overview of the extent and effects of domestic violence in the workplace by focusing on three key topics. First, we present statistics documenting that domestic-related homicide, sexual and physical assault, and stalking spill over into the workplace. Second, we discuss the measurement limitations inherent in the current domestic-related workplace violence data collection systems. Third, we provide a summary of the research showing the negative toll domestic violence has on victims, perpetrator-employees and co-workers, while increasing legal obligations and healthcare costs for employers and, ultimately, undercutting profits. In the second section, we discuss the strengths and limitations of key current recommendations for reducing the threat and incidence of domestic violence within the workplace. Here we present the results from our content analysis of web-based domestic violence in the workplace information and recommendations that are publicly available.

We conclude by discussing the gaps in our knowledge about these issues, with a particular focus on the gaps in the identification and prevention of and response to domestic violence by employers and their organizations.

The scope of the problem: the extent of workplace domestic violence and related measurement issues

A perennial question arises in any discussion of issues surrounding the nexus of domestic violence* and the workplace: how many violent acts are perpetrated by intimates each year in a workplace or during the course of work? This is a question that no one government agency, private firm or research study can answer with certainty. However, several data sources can shed some light on the frequency of workplace domestic violence.

The extent of workplace domestic violence

Although incomplete, broader surveillance efforts for workplace illness and injury and for violent events can provide some information. With approximately 140 million employees in the United States working around-the-clock, seven-days-a-week, it is not a surprise that many experience violent acts while on the job. Workplace violence has been one of the leading causes of occupational death since the Bureau of Labor Statistics began the Census of Fatal Occupational Injuries in 1992 (Bureau of Labor Statistics 2004). However, following trends in general violent crime and intimate partner violence, workplace homicides have decreased dramatically since their peak in 1994 and remained rather steady from 1999 to 2003 (Rennison 2001; Fox and Zawitz 2004).

Men and women are not equally likely to be workplace homicide victims. In 2003, women comprised 47 per cent of the total labour force, yet they were at a disproportionately high risk for workplace homicide (http://www.dol.gov/wb/welcome.html, 2004). While homicides comprise 10 per cent of all occupational fatalities among males, they comprise 27 per cent among women (http://www.bls.gov/news.release/cfoi.t04.htm).

*For this chapter, domestic violence will be defined as a pattern of behaviour between two heterosexual or same-sex partners in which one partner (or possibly both) uses emotional or psychological abuse, economic abuse, sexual or physical violence, threats, stalking, cyberstalking or other harassing behaviour to control, intimidate or coerce the other partner in the relationship. Homicide is also included. A partner includes a spouse, ex-spouse, boyfriend/girlfriend, ex-boyfriend/ex-girlfriend, or date. This type of workplace violence is an example of relationship violence (Type 3) found in Bowie's expanded workplace violence typology (see Bowie, this volume).

Each year, an estimated 1,200 women and 400 men are killed by their intimate partner (Federal Bureau of Investigation 2004). Given the sheer number of women and men who work, it is quite likely that some of these homicides will happen in the workplace. In fact, each year approximately 3 per cent of workplace homicides are known to be perpetrated by an intimate partner. Of the workplace homicides committed by an intimate, 62 per cent were committed by a husband (n = 122) and 37 per cent were committed by a boyfriend (n = 72). Far fewer homicides, 2 per cent (n = 3), were committed by a wife (Rugala and Isaacs 2004; 42).

According to NCVS data, an annual average of over 1.7 million workplace violent victimizations (i.e. rape, sexual assault, robbery and simple and aggravated assault) occur each year. A larger proportion of female employees experienced rape and sexual assault than men (80 per cent compared to 20 per cent, respectively) (Duhart 2001). In contrast, a larger proportion of male employees were robbed (70 per cent versus 30 per cent), and assaulted (71 per cent versus 29 per cent for aggravated assault and 69 per cent versus 36 per cent for simple assault). Intimate partners (i.e. current or former spouse or boyfriend/girlfriend) were reported to be the perpetrators in an average of 1.1 per cent of these violent acts each year, yielding an estimate of approximately 19,000 workplace violence victimizations by intimates each year.

The National Violence Against Women (NVAW) study reported that women are significantly more at risk of being assaulted by an intimate partner than are men (Tjaden and Thoennes 1998). To illustrate, 25 per cent of the women reported being raped and/or physically assaulted by an intimate partner in their lifetime compared to 8 per cent of the men. Along the same lines, women reported being victims in 85 per cent of the 790,000 intimate partner victimizations reported by the NCVS in 1999 (Rennison 2001).

Looking at workplace-specific results, data from the 1987–92 NCVS confirm that a larger per cent of female employees were victimized by an intimate than their male counterparts. Five per cent of the women victimized at work were attacked by a current or former spouse or boyfriend, compared to 1 per cent of the men (Bachman 1994). Supportive of these national-level results, a small pilot study of working battered women in New York City revealed that as many as 74 per cent had been harassed by an abusive partner face to face or over the telephone on the job (Friedman and Couper 1987).

These estimates, however, are likely to underestimate drastically the extent of the domestic violence and workplace nexus for several reasons. As we discuss further below, coding schemes may fail to identify an intimate partner homicide as being work-related, even if it occurs in the workplace. In addition to coding problems within established data sources, many violent incidents that happen while on the job go unreported to the police or to other work-related officials (Duhart 2001). Reasons for not reporting include concern over loss of employment, as well as worries about stigma, embarrassment and judgement about experiencing domestic violence.

Measurement issues

While there are data systems that can be used to identify work-related deaths (e.g. Bureau of Labour Statistics Census of Fatal Occupational Injuries), work injuries resulting from being victimized (e.g. Employer's Reports of Injury and Illness or OSHA logs), homicides (e.g. Federal Bureau of Investigations Supplemental Homicide File) and violent victimizations (e.g. National Crime Victimization Survey, NCVS), none of these sources was specifically designed to identify the intersection between domestic violence and the workplace or while at work. This inability to measure workplace domestic violence is, in part, because of two basic measurement limitations inherent in the objectives of the existing databases. First, the reporting systems that collect occupational safety and health information include all types of work-related illnesses and injuries. They rarely identify the victim-offender relationship because only the violent events, which are usually a small proportion of the events collected, involve a perpetrator. The California Occupational Safety and Health Administration developed a classification scheme to identify workplace violence by the perpetrator's relationship to the business (California Department of Occupational Safety and Health 1995). This classification includes a category for interpersonal violence, which includes violence perpetrated by employees as well as personal acquaintances. This scheme has been modified to include a category exclusively for workplace violence perpetrated by a personal acquaintance of the victim (Peek-Asa *et al.* 1997), and this modified system could be adapted to serve most data-collection systems.

The second reporting systems are designed to describe violent events, and therefore have information on victim-perpetrator relationships. However, these typically have not utilized a sample drawn from the labour force and also do not always identify if the event was work-related or occurred in a place of work. For example, the NCVS incident-level reports do identify the victim-offender relationship (e.g. spouse, boyfriend). However, the NCVS estimates are based on a probability sample of housing units and not from a sample drawn from employed individuals. Hence, its annual estimates of domestic violence in the workplace have high sampling variation. Among the consequences of these two measurement limitations is that our current reporting systems in the US may under-recognize acts involving intimate partners, and hence, underestimate the extent of domestic violence that occurs in the workplace.

The effects, consequences and costs of domestic violence on the workplace

Research has documented that there are a number of negative consequences from domestic violence experiences that permeate the work environment. Although this body of research is in its infancy, a clear theme is emerging: the effects of domestic violence collectively impact the safety and wellbeing of many parties – the abused employee, the perpetrator employee, co-workers and the organization.

The effects of domestic violence on the abused employee at work

Experiencing domestic violence takes a severe toll on the physical and mental health of its victims. Research has consistently reported that domestic violence is associated with a host of short- and long-term problems, including physical injuries from bruises to concussions, psychological symptoms such as fear, depression, fatigue, suicidal thoughts and post-traumatic stress disorder, and conditions such as chronic pain or high blood pressure (Burgess and Crowell 1996).

Workplace-focused studies confirm that domestic violence has negative effects on the victim's job performance. Many domestic violence victims miss days of work or are tardy due to the physical and psychological abuse their bodies endure. Friedman and Couper (1987) interviewed 50 working women who were victims of domestic violence and found that they were late for work five times a month, 28 per cent left work early at least five days a month, 54 per cent missed at least five full days of work a month, and 20 per cent lost their jobs. In a comparable study, Shepard and Pence (1988) found that although 58 per cent were working at the time of the study, the battered women reported that their work performance was severely compromised because of the physical abuse that they had experienced. A 1997 national study reported that 24 per cent of women between the ages of 18 and 64 years old who had experienced domestic violence indicated that the abuse caused them to arrive late at work or miss days of work (as cited in www.endabuse/org 2004). Overall, Farmer and Tiefenthaler (2003) estimated that there are between 3 million (using NVCS data) and 7 million (using NVAW data) lost work days per year, with a lower bound estimate of losses of $192 million shared by the victims and their employers.

The examination of the relationship of domestic violence and women's employment has also uncovered several significant results. First, abused women may lose their jobs or earn lower wages as a consequence of their violent experiences and the resulting absenteeism or poor performance (Farmer and Tiefenthaler, 2003; Lloyd 1997; Lloyd and Taluc 1999). Second, contrary to expectations, two studies reported that domestic violence does not reduce women's labour force participation. Using three national-level data sets to build game theoretic models, Farmer and Tiefenthaler (2003) showed that domestic violence has a positive effect on labour market participation. In other words, abused women are more likely to work than women who are not abused. Lloyd's (1997; 1999) interviews with and survey of randomly selected women in a Chicago neighbourhood echo Farmer and Tiefenthaler's results: women who experienced intimate partner violence were employed at a rate that was not significantly different from women who were not abused. One explanation is that abused women work to maintain or regain economic independence. Another reason could be that abused women feel safer at work than at home, although the workplace domestic violence research suggests that this may not always be true for some women.

The abused employee's legal rights

Working abused women face additional work-related issues: taking time off work to participate in criminal proceedings or secure a civil restraining or protection order. Understanding that the abused is fearful of being fired because of the missed time at work, 27 state legislatures (and the Virgin Islands) have passed statutes 'that make it illegal for an employer to fire or otherwise discriminate against a crime victim for taking time off to testify in criminal court' (NOW Legal Defense and Education Fund 2001). There is much variation in these laws, which range from those that require employers to give a day off for the employee-victim to attend the court proceedings to those that generally require employers to make a 'reasonable' accommodation within the employment context to help the victim address the abuse (Legal Momentum 2004). Fifteen additional states 'encourage employers to cooperate with employees who were victimized by crime', but do not require employers to permit employee victims time off from work to testify (NOW Legal Defense and Education Fund 2001).

Recently, the legality of state-level legislation to protect abused employees has been challenged in the courts (Weiser and Widiss 2004). In a precedent-setting case, a Massachusetts Superior Court ruled that a reporter, Sophia Apessos, was wrongfully terminated by her former employer, Memorial Press Group, when she took time off from her job to obtain a permanent abuse prevention order against her abusive husband (*Apessos v. Memorial Press Group*, No. 01-1474-A 2002). The court sent a strong message to employers in Massachusetts when it wrote that Memorial Press Group's decision to fire Ms Apessos 'violates the Commonwealth's clearly defined public policy to promote health, physical safety, and economic self-sufficiency of individuals victimized by domestic violence'. (www. legalmomentum.org/issues/vio/complaint-Apessos,pdf,p.2).

The process of obtaining a civil restraining or protection order has not been awarded the same legal protection as participation in criminal proceedings. Just over a handful of states and even fewer municipalities have laws that protect domestic violence victims who take time off work to obtain a civil order. Close to 20 states have adopted laws or proposed bills that allow employers to apply for restraining orders to prevent violence, harassment or stalking against their employees that can be carried out in the worksite (NOW Legal Defense and Education Fund 2004). In addition, the Victims' Economic Security and Safety Act (VESSA) is currently pending before US Congress (S. 1249; H.R. 2670). VESSA would require private employers to provide support and protection to employed victims of domestic violence and encourage employers to address domestic violence in the workplace, including co-worker issues. Included in proposed legislation are provisions for unpaid emergency leave, eligibility for unemployment insurance, and protection from employment and insurance discrimination for victims of domestic, sexual and dating violence and stalking. It also would establish a clearing house to promote model workplace guidelines, programmes and polices, and a tax credit to employers who implement initiatives to create a safe and supportive work environment (see also NOW Legal Defense and Education Fund 2004).

The impact of perpetrator-employee on the job

The behaviour of the perpetrator-employee who uses job-related resources to execute his/her abuse against a partner has been given very limited attention by researchers. A recent study sponsored by the Maine Department of Labor and Family Crisis Services interviewed participants in domestic abuse intervention programmes in six cities (Reckitt and Fortman 2004). Participants were asked how they used job-related resources to facilitate their abusive behaviour against a partner and how their behaviour affected workplace safety and health, productivity and lost work time.

Their results confirmed what many domestic violence advocates have been articulating: domestic violence offenders use work time and resources to manipulate and intimidate their partner. Eighty-five per cent reported that they had used company resources to contact their partner while on the job. Seventy-seven per cent used the company phone and 24 per cent used the company cell phone to check up on, pressure, threaten or express remorse/anger to the victimized partner. A quarter of the abusers used the company's car during working hours to drive to the victim's residence.

Job performance was also affected; 41 per cent of the abusers reported that their abusive behaviour towards their partner had a negative effect on their job performance. When on the job, nearly half (48 per cent) admitted that it caused them to have difficulty concentrating on their work because they were thinking about their relationship. Slightly fewer (19 per cent) provided anecdotes of accidents or near-miss accidents that were brought on by their abusive behaviours toward a loved one. Their abusive behaviour, while not at work resulted in over 15,000 hours of work time lost because they were in police custody.

In an attempt to hold the abuser accountable through his/her employment, the mayor of the city of Boston in 1997 issued an executive order directed at all city employees arrested for domestic violence. To lessen the risk of the effects of domestic violence both outside and inside the workplace, any city employee arrested for domestic violence is required to undergo counselling or face unpaid administrative leave (Gomstyn 2002).

The consequences for co-workers

When an employee is the target of domestic violence outside or inside the workplace, other employees can suffer too. If a domestic violence event does occur within a workplace, security fears may become an issue for other employees. If there is public knowledge of a violent event, this fear can extend to customers and clients as well. Even without an actual event, domestic violence that is unaddressed within a workplace can affect employees. The stresses that affect one victim, which can lead to lost individual productivity, absences and poor communication, can lead to increased stress on other workers. If problems and potential threats are talked about among employees but not formally addressed by the business leadership, morale may be affected because employee needs are not being addressed. This presents an important problem for employers because they must create an atmosphere in which potential problems are identified, and then they must ensure that steps are in place to address them.

Costs to businesses

Only recently has domestic violence become an issue on the business community's agenda, yet very few have adopted policies or developed innovative programmes to address workplace domestic violence (for exception see promising practices in 2002 National Victim Assistance Academy 2004). This seems almost contradictory as business executives and managers are well aware of the effects of domestic violence on the operation of their firm.

In a 2002 survey of 100 senior executives and managers from Fortune 1000 companies, 56 per cent were aware of employees who had experienced domestic violence. A large proportion of them believed that domestic violence took a toll on employees and this eventually had an impact on the firm. Among the harmful effects noted by a substantial proportion of respondents were psychological wellbeing of employees (60 per cent of the executives), physical safety (52 per cent), productivity (48 per cent), and attendance (42 per cent). Half of them recognized that domestic violence had a negative effect on their company's insurance and medical costs (as cited in Randel and Wells 2003).

The costs of domestic violence for businesses is staggering. Medical costs alone are high. One domestic violence victim can cost an employer, on average, $1,775 more in medical expenses than an employee who is not abused (as cited in Partnership for Prevention 2004). Medical costs coupled with a decrease in employee productivity add to the escalating costs of domestic violence. The Bureau of National Affairs estimated in 1990 that domestic violence cost firms between $3 and $5 billion in absenteeism, medical bills, employee turnover and lost productivity (Bureau of National Affairs 1990). More recently, Zorza (1994) estimated this loss to be closer to $13 billion annually. An estimated $100 million in lost wages, paid sick leave and absenteeism linked to domestic violence is also spent by businesses (as cited in Partnership for Prevention 2004).

Businesses also can incur steep costs associated with legal liability, in particular negligence, should they fail to act when domestic violence issues enter the workplace. For example, 'Courts have held companies liable for negligent hiring, negligent retention and for failure to warn because domestic violence that crosses over into the workplace may be predictable and preventable' (Braun Consulting News 2004). Businesses may incur additional legal liability under various laws governing their response to workplace domestic violence, including Occupational Safety and Health Administration regulations, the American Disabilities Act and anti-discrimination laws (Dougan 2004).

Despite the documented negative effects and escalating costs associated with workplace violence committed against one partner, little is known about the content of the information that is publicly available to employers. Examining this topic reveals much variation in the content of the information that is publicly available.

Current synopsis of publicly available information and recommendations about domestic violence in the workplace

Using two popular search engines, Google and Yahoo, we searched the Internet for publicly available documents that addressed the issue of domestic violence in the workplace and that made recommendations about different approaches to addressing the issue. We limited our search to materials that are published by organizations or agencies based in the United States. Our search included the key words 'domestic violence', 'workplace' and 'workplace violence', and we examined documents that included at least two of these three terms. We excluded documents that mentioned only one specific policy or that described a specific programme of a state government. The search yielded 19 documents that directly addressed workplace domestic violence. A list of these documents and their web addresses is included in Appendix 6.1.

The documents came from many sources and provided several perspectives. Six (31.6 per cent) of the documents were produced by federal agencies and seven (36.8 per cent) by national organizations. Unions and legal agencies were the source for three (15.8 per cent) each. The majority of documents (90 per cent) made recommendations for employers, and three of these were developed for specific types of employers (federal agencies, small businesses). One document was developed specifically for union stewards and one was developed for victims of domestic violence in any type of work setting.

We examined whether or not the documents focused on domestic violence victimization that occurred specifically within the workplace and/or victimization that occurred outside the workplace. Ten (52.6 per cent) focused on both. Five (27.8 per cent) focused only on victimization in the workplace, thus providing no information about how to assist victims in their personal lives. Three (16.7 per cent) focused only on victimization outside the workplace, thus providing no information about how employers or co-workers could assist victims while at work. One document was not specific about the location of victimization with regard to the workplace. A definition for the term 'domestic violence' was provided in only five (25.4 per cent) of the documents, and a definition for 'workplace violence' was provided by only one. Thus, there may be some conceptual differences between the documents in the intended audiences and the types of acts considered as either domestic or workplace violence.

We reviewed these documents for several points. First, we wanted to identify the types of recommendation made and see how they varied across documents. Second, we wanted to determine if the recommendations formed a complete approach to responding to domestic violence in the workplace, using general guidelines for workplace violence prevention programmes as a model. Finally, we wanted to determine if the recommendations provided were consistent across documents, especially with regard to documents that have different focuses. For example, it would be very confusing if a document recommended one course of action for an employer, while a victim-based document recommended something contradictory. To examine these issues, we did a content analysis of each of the documents.

Recommendations to prevent or intervene on domestic violence in the workplace

Table 6.1 shows the recommendations that were most commonly found in the reviewed documents. The two recommendations most frequently mentioned, both by over 70 per cent, were administrative approaches that involved offering schedule flexibility and leave options for the victim-employee.

Recognizing signs of domestic violence was commonly mentioned, but there was variation in what these signs are. The most common types of sign were related to work productivity (63.2 per cent of all documents), including absenteeism, poor work performance and frequent phone calls. Psychological signs such as changes in behaviour, inability to focus and

Table 6.1 Recommendations made to address domestic violence in the workplace

Specific recommendation	Proportion of documents making recommendation N (%)
Offer flexibility in the victim-employee work schedule	15 (79.0)
Offer leave options for the victim-employee	14 (73.7)
Train employers/managers how to talk with an employee who is a victim of domestic violence	13 (68.4)
Recognize warning signs of domestic violence victimization	
Work productivity signs	12 (63.2)
Psychological signs	10 (52.6)
Physical signs	9 (47.4)
Escort victims to parking lots or public transportation	11 (57.9)
Disseminate any domestic violence policies to managers and supervisors	9 (47.4)
Advocate for the victim to get legal services and contact law enforcement	9 (47.4)
Advocate for the victim to get in-house services, such as counselling, if available	9 (47.4)
Conduct environmental surveillance, e.g. keeping intruders easily observable, keeping areas such as parking lots visible	9 (47.4)
Develop a personal safety plan for the victim	8 (42.1)
Recognize warning signs of domestic violence perpetration	2 (10.5)

depression were mentioned by ten (52.6 per cent) documents, and physical signs such as bruising were mentioned by nine (47.4 per cent). Only two documents (10.5 per cent) mentioned training to recognize potential signs of domestic violence perpetration.

Most of the documents did not mention specifically who should be trained to identify these signs or to have knowledge of domestic violence (for example, human resources personnel, managers, executives or employees). Among documents that did mention who should receive domestic violence training, ten (53 per cent) recommended training for managers/supervisors, five (26 per cent) recommended training for human resources personnel, five (26 per cent) recommended training for all employees and three (16 per cent) mentioned training for employers.

The majority (68.4 per cent) of documents recommended that employers talk to domestic violence victims about work-related issues when victims are identified. When talking to victims, the documents mentioned the following elements: maintain confidentiality (52.6 per cent), offer potential for work relocation or shift change (47.4 per cent), do not discriminate or retaliate, and provide information on how absences from work will be handled (36.8 per cent).

It is noteworthy that there was not a single recommendation that was made in all documents. While this might be a reflection of the different audiences for the documents, it is also a reflection of the scarcity of research identifying what information needs to be communicated, for example the victim's legal rights in the organization's programmes and policies. There is also a scarcity of information about which strategies have been effective in reducing or responding to domestic violence in the workplace.

There are also other noteworthy omissions in the recommendations. For example, only four (21.1 per cent) of the documents mentioned the potential for identifying perpetrators of domestic violence in the workplace. While 16 (68.4 per cent) of the documents recommended that employers receive training in the best methods to talk with a domestic violence victim, only three (15.8 per cent) recommended such training in how to speak with a domestic violence perpetrator-employee. Since perpetrators have already exhibited violent behaviour, methods to discuss this sensitive issue with them might be an important element of training. Documents that addressed steps to take when a perpetrator was identified focused on the process of taking legal action against the perpetrator. For example, all four of the documents that addressed the potential for an employee to be a perpetrator mentioned steps for taking disciplinary action or to inform law enforcement.

All but one of the documents provided background information on domestic violence in the workplace. However, two provided references only from non-technical sources such as newspaper articles, and almost a third (31.6 per cent) provided no references at all. Nearly 32 per cent of the documents discussed the effects of domestic violence on co-workers, and 63.2 per cent discussed the benefits of employers addressing domestic violence in the workplace.

It is well known that domestic violence is a criminal offence in every state. It is, therefore, striking that only one of the documents included suggestions on how to collaborate with local law enforcement and only nine (47.4 per cent) of the documents recommended that employers learn about specific laws within their state. Equally noteworthy, especially in light of the Violence Against Women Act's focus on developing local outreach to victims of domestic violence and stalking, is that only seven (36.8 per cent) of the documents provided suggestions on how to collaborate with local organizations for services or resources and 12 (63.2 per cent) suggested making referrals to local area domestic violence centres. One suggestion was for the organization to schedule lunch programmes with speakers from local family violence shelters and programmes to raise managerial and employee awareness about the causes and effects of domestic violence. Another document encouraged employer participation as a volunteer in domestic violence shelters.

Types of recommendations made by documents from different sources

The general types of approach involved in a comprehensive workplace violence prevention programme need to include, at a minimum, the following (Howard 1996; Randel and Wells 2003):

- Conduct a hazard assessment to identify vulnerabilities within the specific workplace.

- Implement behavioural strategies, such as education and training, recognizing signs of victimization or perpetration, encouraging good communication, and advocating for services.

- Implement administrative policies, such as work accommodations for victims, policies that prohibit retaliation or discrimination against victims, requiring reporting of potential violent events, and ensuring appropriate legal response.

- Implement strategies to control the environment, including good surveillance and visibility, access control and target hardening.

As can be seen in Table 6.2, the 19 documents varied in the number and types of components that were included in their recommendations.

Table 6.2 Prevention strategies for reduction of domestic violence in the workplace

Type of prevention strategy	Proportion of documents that mentioned the type of prevention strategy			
	Federal agencies	Legal organiza- tions	National organiza- tions	Unions
	N = 6	N = 3	N = 8	N = 2
	N (%)	N (%)	N (%)	N (%)
Conduct a hazard assessment	0 (0.0)	0 (0.0)	2 (25.0)	2 (100)
Behavioural strategies	5 (83.3)	3 (100)	8 (100)	2 (100)
Administrative strategies	5 (83.3)	3 (100)	7 (87.5)	2 (100)
Environmental strategies	3 (50.0)	1 (33.3)	6 (75.0)	2 (100)
Security/law enforcement strategies	4 (66.7)	2 (66.7)	8 (100)	1 (50.0)

Conducting a needs or hazard assessment was recommended by only four of the 19 documents (21.1 per cent), none of which was a document from a federal agency or legal organization. In contrast, most documents mentioned components of behavioural (i.e. describing how-to training, reporting, etc.) and administrative (i.e. policies and procedures such as policies to report, communicate, mandate training) interventions. From 83 per cent to 100 per cent of the documents included behavioural and administrative strategies. Environmental approaches (i.e. changing the physical environment, surveillance, access control, etc.) were more frequently mentioned in documents from unions (100 per cent) and national organizations (75 per cent) than from federal agencies (50 per cent) or legal organizations (33.3 per cent).

We also collected and analysed information from the documents about recommendations for integrating in-house/internal security and law enforcement into a workplace domestic violence programme. These strategies included collaboration between security and local law enforcement, using resources available from local law enforcement, and employing security personnel to help identify and restrict access to potential outside perpetrators. Two-thirds of the documents mentioned some of these strategies. The most common security-related recommendations were for programmes to escort victims to parking lots or public transportation (57.9 per cent) and to maintain photos of known perpetrators (52.6 per cent). However, less than a third of the documents making these recommendations specified that security personnel would be appropriate to conduct these tasks. Surprisingly, only 21 per cent of the documents mentioned the importance of training in-house/internal security about domestic violence in the workplace. Again, given that state-level statutes cover domestic violence, only 11 per cent of the documents mentioned collaboration between in-house/internal security and local law enforcement. The documents sponsored by legal organizations were the only sources to mention resources from local law enforcement, such as workplace restraining orders.

Overall, only four (21.1 per cent) documents made recommendations from all of the components of a comprehensive workplace violence programme. Furthermore, only 37 per cent of the documents integrated their workplace domestic violence plans into the structure of a larger workplace violence or workplace security plan. This is an indication that workplaces may continue to see domestic violence as a security issue separate from violence from criminals, customers/clients or other employees. However, two-thirds of the documents included recommendations that could both prevent a domestic violence event from occurring and how to intervene should an event take place.

Although most of the documents did not fully address each component of a comprehensive security plan, together they addressed a wide range of approaches. The recommendations were generally very consistent across documents, in part because many drew from the same limited references. Fewer than half of the documents included details as to how the recommendations should be implemented or exactly who should be responsible for each step. For example, several documents mentioned maintaining a photo of any known perpetrators of domestic violence against an employee, but it was not clear who should collect it or where such information should be housed.

The recommendations were largely focused on large employers that have human resource departments and benefits plans (for exception see Legal Momentum 2004). Implementing some of the recommendations would be very difficult for small businesses, those that involve off-site work, and those that don't offer their employees benefits such as health insurance or paid leave.

Discussion

Research has documented that domestic violence does not stay at home with the victim/employee or the perpetrator/employee. When either party enters the worksite, the potential for violence becomes a reality not only for the victim and the offender but also for other personnel. Even without a plethora of studies, there is enough evidence documenting the impact of domestic violence in the workplace that employers will be lax and possibly held legally responsible should they not take action. Furthermore, evidence that domestic violence will affect individual and overall employee morale and productivity provides more incentive to address this problem. Clearly, domestic violence in the workplace and its effects are problems that warrant more attention, so that employers can have information about which steps will be effective, which will fit best with ongoing business practices and resources, and which will be the most beneficial to employees.

These empirical patterns have implications for the development, implementation and evaluation of domestic violence policies and programmes in the workplace. Below we address two relevant issues. First, is more domestic violence workplace information needed? Second, when such policies and programmes are undertaken, what should their content be?

Is more domestic violence workplace information needed?

Given the ease of availability of workplace domestic violence information on the Internet, is more information needed? An increase in the number of publications may not be the answer, in part because much of the existing information stems from the same limited sources. More of the same, mostly unevaluated information will not greatly advance our knowledge and is not likely to create strong incentives to establish programmes. What will help are documents that will serve as incentives to employers, and such information needs to include current research from a variety of disciplines.

Rather than repeating the same workplace domestic violence information across more documents, one option for employers to use current information more effectively is to collaborate with state or local women's advocacy groups and law enforcement to tailor information to their workplace needs and make referrals to community domestic violence services and resources. This may be particularly advantageous to small businesses (we only uncovered one document that directed information to this type of business) that do not have the in-house resources of bigger businesses.

How preventable these victimizations and perpetrations are remain important research, practical and legal considerations. Although groundbreaking policies have been implemented by companies such as the Polaroid Corporation, Liz Claiborne, Inc., Aetna, Inc., the Gap, Marshalls, American Express, The Body Shop and Kaiser Permanente, there is little information available as to what these policies entail, how they are best implemented, and how effective they are (see for brief description, Office for Victims of Crime 1998; Family Violence Prevention Center 2004) (for a more detailed description of the Liz Claiborne programme, see Randel and Wells 2003). Most employers would welcome knowledge about effective strategies used in a variety of work settings.

The content of workplace domestic violence policies and programmes

If the availability of more of the same information is not the priority, then what is? The priority for future documents needs to be on comprehensive content – on recommendations that form a pro-active approach to domestic violence (including stalking) that includes designing, implementing and evaluating specific workplace policies that focus on reducing opportunities for workplace domestic violence victimization and perpetration, and having reactive policies should a domestic violence incident occur in the workplace. Such policies could stand alone but should be integrated and coordinated with general workplace security programmes. Although integration and coordination are vital, it is also important for employers to develop a specific domestic violence policy to establish the organization's position on and commitment to workplace domestic violence as being distinct from more general workplace violence. This distinction is needed because the causal dynamics underlying workplace domestic violence and its impact are in many ways unlike those perpetrated by strangers, clients, customers or co-workers.

Our review of the documents also revealed that recommendations were not always well focused on the specific roles of employers, supervisors, human resources personnel, union stewards, security or co-workers. In this regard the documents did not provide employers with a roadmap to implement the key activities that will result in a comprehensive response, spanning the range of activities from pro-active to reactive (e.g. education and awareness, training, leave options).

We did find two exemplary documents: 1) a template, Sample Policy of Domestic Violence, for developing a comprehensive domestic violence workplace policy developed by the National Center on Domestic and Sexual Violence (2004), and 2) a resource guide for employers, unions and advocates developed by the Family Violence Prevention Center (2004). A range of topics are included in these timely guides: guidelines for supervising victims of domestic violence, pointers on how to talk with an employee who is a perpetrator of abuse, designing personal and workplace safety plans, securing the work area, identifying and treating domestic violence, legal issues and union responses to domestic violence.

The Sample Policy of Domestic Violence is relevant to developing a workplace domestic violence policy as it covers several key topics that our analysis revealed were not universally addressed. For example, the majority of the documents did not specify who should receive domestic violence awareness training. The Sample Policy of Domestic Violence clearly states, '[Company name] will ensure that all supervisors, managers and employees are trained in safety planning and the handling of emergencies, such as the offender showing up at the workplace, armed and threatening the victim and co-workers (www.ncdsv.org/images/sample-policy.pdf,p4).'

In addition, fewer than one in five documents reviewed included perpetrator-related issues such as identifying a domestic violence perpetrator/employee or learning how to talk with that person. Both documents provide a comprehensive approach to addressing such issues. To illustrate, the resource guide provides recommended model policy guidelines for disciplining acts or threats of domestic violence at and off the worksite (see Family Violence Prevention Fund pp. 46–47).

We recognize that no single document can address all domestic violence issues for all types of workplace. Furthermore, programmes and policies for individual businesses will need to be designed for each specific work environment. However, as the information on this topic grows it will benefit from concerted efforts to focus recommendations for specific situations and for specific workplaces; in sum, to become a cohesive and comprehensive body of practical guidelines, programmes and policies informed by high-quality needs assessments, and process and outcome evaluations.

Conclusion

In closing, the data show that workplace domestic violence victimization or perpetration and their effects are realities of the labour market. Effectively addressing workplace domestic violence is more than just creating additional publicly available documents that rehash the same limited amount of information, or creating policies and practices with little, if any, substantive content. This approach produces too much of nothing that, in both the short term and long term, does very little to reduce the incidence and effects of domestic violence victimization and perpetration in the workplace or create a safe workplace for all employees.

Information about programme development, implementation and effectiveness is the critical gap that needs to be filled. Such information may provide models and incentives for employers effectively to address the incidence and effects of domestic violence in their workplace, and move beyond knowing too much of nothing.

Appendix 6.1 Documents reviewed that address workplace domestic violence

Title of document	Title of agency	Website
Federal agencies		
Workplace Violence: Issues in Response	FBI Critical Incident Response Team	http://www.fbi.gov/publications/violence.pdf
Domestic Violence: A Workplace Issue	US Department of Labor Women's Bureau	http://www.eurowrc.org/06.contributions/1.contrib_en/10.contrib.en.htm
Responding to Domestic Violence: Where Federal Employees Can Find Help	US Office of Personnel Management: The Federal Government's Human Resources Agency	http://www.opm.gov/ehs/workplac/html/asp
Violence in the Workplace	US Department of Health and Human Services: CDC/NIOSH	http://www.cdc.gov/niosh/violcont.html
What Employers Can Do to Make a Difference	National Advisory Council on VAW, Office of VAW	
Domestic Violence in Workplace	National Institute of Health	http://civil.nih.gov/resources/domestic.html
Legal organizations		
A Guide for Employers: Domestic Violence in the Workplace	American Bar Association	http://www.abanet.org/somviol/workviolence.html
Domestic Violence in the Workplace	Texas Lawyers Association	http://www.tyla.org/pdfs/workplace.pdf
Family Violence: The Role of Employers in Curbing Domestic Violence	Texas Prosecutor	http://www.ncdsv.org/images/roleofemployers.pdf

National organizations

Combating Workplace Violence	http://www.theiacp.org/pubinfo/pubs/pslc/pslc1.toc.htm
Chapter 22: Special topics: Section 5, Workplace Violence	www.ojp.usdoj.gov/ovc/assist/nvaa2002/chapter22_5.html
International Association of Chiefs of Police	
National Victim Assistance Academy	
Small Business Intiatives on Domestic Violence	http://www.legalmomentum.org/issues/vio/smallbusinessinitiative.shtml
Legal Momentum: Small Business Initiative – project of Safe@Work Coalition	
Getting Help: Workplace Guidelines	http://www.ncadv.org/gettinghelp/workplace.html
National Coalition Against Domestic Violence	
Violence Against Women: Domestic Violence Workplace Policies	http://www.legalmomentum.org
Legal Momentum: formerly NOW Legal Defense and Education Fund	
Domestic Violence and the Workplace	http://www.ncadv.org/gettinghelp/workplace.html
National Center on Domestic and Sexual Violence	
Facts on Workplace and Domestic Violence; 10 Things Employers Can Do	www.endabuse.org
Family Violence Prevention Fund	
Domestic Violence in the Workplace	http://www.ndvh.org
National Domestic Violence Hotline	

Unions

Domestic Violence: What Unions Can Do	http://www.afscme.org/wrkplace/domvio.htm
American Federation of State, County and Municipal Employees (AFSCME); the Family Violence Prevention Fund	
Prevent Workplace Violence: Chapter 6: Domestic Violence in the Workplace	http://www.afscme.org/health/violtc.htm
AFSCME's Women's Rights Department	

References

American Institute on Domestic Violence (2004) 'The Corporate Cost of Domestic Violence', http://www.aidv-usa.com/Statistics.htm (accessed 20/10/04).

Apessos v. Memorial Press Group No. 01-1474-A, 2002 Mass. Super. LEXIS 404 (Mass. Super. Ct. Sept. 30, 2002).

Bachman, R. (1994) 'Violence and Theft in the Workplace', NCJ 148199, Washington, DC: US Department of Justice.

Bowie, V. (2005) 'Organizational violence: a trigger for reactive terrorism', see this volume.

Bureau of Labor Statistics (2004) 'National Census of Fatal Occupational Injuries in 2003', USDL 04-1830, Washington, DC: US Department of Labor.

Braun Consulting News (2004) 'Domestic Abuse & Workplace Violence – A Liability Issue For Employers', http://www.braunconsulting.com/bcg/newsletters/spring2.html (accessed 11/11/04).

California Department of Occupational Safety and Health (1995) 'Cal/OSHA Guidelines for Workplace Security', Sacramento, CA: California Division of Industrial Relations.

Campbell, J.C., Webster, D., Koziol-McLain, J., Block, C., Campbell, D., Curry, M.A., Gary, F., Glass, N., McFarlane, J., Sachs, C., Sharps, P., Ulrich, Y., Wilt, S.A., Manganello, J., Xu, X., Schollenberger, J., Frye, V. and Laughon, K. (2003) 'Risk factors for femicide in abusive relationships: results from a multisite case control study', *American Journal of Public Health*, 93(7), pp. 1089–97.

Coker, A.L., Smith, P.H., Thompson, M.P., McKeown, R.E., Bethea, L. and Davis, K.E. (2002) 'Social support protects against the negative effects of partner violence on mental health', *Journal of Women's Health & Gender-Based Medicine*, 11(5), pp. 465–76.

Crowell, N. and Burgess, A. (eds) (1996) *Understanding Violence Against Women*. Panel on Research on Violence Against Women, Committee on Law and Justice, Commission on Behavioral and Social Sciences and Education, National Research Council. Washington, DC: National Academy Press.

Di Martino, V. (2005) 'A Cross-National Comparison Of Workplace Violence and Response Strategies.' See this volume.

Dougan, S. (2004) 'Employers May Face Liability When Domestic Violence Comes to Work', *Employee Benefit Plan Review*, February 2003, http://www.gtlaw.com/pub/articles/2003/dougans03a.asp (accessed 11/11/04).

Duhart, E. (2001) 'Violence in the Workplace 1993–1999 Bureau of Justice Statistics Special Report', NCJ 190076, Washington, DC: US Department of Justice.

Family Violence Prevention Fund (2004) 'The Workplace Responds to Domestic Violence: A Resource Guide for Employers, Unions, and Advocates', San Francisco, CA: Family Violence Prevention Fund,
http://www.mag.maricopa.gov/detail.cms?item=1983 (accessed 31/10/04).

Farmer, A. and Tiefenthaler, J. (2003) 'The Employment Effects of Domestic Violence', *Research in Labor Economics*, 23, pp. 301–334.

Federal Bureau of Investigation (2004) 'Crime in the United States: 2003. Uniform Crime Reports', Clarksburg, WV: Federal Bureau of Investigation.

Fox, J. and Zawitz, M. (2004) 'Homicide Trends in the US. US Department of Justice', Washington, DC: US Department of Justice,
http://www.ojp.usdoj.gov/bjs/pub/pdf/htius.pdf (accessed 2/11/04).

Friedman, L., and Couper, S. (1987) 'The cost of domestic violence: A preliminary investigation of the financial costs of domestic violence', New York: New York City Victim Services Agency.

Gomstyn, A. (2002) 'Abusers' Effect on Workplace Tracked', *Boston Globe*, C2, 22 October 2002.

Howard, J. (1996) 'State and local regulatory approaches to preventing workplace violence', in R. Harrison (ed.) *Workplace Violence. Occupational Medicine: State of the Art Reviews*, Philadelphia: Hanley and Belfus, Inc.

Legal Momentum (2004) 'Small Business Initiative on Domestic Violence',
http://www.legalmomentum.org/issues/vio/smallbiz.pdf
(accessed 20/10/04).

Lloyd, S. (1997) 'The Effects of Domestic Violence on Women's Employment', Law Society, 19(2), pp. 139–67.

Lloyd, S. and Taluc, N. (1999) 'The Effects of Male Violence on Female Employment', *Violence Against Women*, 5(4), pp. 370–92.

National Center on Domestic and Sexual Violence (2004) 'Sample Policy of Domestic Violence'
http://www.ncdsv.org/images/sample_policy.pdf (accessed 25/10/04).

National Victim Assistance Academy (2004). Foundations in victimology and victims' rights and service.
http://www.ojp.usdoj.gov/ovc/assist/nvaa99/chap21-5.htm
(accessed 24/11/04).

NOW Legal Defense and Educational Fund (2001) 'Domestic Violence at Work: Survivors' Right to Take Time From Work to Participate in Criminal Proceedings',
http://www.nowldef.org/html/issues/work/StateLawFactshts/
Criminal%20Proceedings.PDF (accessed 20/10/04).

NOW Legal Defense and Educational Fund (2004) 'Victims' Economic Security and Safety Act "VESSA" Fact Sheet',
http://www.nowldef.org/html/issues/vio/VESSA_FactSheet.pdf
(accessed 21/10/04).

Partnership for Prevention (2004) 'Domestic Violence and the Workplace',
www.prevent.org (accessed 20/10/04).

Peek-Asa, C., Howard, J., Vargas, L. and Kraus, J.F. (1997) 'Incidence of non-fatal workplace assault injuries determined from employer's reports in California', *Journal of Occupational and Environmental Medicine*, 39(1), pp. 44–50.

Office of Victim of Crime (1998) 'New Directions from the Field: Victim's Rights and Services in the 21st Century', NCJ 172823, Washington, DC: US Department of Justice.

Randel, J. and Wells, K. (2003) 'Corporate approaches to reducing intimate partner violence through workplace initiatives', in C. Wilkinson and C. Peek-Asa (eds) *Violence in the Workplace: Clinics in Occupational and Environmental Medicine*, Philadelphia: W.B. Saunders Company.

Rickett, L. and Fortman, L. (2004) 'Impact of Domestic Offenders on Occupational Safety and Health: A Pilot Study', Augusta, ME: Maine Department of Labor, Family Crisis Services.

Rennison, C. (2001) 'Intimate Partner Violence and Age of Victim 1993–1999', NCJ 187635, Washington, DC: US Department of Justice.

Rugala, E., Isaacs, A. and Arnold, R. (2004) 'Workplace Violence: Issues in Response', Washington DC: US Department of Justice and Federal Bureau of Investigation, http://www.fbi.gov/publications/violence.pdf (accessed 11 July 2005).

Shepard, M. and Pence, E. (1988) 'The Effect of Battering on the Employment Status of Women', *Affilia*, 3(2), pp. 55–61.

Tjaden, P. and Thoennes, N. (1998) 'Prevalence, Incidence, and Consequences of Violence Against Women: Findings From the National Violence Against Women Survey', NCJ 172837, Washington, DC: US Department of Justice.

Victims' Economic Security and Safety Act (2004) S. 1249; H.R. 2670.

Wathen, C. and MacMillan, H. (2003) 'Interventions for violence against women: scientific review', *Journal of American Medical Associations AMA*, 289(5), pp. 589–600.

Warchol, G. (1998) 'Workplace Violence 1992–1996', NCJ 169634, Washington, DC: US Department of Justice.

Weiser, W. and Widiss, D. (2004) 'Employment Protection for Domestic Violence Victims', Clearinghouse Review, May–June 2004, pp. 3–11.

Zorza, J. (1994) 'Women Battering: High Costs and the State of the Law', *Clearinghouse Review*, 28(4), pp. 383–95.

Chapter 7

Caring for those who care – aid worker safety and security as a source of stress and distress: a case for psychological support?

Ros Thomas

Introduction

Each day news reports describe deliberate targeting in Sudan, bombings in Iraq and shootings in Afghanistan. They attest to intentional robbery, banditry, kidnapping and murder in Chechnya, Bosnia, West Timor and Iraq, crossfire in Angola, hostage-taking in Liberia and hijacking in Somalia (AFR/851 IHA/874 2004; Helton 1997; Slim 1995). These are just some examples of the growing security hazards faced by aid workers in the workplace known as the 'field'. Ironically, on 12 August 1999, as the 50th anniversary of the Geneva Convention was being celebrated in Geneva with the signing of a declaration for combatants to respect these treaties, six medical relief workers from Norway, the UK and Italy were held hostage by an alleged rebel faction in Liberia.

Such security events are all too commonplace. Indeed, there is near universal agreement that political realities of the last two decades have created a context so that aid workers are placed in unprecedented proximity to the violence of war (Ditzler 2001; Potter 2004; Sheik *et al.* 2000; Martin 1999; Vaux 2002). A commonly articulated rationale for aid worker stress is that exposure to risks in this work is inevitable, and may even be necessary to get the job done (Sheik *et al.* 2000).

Most relief organisations recognize that injuries and deaths to aid workers are rising (Martin 1999; McFarlane 2004). A 2000 study by Sheik *et al.* (2000) documents this belief that deaths among aid workers have risen since the early 1990s. Ditzler (2001) shows too, that in environments such as Rwanda in 1994, Kosovo in 1999 and in Sudan, aid workers have and do face intense stress and threats in much the same way as the local people. Even though the suffering of victims will always be the primary concern for relief organizations, aid workers share many risks with those they try to help. They also face moral and operational dilemmas and are often at considerable physical and psychological risk. As 'doers' who seldom have the time to reflect and ponder, their security has been largely disregarded as a subject for serious study (Bergman 2003).

Much of the research has identified that dangerous working environments put the physical security of aid workers on the line. But what of their psychological health?

This chapter will first consider the aid workers themselves and then outline the security issues they face in the 'field'. It will then raise awareness of the potential mental health consequences of work under war conditions and how to best manage these. It is essential that aid workers are equipped to do more than just survive physically. Finally, it will suggest some practical steps that can be tailored by organizations to provide support systems that attend to the mental health of their staff before, during and after work in the field.

Entry into aid work

So who are these aid workers and what are the potential mental health consequences for them in the work they do under war conditions? What is the best way to manage these and what practical steps can be tailored to provide support systems that attend to the mental health of people before, during and after work in the field?

Most aid workers start their careers in their twenties when with raw energy and few expectations they move willingly into the world's trouble spots. Many soon find the pressures of 'normal life' stressful and complain jokingly of the need for the adrenaline rush of the field. Some are professionals and view this work as a career choice with good financial rewards. All seek adventure, travel and to engage in something different. They are motivated by a wish to engage in meaningful activities that contribute to securing a better life for those in distress.

In the field they are given responsibility, independence and freedom. They drive land cruisers, report land mines, conduct risk assessments, negotiate with militia at checkpoints, set up clinics and schools, deliver babies in fields and tend to the wounded. These aid workers share a concern for the world's victims. They are not saints but are a rare breed much needed. Sometimes they can be seen as misfits, sometimes as adrenaline junkies, sometimes they are nomads, sometimes they are institutionalized functionaries, but most often they are humble, practical and committed people determined to do the decent thing. They feel useful, needed and recognized. They have chosen to work in the most dangerous, demanding and in the end rewarding parts of the world. Overseas aid work is often totally engaging and the urgency and adrenaline can be addictive (Fawcett 2000). Soon most are hooked.

Security issues faced by aid workers in the field

Sadly, this is an incomplete picture. While it may be meaningful, aid work is a dangerous business for wars are fought without rules. Once deployed, many workers find on-site support limited by factors like financial constraints and lack of adequate resources which are beyond their control (Ditzler 2001; Ehrenreich and Elliot 2004). Aid worker efforts to help civilians may be seen as aiding the enemy or prolonging the conflict, or it may simply be that they are near to relief supplies. Today relief organizations are no longer seen as neutral. Aid workers in these chaotic environments are often deliberate targets of intentional violence and aggression, including robbery, kidnapping and murder, such as in Chechnya (December 1996), Rwanda (October 1999), Bosnia and Herzegovina, West Timor and Afghanistan and as in the bombing of the United Nations headquarters in Baghdad in August 2003 that killed 23 people and wounded 100. Recent tragedies include the shooting of the UNHCR worker in Afghanistan in November 2003 and the ICRC employee in Baghdad in October 2003. Among myriad other examples since January 1992, 214 United Nations staff have lost their lives while in the field and only 22 perpetrators have been brought to justice. Between January 1994 and October 2002 there were 74 instances of hostage-taking and kidnapping involving 261 staff (UNSECOORD 2003). There was public condemnation by UNHCR and WFP at the murder of two humanitarian aid workers in Afghanistan (UNHCR 1998). Among other forms of violence, incidents of armed robbery, rape and attacks on humanitarian convoys continue to occur.

Although statistics change daily, from March 2003 until August 2004, more than 80 workers from Non-Governmental Organizations (NGOs) and UN agencies have been killed in security incidents, with over 108 seriously injured. In Afghanistan and Iraq the hostile conflict environment and the presence of so many different actors in the field has thrown up a host of security threats for aid workers who are vulnerable soft targets. It becomes a challenge to convince all that they are purely humanitarian, for if they are perceived as part of the conflict the risk to their safety rises (Dind 1999). Since March 2003, until August 2004, 44 humanitarian workers have been killed in Afghanistan alone (Peel 2004). Here a tragic contributory factor is the blurring of the lines between independent humanitarian aid and the US-led coalition forces (Collett-White 2004; Peel 2004). The attacks have the aim of halting humanitarian assistance and disrupting the 2004 elections (Collett-White 2004). In a humanitarian space reduced by the logic of 'who is not with me is against me', there remains little room for the humanitarian intermediary who, to help the victims, is simply trying to remain neutral, impartial and independent (Van Brabant 2001). In 2004, ICRC president Jakob Kellenberger also claimed that the repercussions of the 'war on terrorism' declared by the United States (US) administration have speeded up the erosion of humanitarian space. There is a trend toward polarization and radicalization which has meant that certain people associate aid organizations with the Western world, which they reject (Hazan and Berger 2004).

These risks are mirrored in the reality that the cherished qualities of respect and immunity are no longer assured. The light blue laurel wreath of the UN or the protective symbols of the Red Cross and Crescent no longer act as indicators of protection. This erosion of neutrality is described by Hugo Slim (1995) when he suggests that some insignia identify the wearer as the enemy coming from the privileged international community from which many local people perceive themselves as excluded. In the present climate this results in the prized symbol of neutrality coming under attack. The symbol of compassion is replaced by an interpretation of superiority and unconscious paternalism.

Following the bombing of the UN in Baghdad on 26 August 2003, the UN Security Council unanimously adopted a resolution calling attacks against peacekeepers and humanitarian personnel 'war crimes'. Secretary General Kofi Annan stated:

> I can think of no issue about which I feel more strongly, as secretary general – and I believe none should be more important to each of you, as members of the Security Council – than the safety of those brave men and women who serve this organization in the places where it matters most, that is, in zones of conflict and danger. Last week's vicious attack on our headquarters in Baghdad, with all its tragic consequences, has brought this vital issue to the forefront of our priorities. (Aita 2003: 1)

In passing the resolution, Annan said, the council sends 'an unambiguous message to all those who mistakenly believe that, in today's turbulent

world, they can advance their cause by targeting the servants of humanity'
(Aita 2003: 1).

International awareness of security issues and policy development

How then do organizations offer adequate support mechanisms to
safeguard security? How do organizations help staff develop coping
mechanisms to equip them to deal with violent onslaughts and the
aftermath? It is perhaps helpful to consider the historical context of security
concerns.

Concern for security can be found as early as five years after the
Battle of Solferino in 1859, when some attention was paid to conditions
and protection of aid workers. This was followed by the 1864 Geneva
Convention for the Amelioration of the Conditions of the Wounded in the
Field. Here two out of ten articles were elaborated to attend specifically to
the protection of the workers who were tending the sick (Dunant 1986).

Today the instruments of international humanitarian law are the four
Geneva conventions of 1949 and their additional protocols of 1977. The
four Geneva conventions of 1949 enjoy near universal acceptance. They
set out basic standards of treatment for persons who are not, or are no
longer, participating in armed conflict: specifically sick, wounded and
shipwrecked soldiers (conventions I and II), prisoners of war (convention
III), and civilians during armed conflict (convention IV). The conventions
are enhanced by two additional protocols of 1977. Protocol I extends
coverage to wars of national liberation and self-determination 'against
colonial domination and alien occupation and against racist regimes'.
By recognizing such conflicts, protocol I signalled a pragmatic evolution
in defining war. Protocol II supports provisions on non-international
conflicts, but is restricted to cases in which the warring party imposes
control over national territory. In summary, they embody the principle of
respect for individuals and set out humanitarian obligations during armed
conflicts. Unlike the 1949 conventions, these two protocols have not been
universally supported, although they are binding on about three-quarters
of states. Finally, the conventions and protocols are supplemented by other
humanitarian principles and international law, such as the right to be free
from torture, enslavement or murder (Helton 1997; ICRC 1983).

In sum, these conventions offer some legal protection but, as we know,
violators are seldom brought to justice and the onus is on the signatories
to bring violators to justice (The Lancet 1999). The main flaw in these
instruments is that the implementers are the states in conflict that cannot be
relied on to protect their own citizens let alone the aid workers present on
the ground. International experience shows the need for more enforcement

of the conventions through a body such as the International Criminal Court (ICC) established by the Rome Statute of the International Criminal Court on 17 July 1998. This independent international organization has its seat in The Hague and was established to promote the rule of law and ensure that serious international crimes do not go unpunished. Prosecution of offenders through an institution such as the ICC could act as a deterrent and give comfort to aid workers.

At a field level in 1997, the UNHCR noted that its aid staff was increasingly operating in more dangerous environments and that two-thirds of its international and national aid workers worked in security-risk areas and one-third were in hazardous areas. In July 2004 this rising security risk was recognized by Jan Egeland, the UN emergency relief coordinator and undersecretary general for humanitarian affairs, who claimed the greatest challenge faced by aid workers today is avoiding attacks and restrictions on their movements. These attacks are aimed at keeping them from reaching people in need (Hoge 2004). So successful are these tactics that on 28 July 2004 Médecins sans Frontières (Doctors without Borders) reluctantly announced that it was leaving Afghanistan after 24 years following the killing of five colleagues in a deliberate attack on a clearly marked MSF vehicle on 2 June 2004 in north-west Afghanistan (Médecins sans Frontières 2004).

The impact of this growing awareness can also be seen in the domain of the military, peacekeepers, journalists and disaster relief workers where the relationship between exposure to violence and distress is well documented (Britt and Adler 1999; Danieli 2002; Feinstein et al. 2002; Raphael and Wilson 2000; Shay 1994). In a 2003 report, the Overseas Development Institute's Humanitarian Policy Group looked at safety and security management in 20 of the world's major aid agencies. It argued that developing awareness of risk is not enough in a violent world in which respect for relief and development workers is in decline (Cardozo and Salama 2002; Van Brabant 2001). A decade ago humanitarian aid workers were afforded protection by their role in the field. Of note is that in this young field of inquiry only a fledgling literature exists about the moral and psychological dilemmas facing aid workers in situations of security breakdown, and that which does is anecdotal (Cardozo and Salama 2002; Danieli 2002; Ditzler 2001; Ehrenreich 2001; Fawcett 2000; McFarlane 2004).

Organizational responses to security issues

Attempts by international relief organizations to respond to security issues are found in the many publications which show raised willingness to prioritize staff support (ICRC 1999; IRC 2000; Martin 1999; Médecins sans Frontières 2002; Oxfam 2002). In 2000 the United Nations Secretary General detailed a two-year programme for the reinforcement of the UN Security Management System – an example of constructive efforts made in an attempt to deal with escalating security concerns. On 1 August 2002 a full-time United Nations Security Coordinator (UNSECOORD) assumed duties to strengthen security coordination and raise the efficacy of the security management system. Additional professional staff, including counsellors, have been appointed and Minimal Operational Security Standards (MOSS) developed (UNSECOORD 2003).

The organizational tone acknowledging risk is often sombre, as is the acknowledgement that danger is no longer the exception. Zero risk does not exist for wars are fought without rules. The cornerstone of the current attempt at systematic security management is rooted in the same acknowledgement that threats are ever present and an acceptance that traditional rules no longer apply (Humanitarian Affairs Review 2001). The simple fact is that the United Nations sends unarmed aid workers into environments where member governments will not send their own armed troops (Bertini 2002).

Why then, with this growing awareness of the need for physical security, is little immediate psychological help offered to those affected by security incidents? To try to answer this question we need look no further than the tough choices and moral dilemmas faced by humanitarian organizations today. Aid workers in the field may well experience an arena vastly different from the written word. Academics and practitioners alike observe that despite the written idiom of care, this is often more ideological than strictly factual. This written idiom of care is used to rationalize vast disparities between organizational ideology and the reality of operational practice (Barron 1999; Slim 1997, 2002).

While conducting research in February 2004 I witnessed a security incident that highlighted the mismatch between the written idiom of care and the reality of the field. The incident involved a group of eight United Nations and non-governmental staff who were delivering much-needed food and other aid to about 13,500 war-affected people during a relief operation in Nimnim, Western Upper Nile in Southern Sudan. The group was finishing a four-day mission when they were subjected to about 20 minutes of intense and sustained shooting by rifle, machine-gun, rocket-propelled grenade and mortar fire by unknown militia.* All were successfully evacuated and flown to safety in Northern Kenya.

*See full Press Release AFR/851 IHA/874, 'UN Condemns Deliberate and Concerted Attack on Aid Workers in Southern Sudan', Nairobi/Khartoum, 27 February (OCHA) http://www.un.org/News/Press/docs/2004/afr851.doc.htm

Stepping back from this example, it is clear that the rescue was competently organized and the result commendable. No one was injured and all were safely evacuated. But in the immediate aftermath of the evacuation (next 48 hours), no psychological support was offered. No defusing or debriefing took place and help could only be found upon return to Nairobi (72 hours later) if individuals asked for it. Psychological support was not mandatory. Where systematic implementation of such care is not found there was no match between the written idiom of care and the reality of the field. Such security events are all too commonplace and organizations need to train and support aid workers to do more than just survive physically.

Security preparedness

While securing humanitarian workers is ideally the task of the host government, the harsh reality of the precarious political climates in which many aid organizations work is that the humanitarian community cannot rely on state entities to have adequate commitment to protect its staff and property or for governments to arrest the culprits (Médecins sans Frontières 2004). As the humanitarian world shares this worrying realization and unprecedented vulnerability, the challenge becomes how to put into effect support for staff who face security risks as they respond to the urgent needs of disaster-hit communities and countries in conflict (Potter 2004).

For organizations to address security preparedness demands three inter-connected factors; organizational preparedness, individual commitment and accurate risk assessment at every application. This targets staff preparation, pre-briefing, in-service support, aspects of security training, evacuation procedures, provision of mental health services such as counselling, debriefing and ongoing psychological services.

Limiting risks also involves adopting a more technical approach to security issues. In this domain, triggered by the conflicts in the former Yugoslavia, much has been done in the last ten years. Seminars on security, guidelines, security briefings, security manuals, systematic notification of all field movements and targeted dissemination at checkpoints are standard practice today. Such measures do make it possible to work in places where the risks engendered by 'classic' conflicts are a daily reality, but they do little to lessen the new and deliberate threats and acts facing humanitarian workers in these highly polarized contexts (Van Brabant 2001).

Understanding trauma and its mental health consequences

If measures are taken to best protect aid workers physically, how does one survive mentally in the aftermath of facing such dramatic events? Are there means of preventing what we mental health professionals call Acute Stress Disorder (ASD) or, worse yet, Post-Traumatic Stress Disorder (PTSD). Although not every aid worker in the field suffers to such an extent, studies have shown that in the aftermath of security incidents many do, and this occurs regardless of age, sex or cultural origin (Britt and Adler 1999; Britt 2000; Fawcett 2000; Fullerton and Ursano 1997; Gist and Devilly 2002; ICRC 2001; Janoff-Bulman 1985; Jensen 1999; Potter 2004; Raphael and Wilson 2000; Rose and Bisson 1998; Shay 1994). Such anguish is painfully real and has a profound impact on the lives of those afflicted. Terrifying experiences can rupture people's sense of predictability and invulnerability, and ASD and PTSD can prevent intelligent and highly capable people from being fully operational. It can alter the way aid workers deal with their emotions in the public sphere of work and in their private lives (Fawcett 2000; Shay 1994; van der Kolk *et al.* 1995). People with field experience frequently report witnessing such outcomes (Britt and Adler 1999; Fawcett 2002; Fullerton and Ursano 1997; Potter 2004).

So as to appreciate the potential mental health vulnerability of humanitarian aid workers to raised security risks, Ruth Barron (1999) points us to original historical recognition of trauma. It is Herman (1992), in her landmark book *Trauma and Recovery*, who argues that societal examination of trauma has been dependent on the ebb and flow of societal stress and political movements. From the time of antiquity, recognition of stress in military casualties can be found. It was only in the 1920s that early psychoanalytic theory was used to try to understand and treat responses to extreme and cumulative stress. During World War II these insights stayed in the military (except for testimony of Holocaust survivors) and only after the Vietnam War was recognition given to the effect of stress and trauma on the individual, family, community and entire country (Barron 1999). In early studies soldiers suffering from psychological distress were seen as having weakness of character and feminine frailty. In the Western World sustained recognition of psychological distress and trauma only became apparent in the 1970s with a revision of human rights and women's liberation. With this, society became more receptive to learning about victimization and emotional needs of women, children and most importantly men, who had not voiced their suffering because of an unreceptive climate. As victims and survivors gained power there was a growing awareness that it was the event that was abnormal, not the individual (Barron 1999).

A traumatic event, defined as an extreme occurrence outside the realm of normal everyday life, can exert a significant impact on psychological functioning. When aid workers become victims of security incidents this poses a clear threat to their conceptual framework in which they understand the world. Stress arises from a dissonance between the abilities and expectations on one hand and the requirements of the working environment on the other (Ajdukovic and Ajdukovic 2000). Although an occupational hazard, stress can devastate the worldview, spirituality and sense of identity of the aid worker. Furthermore, when aid workers experience trauma it brings to the surface uncertainties, fear and vulnerability in colleagues who have contact with them (Gal 1998). When they experience acute or delayed reactions to their experiences after exposure to significant stressors, this cost of caring is variously referred to as secondary stress and secondary stress disorder, compassion fatigue, empathic strain, event counter transference, compassion stress, vicarious traumatization, soul sadness, burnout and contact traumatization (Figley 1995). Traumatization occurs if the balance between the severity of the stressor factors and the individual protective factors is significantly challenged.

Aid workers may be exposed to *primary* traumatization by being a direct target of a critical incident or traumatic event such as hijacking, banditry, hostage-taking, ambush, assault or rape. Primary traumatization may be diagnosed in an individual who experiences, witnesses or is confronted with a traumatic event and responds with intense fear, helplessness or horror. These may be intentional traumas such as combat, sexual assault, terrorism and mass violence, or unintentional traumas such as natural disasters and accidents, and may cause this pervasive psychiatric condition (Zimering *et al.* 2003). They may be exposed to *secondary* traumatization when close colleagues or friends are targeted. Secondary trauma is also defined as indirect exposure to trauma through a first-hand account or narrative of a traumatic event. The vivid recounting of trauma by the survivor and the clinician's subsequent cognitive or emotional representation of that event may result in a set of symptoms and reactions that parallel PTSD (such as re-experiencing, avoidance and hyperarousal). Families of primary traumatized aid workers may suffer from secondary traumatization as they learn of the events (Figley 1995; Jensen 1999; Pearlman 1999).

Aid workers may be exposed to Re Entry Syndrome (RES) or Reverse Culture Shock when returning home from working in a different culture in the field where they have experienced a security incident. Returning home is a pivotal transition and the psychological response known as RES affects the returning worker's homecoming and also family and friends. After initial euphoria, many returned aid workers experience feelings of loss, bereavement and isolation. Often aid workers feel that no one understands what they have been through and most people aren't that interested. They feel frustrated by not being able to communicate their recent experience – or the sense of loss that they have. They may feel disconnected from their homes and become critical of the values of the people around them. Many miss the strong bonds formed with like-minded colleagues in stressful experiences in the field. This syndrome becomes a problem when it is associated with negative consequences like drug or alcohol abuse, withdrawal and depression or risk-taking behaviour that may affect their health, career and family (McCreesh 2003; van der Kolk *et al.* 1995).

The *stressor factors* affecting aid workers may be divided into: event-related stress, job-related stress (in the field) and organizational stress. Organizational stress is often referred to as basic stress and refers to the emotional reactions arising from tension and inter-personal conflicts with work colleagues and managers in the work environment which are unrelated to the specifics of the humanitarian operation (Ehrenreich and Elliot 2004; ICRC 2001). Poor organization and intolerable workload can also be contributors. In less severe situations, individuals may suffer from general stress symptoms without the more dramatic symptoms of post-traumatic stress disorder.

Protective factors relate to a person's individual psychological strength and ability to cope with stressful situations. They also relate to preparation before arrival, personal life situation (family and network support), age and experience, and preventive measures of self-care during the field mission. They relate to the expectation a person has about their work. Those with highest expectations or with past histories of psychiatric problems often find themselves most vulnerable. When aid workers are confronted with the distress of victims and apparent meaninglessness of much of what they see, they need the ability to find purpose in what they do. From the outset three factors make a crucial difference in adjustment and health in aid workers: (1) the ability to make sense out of external events, (2) the feeling of being in some degree in control of and responsible for events, and (3) an orientation to situations as challenges worthy of commitment and engagement rather than as burdens (Antonovsky 1987, 1993; Barron 1999; McFarlane 2004).

To the above three one can add a crucial variable. This is the strength of relationships in the organization, with colleagues and managers. The strength of individual inter-personal relationships is more an indicator of the likely development of trauma-related conditions than the external event itself (Fawcett 2000, 2002; Hartman 1997; Salama 2000; Shay 1994). When aid workers experience strong emotional reactions in remote locations, usual forms of professional support such as supervision, peer support, team cohesion and consultation may not be a regular part of their activities. Aid workers are seldom in tight-knit, well-trained teams as one might find in military groups where the command chain is clearly defined (Danieli 2002). When communication breaks down and supportive structures are not in place, individual burnout accompanied by bitterness and cynicism occurs. Professional exhaustion known as 'burnout' is referred to as a syndrome of emotional exhaustion, depersonalization and reduced personal accomplishment (Maslach 1979). Kahill identifies five categories of symptoms common in burnout: (1) somatic problems, (2) emotional problems such as irritability, (3) behavioural changes such as raised aggression, anxiety, guilt, defensiveness and a sense of helplessness, (4) work-related performance, and (5) inter-personal difficulties such as poor relationships (1988). When aid workers feel unsupported in security crises they may be less likely to admit what has gone wrong, may not mobilize social support as well, and may be less able to impose limits on demands being made on them. On the other hand, when a sound collegial relationship is in place with staff feeling free to talk, understanding is reached and severe trauma can often be avoided. These workers will be expected to adopt attitudes that are functional for coping. They are able to activate the proper resources when the need arises (Antonovsky 1987; Fawcett 2002).

Security risks that threaten personal safety lead to many modern-day aid workers going through a range of emotions. Their individual appraisal of threat is crucial for the stress reaction to occur. To understand the needs of others, to be present and open, calls for emotional availability. To be receptive as a listener presupposes freedom from preoccupation with personal issues and an awareness of what one can offer and what one cannot. It calls for an ability to identify one's own reactions to interacting with stressful situations and to know ways to deal with these reactions. When faced with direct personal attack, many with beliefs grounded in personal philosophies, sometimes strongly spiritual, are faced with contradictions and a destruction of a worldview (Salama 2000). In practical terms, the lens with which aid workers appraise the conflict shapes the way they interpret their exposure to the field, their own conceptual and analytical frameworks, their own histories, beliefs, worldview and organizational philosophy.

ASD is the most typical reaction when the person has experienced, witnessed or is confronted with a security issue that involves actual or threatened death or serious injury or a threat to the physical integrity of the self or others (American Psychiatric Association (APA) 1994). The relationship between exposure to violence and distress is well documented (Danieli 2002; Mitchell and Everly 2000; Raphael and Wilson 2000). If the aid worker experiences intense fear, helplessness or horror, and debriefing as part of an overall process of support is not offered, this condition may turn into PTSD. I emphasize the overall process of support, as Mitchell shows that the debriefing component of post-incident care needs to be part of an overall process of support to be effective (2000). Care becomes a process, not an event (Ditzler 2001).

The most dramatic event-related stress reactions are often easiest to recognize by the traumatized individual and those closest to the event. Far more difficult to spot are behavioural changes in working relationships: raised risk-taking, substance use or abuse, promiscuity, overwork or withdrawal. Acknowledgement of vulnerability still results in stigma. A study conducted by Britt among US peacekeepers returning from a peacekeeping mission in Bosnia found conclusively that stigma associated with acknowledgement of psychological problems led to a differential perception and treatment by others. People going through psychological difficulties are seen to have characteristics that make them undesirable and therefore the risk of disclosure is considered too costly by many (2000).

A final serious contributing factor is that aid workers active in many of today's complex emergencies are soon also aware that they are unlikely to be able to invoke the law to protect either themselves or the people they serve (The Lancet 1999; Straker and Moosa 1994). This promotes a sense of hopelessness and helplessness in those affected, as they have no possibility for redress.

Future directions for psychological support

Before his tragic death in the Baghdad bombings in August 2003, the late Arthur Helton, a prominent refugee advocate, challenged the international community to review how best to develop security plans so that this would become a source of support to organizations rather a source of stress (1997).

Returning to the examples of security incidents referred to in this paper, it is clear there is not only a physical risk, but also a psychological one to security incidents. Equally clear is that as part of a programme of overall support in the immediate aftermath of these events, psychological follow-up is needed. Employees need to have confidence they can safely request help in disclosing emotional vulnerability. The mental health costs following inaction are potentially grave and merit review.

Firstly, these costs link to Davidson's 1998 statement, 'Good management and support costs money but poor management and support costs more' (WHO/EHA/98.3, 1998: 7). It makes good economic sense to ensure that security policies are explicitly regular features of programming. It makes good economic sense to protect the considerable financial investment made in human assets. There is logic in protection that results in fewer casualties and fewer health claims – both physical and psychological.

Secondly, it also makes good sense to adopt a balanced view that takes into account a crisis response strategy that attends equally to physical safety and mental health during critical incidents and provides access to long-term support if needed.

Organizational strategies

The organization should be able to respond to questions like:

- What do we do if a staff member is exposed to a significant traumatic event?

- What types of support and preventive structures are there for aid staff to prevent mental health problems because of deployment?

- How do we work within a culture that has a strong norm of psychological health, coping and resiliency to ensure that disclosure of a psychological problem is tolerated without stigmatization?

- How do we create an organizational climate where aid workers can have confidence that disclosure of emotional vulnerability will no longer be more stigmatizing than admission of a medical one?

At an organizational level some suggested actions include:

- Strengthen management and leadership in the field and at headquarters so that psychological support is a systematic part of security management. Management of people is not an exact science, and management and staff are in need of professional tools to handle work-related stress and cope with life-threatening situations. This raises awareness and gives credibility to aid worker experience.

- Given the unique and stressful nature of work in security situations, extra time is needed to prepare staff for what they may experience. Pre-deployment training can obviate the need for much post-deployment intervention and aim to cut worker attrition. This preparation also heightens awareness of the realities of the emergency staff will work in, so leading to a greater sense of predictability and control.

- Provide clear training on safety and security protocols, including personal health and medical evacuation procedures, methods of analysis of security issues, contextual analysis, risk analysis, safety and security on stress management and behaviour with partner organizations, counterparts, rebels and militia.

- Provide training tailored to grasp acute stress. Armed with this knowledge, aid workers can identify their own psychological and social vulnerabilities and have the basic skills to identify colleagues at risk.

- Ensure that there is adequate budgetary provision for well-structured support services. Where possible these should not be subject to unrealistic budgetary restrictions.

- Make present competent, trained senior personnel who are emotionally and physically available. This provides social support often provided by families at home. As long as social support networks are intact, most mature adults are amazingly resilient (van der Kolk *et al.* 1995).

- Involve those who have personal experience of security incidents to capture knowledge and improve the validity of psychological support.

- Identify an empathic field manager who can take charge without taking over and place a metaphorical arm around the aid worker. We know that emotional attachment is the primary protection against difficult experiences and aids rapid recovery.

- Encourage group and team cohesion to protect against difficult experience.

Individual strategies

On an individual level, aid workers can aim to develop a self-schema of 'mental readiness' in the work they do. This will support their coping skills. How do they acquire this? In part, by self-selection and screening, pre-field preparation and the knowledge that even when in difficult and remote areas their organizations support them.

Steps that can be taken in this regard include:

- Establish a careful process of screening before employment and deployment. Individuals should ask themselves questions about their personal traits, expectations and physical and mental health. This will identify applicants with unresolved personal issues and past histories of psychiatric problems that make them far more suggestible to adverse emotional and physical reactions.

• Actively encourage personal self-care. If aid workers take care of themselves they will be better able to take care of others.

• Although sensible self-care measures will help, some who find it inadequate may need referral to a structured experience of defusing, debriefing, spiritual counselling, crisis counselling or psychotherapy to re-establish equilibrium.

• Normalize discussions on mental health and stress-related problems among colleagues and in the organization to diminish stigma associated with acknowledgement of difficulties.

• Aim to prevent re-entry syndrome (RES) by raising awareness of the need to put experiences, cognitions and feelings into words. This creative tool helps tell the story, lessen feelings of helplessness and regain hope.

Conclusion

This chapter has outlined security issues faced by aid workers in the workplace known as the 'field'. It recognizes that while it is unlikely that security situations can ever easily be prevented there are strategies that encourage an organizational climate in which security-promoting behaviours can be fostered. It stresses that mental health care of aid workers exposed to the consequences of work under war conditions is a process not an event. It provides suggestions for future psychological support so that in the event of security incidents importance is attached to more than just physical survival.

How we do things is important. How we develop the best processes for psychological support is important. How we support aid workers on their journey to wellness in the aftermath of security incidents is a challenge worth reflection and action. How we match the written idiom of care with the reality of operational practice is important. Challenging environments merit security policies and procedures that attend to the physical and psychological needs of their staff with equal care.

References

AFR/851 IHA/874 (2004) 'UN Condemns Deliberate and Concerted Attack on Aid Workers in Southern Sudan'. Press Release Nairobi/Khartoum (OCHA) 27 February http://www.un.org/News/Press/docs/2004/afr851.doc.htm (accessed 3 June 2004).

Ahearn, F. (ed.) (2000) *Psychosocial Wellness of Refugees: Issues in Qualitative and Quantitative Research*, London: Berghahn Books.

Aita, J. (2003) UN security council focuses on protecting aid workers (resolution calls attacks on workers 'war crimes') (920). US Department of State. International Information Programs http://usinfo.org/wf-archive/2003/030827/epf307.htm. 26 August 2003 (accessed on 5 September 2003).

Ajdukovic, D. and Ajdukovic, M. (eds) (2000) *Mental Health Care of Helpers*, Zagreb, Croatia: Society for Psychological Assistance.

American Psychiatric Association (APA) (1994) *Diagnostic and Statistical Manual of Mental Disorders*: DSM-IV, Washington, DC: American Psychiatric Association.

Antonovsky, A. (1987) *Unravelling the Mystery of Health: How People Manage Stress and Stay Well*, San Francisco, CA: Jossey-Bass.

Antonovsky, A. (1993) 'The structure and properties of the sense of coherence scale', *Social Science and Medicine*, 36, 6: 725–33.

Barron, R.A. (1999) 'Psychological trauma and relief workers', in J. Leaning (ed.) *Humanitarian Crises: The Medical and Public Health Responses* (pp. 143–75). Cambridge, MA: Harvard University Press.

Bergman, C. (2003) *Another Day in Paradise: Front Line Stories from International Aid Workers*, London: Earthscan.

Bertini, C. (2002) Security of UN Humanitarian and Associated Personnel. http://gos.sbc.edu/b/bertini.html. 9 February 2002.

Britt, T.W. (2000) 'The stigma of psychological problems in the work environment: evidence from the screening of service members returning from Bosnia', *Journal of Applied Social Psychology*, 30, 8: 1599–1618.

Britt, T.W. and Adler, A.B. (1999) 'Stress and health during medical humanitarian assistance missions', *Military Medicine*, 164 (4), April: 275–9.

Cardozo, B.L. and Salama, P. (2002) 'Mental health of humanitarian aid workers in complex emergencies', in Y. Danieli (ed.) *Sharing the Front Line and the Backhills: Peacekeepers, humanitarian aid workers and the media in the midst of crisis*. Amityville, NY: Baywood Publishing Company, Inc.

Collett-White, M. (2004) *Gunmen kill two Afghans from German aid group*. Reuters Foundation AlertNet http://www.alertnet.org/thenews/newsdesk/SP156340.htm (accessed 10 July 2004).

Danieli, Y. (ed.) (2002) *Sharing the Front Line and the Back Hills. International Protectors and Providers: Peacekeepers, Humanitarian Aid Workers and the Media in the Midst of Crisis*, Amityville, NY: Baywood Publishing Company, Inc.

Dind, P. (1999) 'Security in ICRC field operations', *Forced Migration Review*, 4, April: 13–15.

Ditzler, T. (2001) 'Mental health and aid workers: the case for collaborative questioning', *The Journal of Humanitarian Assistance*, 7 January. http://www.jha.ac/articles/a063.htm (accessed on 12 December 2002).

Dunant, H. (1986) *A Memory of Solferino*, Geneva: International Committee of the Red Cross.

Ehrenreich, J. (2001) *Coping with Disaster: A Guidebook to Psychosocial Intervention*, Center for Psychology and Society. http://www.mhwwb.org/disasters.htm (accessed 6 June 2002).

Ehrenreich, J. and Elliot, T. (2004) 'Managing stress in humanitarian aid workers: a survey of humanitarian aid agencies' psychosocial training and support of staff. Peace and Conflict', *Journal of Peace Psychology*, 10, 1: 53–66.

Fawcett, J. (2000) 'Managing staff stress and trauma', in M.Janz and J. Slead (eds) *Complex Humanitarian Emergencies: Lessons for Practitioners*. Monrovia, CA: World Vision, pp. 92–125.

Fawcett, J. (2002) 'Preventing broken hearts, healing broken minds', in Y. Danieli (ed.) *Sharing the Front Line and the Back Hills: International protectors and providers: peacekeepers, humanitarian aid workers and the media in the midst of crisis*. Amityville, NY: Baywood Publishing Company, Inc, pp. 223–32.

Feinstein, A., Owen, J. and Blair, N. (2002) 'A hazardous profession: war, journalists and psychopathology', *American Journal of Psychiatry*, 159, 9: 1570–75.

Figley, C.R. (ed.) (1995) *Compassion Fatigue. Coping with Secondary Traumatic Stress Disorder in Those Who Treat the Traumatized*. Florence, KY: Brunner/Mazel.

Fullerton, C.S. and Ursano, R.J. (eds) (1997) *Posttraumatic stress disorder: acute and long-term responses to trauma and disaster*. Washington, DC: American Psychiatric Press.

Gal, R. (1998) 'Colleagues in distress', *International Review of Psychiatry*, 10, 3: 234–8.

Gist, R. and Devilly, G.J. (2002) 'Post-trauma debriefing: the road too frequently travelled', *The Lancet*, 530, 9335: 741.

Hartman, J. (1997) 'The manager's role in promoting recovery from workplace trauma', Joint National Conference of Australian Society for Traumatic Stress Studies (ASTSS), Australian Critical Incident Stress Association (ACISA), and National Association for Loss and Grief (NALAG), Australia.

Hazan, P. and Berger, J.-F. (2004) *Humanitarian Action. From risk to real danger*. International Committee of the Red Cross. http://www.redcross.int/EN/mag/magazine2004_1/4-9.html (accessed 1 November 2004).

Helton, A.C. (1997) *Protecting Aid Workers: Prospects and Challenges. The Forced Migration Projects. Special Report*, Open Society Institute, September.

Herman, J.L. (1992) *Trauma and Recovery*. New York: Basic Books.

Hoge, W. (2004) 'UN aid chief takes on the world's troubles', *International Herald Tribune*, 10–11 July.

Humanitarian Affairs Review (2001) 'Aid workers can protect themselves', ReliefWeb. http://www.reliefweb.int/w/rwb.nsf/0/09c02d7bff64943ac1256a7800574629?Open (accessed 26 June 2001).

ICRC (1983) *Basic Rules of the Geneva Conventions and Their Additional Protocols*, International Committee of the Red Cross, Geneva, September.

ICRC (1999) *Staying Alive. Safety and Security Guidelines for Humanitarian Volunteers in Conflict Areas*, International Committee of the Red Cross, Geneva.

ICRC (2001) *Humanitarian action and armed conflict. Coping with stress*, July 1–28.

IRC (2000) *Security Management Plan Workbook*, International Rescue Committee, 1 October.

Janoff-Bulman (1985) 'The aftermath of victimization: Rebuilding shattered assumptions', in C.R. Figley (ed.) *Trauma and Its Wake*. New York: Brunner/Mazel.

Jensen, S.B. (1999) *Taking Care of the Caretakers Under War Conditions. Who Cares?* European University Centre for Mental Health and Human Rights.

Kahill, S. (1988) 'Interventions for burnout in the helping professions: A review of the empirical evidence', *Canadian Journal of Counseling Review*, 22: 310–42.

Martin, R. (1999) 'NGO Field Security', *Forced Migration Review*, 4: 4–7.

Maslach, C. (1979) 'Burnout: The loss of human caring', in A. Pines and C. Maslach (eds) *Experiencing Social Psychology*. New York: Random House.

McCreesh, M. (2003) *Re-Entry Syndrome. 6 August*. Aid Workers Network. Aid Workers Exchange. http://www.aidworkers.net/exchange/20030806.html (accessed 6 August 2003).

McFarlane, C.A. (2004) 'Adjustment and risks of humanitarian aid workers', *Australasian Journal of Disaster and Trauma Studies*. http://www.massey.ac.nz/~trauma/issues/2004-1/mcfarlane.htm (accessed 12 December 2004).

Médecins sans Frontières (2002) MSF Charter. http://www.doctorswithoutborders.org/about/charter.shtml (accessed 2 December 2002).

Médecins sans Frontières (2004) 'MSF pulls out of Afghanistan', MSF Press Release. http://www.msf.org/countries/page.cfm?articleid=8851DF09-F62D-47D4-A8D3EB1E876A1E0D (accessed 28 July 2004).

Mitchell, J.T. and Everly, G.S. (2000) 'Critical incident stress management and critical incident stress debriefing: evolutions, effects and outcomes', in B. Raphael and J.P. Wilson (eds) *Psychological Debriefing. Theory, practice and evidence*. Cambridge: Cambridge University Press, pp. 71–90.

Oxfam (2002) *Preparation and support of staff working on conflict areas: Guidance for managers* (ed. Oxfam). Oxfam, UK, 9 pages.

Pearlman, L. (1999) 'Self-care for trauma therapists: ameliorating vicarious traumatization', in B.H. Stamm (ed.) *Secondary Traumatic Stress. Self-Care Issues for Clinicians, Researchers, and Educators*. Baltimore: Sidran Press.

Peel, Q. (2004) 'Keeping Humanitarian Aid Neutral', *Financial Times* http://news.ft.com/cms/s/9708fdac-e67c-11d8-9bd8-00000e2511c8.htm (accessed 5 August 2004).

Potter, J. (2004) 'Securing the safety of aid staff', OneWorld Network, 5 April. http://www.oneworld.net/article/view/75669/1/ (accessed 5 April 2004).

Raphael, B. and Wilson, J.P. (eds) (2000) *Psychological Debriefing. Theory, practice and evidence*. Cambridge: Cambridge University Press.

Rose, S. and Bisson, J. (1998) 'Brief early psychological interventions following trauma: A systematic review of the literature', *Journal of Traumatic Stress*, 11 (4): 697–710.

Salama, P. (2000) *The Psychological Health of Relief Workers: Some Practical Suggestions*. Concern Worldwide, Dublin, Ireland www.reliefweb.int/library/documents/psycho.htm (accessed 20 May 2002).

Shay, J. (1994) *Achilles in Vietnam. Combat Trauma and the Undoing of Character*. New York: Atheneum.

Sheik, M., Gutierrez, M.I., Bolton, P., Spiegel, P., Thieren, M. and Burnham, G. (2000) 'Death among humanitarian workers', *British Medical Journal*, 321: 166–68.

Slim, H. (1995) 'The continuing metamorphosis of the humanitarian practitioner: some new colours for an endangered chameleon', *Disasters*, 19 (2): 110–26.

Slim, H. (1997) 'Doing the right thing. Relief agencies, moral responsibility in political emergencies and war', *Nordiska Afrikainstitutet. Studies on Emergencies and Disaster Relief. No. 6.*

Slim, H. (2002) 'Claiming the humanitarian imperative: NGO's and the cultivation of humanitarian duty', *Refugee Survey Quarterly*, 21 (3): 113–25.

Straker, G. and Moosa, F. (1994) 'Interacting with trauma survivors in contexts of continuing trauma', *Journal of Traumatic Stress*, 7 (3): 457–65.

The Lancet (1999) 'Thought for safety of aid workers in dangerous places', *The Lancet. Editorial*, 354 (9179): 609.

UNHCR (1998) *UNHCR and WFP condemn murder of aid workers in Afghanistan*. 20 July, Geneva, 1 page.

UNSECOORD (2003) UNSECOORD ReliefWeb. http://www.reliefweb.int/appeals/2003/briefingkits/UNSECOORD.pdf (accessed 12 July 2004).

Van Brabant, K. (2001) *Mainstreaming the Organisational Management of Safety and Security. A review of aid agencies' practices and a guide for management*. www.odi.org.uk/hpg (accessed 10 August 2004).

van der Kolk, B., van der Hart, O. and Burbridge, J. (1995) *Approaches to the Treatment of PTSD*, Trauma Clinic Harvard Medical School. http://www.trauma-pages.com/vanderk.htm (accessed 20 March 2003).

Vaux, T. (2002) *The selfish altruist; relief work in famine or war*. London: Earthscan.

WHO/EHA/98.3 (1998) Consultative Meeting on the Management and Support of Relief Workers (ed, The Division of Emergency and Humanitarian Action WHO UN Joint Medical Services International Centre for Migration and Health), Geneva, 8–9 July.

Zimering, R., Munroe, J. and Bird Gulliver, S. (2003) 'Secondary traumatization in mental health care providers', *Psychiatric Times*. http://www.psychiatrictimes.com/p030443.html (accessed 12 November 2003).

Chapter 8

Not off the hook: relationships between aid organization culture and climate, and the experience of workers in volatile environments

Barb Wigley

Introduction

Over the past two to three decades there has been a significant growth in the number of international humanitarian relief organizations, in part as a response to a perceived rise in the number of complex humanitarian emergencies (those involving both natural and human-made disaster, including wars) (Macnair 1995; Eriksson 2001; Small 1996; McCall 1999; Terry, 2002). Aid channelled through international organizations is increasingly being relied upon as a significant part of the international response to complex humanitarian emergencies, having the effect of both positioning these organizations in a more politically charged operational environment and placing their workers in more precarious and demanding circumstances (Small 1996; Walkup 1997(2); Vaux 2001). This politicization of aid has seen an increase in the potential for aid workers to become either targets for, or witnesses to, violence, in addition to an increase in their exposure to the trauma experienced by others (Barron 1999; Eriksson 2001; Figley 1995; Smith 1996).

There is currently an increasing focus upon the psychological impact of work within an emergency environment, but less emphasis has thus far been placed upon the broader role of organizations in either contributing to or ameliorating the stressful and detrimental experiences of their workers. This paper argues that the culture, climate and dynamics of humanitarian organizations impact upon aid worker experience even to a greater extent than events and incidents as a result of the environments in which they work, and additionally, influence their ability to cope with the violence and trauma inherent in their roles. It is proposed that aid organizations have a responsibility to attend to problems of organizational functioning in order to ameliorate the detrimental effects of organizational culture and climate upon their workers. Not only would this enable aid workers to face external risk and trauma with greater resilience, but also overall outcomes of aid interventions are likely to be considerably improved.

Organizational research clearly indicates the influence of organization dynamics and culture upon the experience of employees. For example, Krantz (1998: 5) argues that organizational culture, structure, policies and procedures 'interact with and shape the way individuals handle their emotional experiences'. Organizational 'climate', referring to employee perceptions about the way in which their workplace functions, has been identified as the strongest determinant of individual morale, and after personality is also the strongest determinant of individual distress. Factors including the experience of leadership and managerial practices and policies play a key role in occupational wellbeing, and have been found to be more influential in morale and distress than adverse events or work-related incidents across numerous occupational groups (Cotton 2003). These findings agree with research conducted within the humanitarian aid and emergency services industries where it was found that organizational and inter-personal issues are among the greatest sources of stress for workers, with one study outlining organizational issues, security, workload, communications, witnessing suffering and inter-personal problems with colleagues as the top factors in order (Barron 1999; McDaniel 1988; Raphael 1994; Robbins 1999; Macnair 1995; Bierens de Haan 2002).

Improved organizational functioning cannot be sufficiently achieved through the use of remedies that address only part of the problem, such as recruitment practices, debriefing, stress management programmes or written guidelines, as these focus predominantly on the individual and fail to address the role of deeper and systemic dynamics. As the first review of the People in Aid 'Code of Best Practice in the Management and Support of Aid Personnel' found, implementing improvement initiatives is 'not always easy' and one of the particularly difficult aspects of introducing change was the attempt to 'embed the Code in their organization's thinking and practice' (Davidson 2001: 2). This complaint alludes to the intransigent nature of organization culture and the virtual impossibility of succeeding in structural changes when there is little or no recognition of the depth and power of organization dynamics.

This chapter begins with an exploration of organization culture and the interaction between culture and psycho-social aspects of organizations, including social defences. It considers some of the factors at different levels, from external to intra-personal, that define and shape humanitarian organization culture in particular. Drawing upon the author's qualitative and quantitative research conducted with two international, inter-governmental humanitarian organizations (referred to as IGO1 and IGO2) and with Australian-based returned humanitarian aid workers attached to four international non-government organizations (INGOs), it then examines some of the ways in which culture is experienced by workers, particularly in reference to leadership and organizational and incident-related stress. Finally, interventions and strategies are discussed in terms of their effectiveness, according to current organizational research, and some specific strategies are proposed.

Organization culture

Both systems-psychodynamics and anthropological frames propose models that aim to understand the influence of hidden and more complex elements of organizational life at a deep dimension (Schein 1992). Culture in organizations is associated with language and power, with systems of ideas and the ways they are expressed in interactions. It forms the frame of reference by which individuals and groups create meaning regarding their daily work and make sense of the challenges and changes they are required to manage (Wright 1994). In essence, organization culture guides and influences at every level 'how we see things here' and 'how we do things around here'. This includes how people view and respond to each other, how they respond to their external environment and how they interpret and respond to the stressors they face.

Unconscious assumptions, attitudes and beliefs become embedded in people's thinking and feeling, and shape understanding of the work task and how to perform it. Assumptions usually have at least an element of truth in them, but when they become a universal truth in themselves that disallows for other possibilities, they become restrictive and often counterproductive. For example, in IGO1, one of the most prevalent and influential unquestioned assumptions was that the need for policy and practices to appear fair and be applied equally to all should take precedence over most other issues and policy decisions. This served to set an unstated benchmark according to the needs and values of white men and had the effect of rapidly repressing discussion regarding the particular needs of women, parents and any other groups with unique or different needs. The collective taking up of attitudes and beliefs within groups contributes to the atmosphere of the workplace and the emotional experience of being a part of it. 'People are often dissatisfied and frustrated in institutions, but very often the reasons remain obscure, and what is bemoaned may have little or nothing to do with the deeper reasons for their frustration'(Hinselwood 2000: 27).

Organizational defences

Culture both influences and is influenced by the organizational or social defences that reflect the internal states of mind and the patterns of interactions of the individuals and groups participating within the system. In a similar way to individuals, the groups of people within organizations develop unconscious defence mechanisms against difficult emotions that are experienced as too threatening or painful to acknowledge. These emotions may be stimulated as a response to external threats or conditions, internal conflict and dynamics, or through the nature of the work itself and the experiences of the client group (Halton 1994). All of these factors are highly influential across the aid industry and are exacerbated by conflict between 'bigger picture' imperatives and the needs and goals of workers at the front lines, for example.

People, groups and organizations tend to retreat to more basic, or primitive, emotional responses when under stress, threat or increased pressure, or during times of change. Under heightened pressure, even the most intelligent and professionally skilled can tend to see things in black and white terms where people and ideas can be experienced as all good or all bad (Halton 1994). When groups are operating in this mode, the effectiveness and outcomes of their organization are undermined, since capacity for problem solving and creative and productive thought are reduced (Krantz 1998). 'Splitting' and 'projection' form a pair of defences that have been observed to occur commonly within organizations operating under conditions of pressure or stress. These terms refer to the process whereby disliked parts of the self, team or larger group are unconsciously split off and attributed to others. These 'others' are then perceived as the ones who have the unwanted characteristics and are experienced as bad, threatening or incompetent.

Organizational defences such as splitting and projection, blame, competition and contempt were found to be prevalent in both IGO1 and IGO2 and were the source of much distress and discontent within these organizations. Although all staff did not experience them all of the time, there were many examples of consistent conflict and feelings of disenfranchisement, competition and blame occurring at each level of these organizations and between many of the significant and contrasting interest groups. For example:

She said that as a reaction to the current climate, people have become more secretive and withholding of information. There is a culture of not being able to admit when one doesn't know something, which interferes with learning.

There's always a struggle between HQ and the field and then in the field between branch and sub offices. People never feel understood from wherever they are.

People group themselves and in a corporate culture it might be acceptable for social groups to further their agenda, but in this organization groups are based on the basis of colour, race, religion, language. It's not a nice feeling.

It needs to be stressed that defences have a useful purpose when they allow staff to manage the stress of their work environment and to carry on in highly challenging circumstances. In this case, defences may allow for creative engagement in the core task and assist in the mobilization of energy to get the work done, and to keep going. For example, in order to function effectively, staff in the field need to protect themselves from becoming overwhelmed by grief or terror during crisis situations, or from identifying too strongly with beneficiaries in long-term and desperate situations. When defences gain the power to distort reality and get in the way of growth, reflection, change and the fulfilment of task, however, they can become even more problematic than the factors they have arisen to protect against (Halton 1994).

Further influences upon culture and climate in humanitarian organizations

A vast array of factors and variables influence and shape the culture and functioning of each organization. The four aspects discussed here represent influences at different levels.

The external environment

An increasingly political role, conflicting agendas and increasing competition provide additional layers of complexity and tension sourced from the external environment. In addition, funding earmarked for operations of concern to donors, increasing accountability and reporting requirements, and increasing involvement by donors in determining policy and operational decisions can tend to create not only tension but also some resentment in the relationship between humanitarian organizations and their donors.

Fear of losing funding leads to considerable energy being directed in the service of pleasing donors. This can mean that energy is often directed away from the core task of the organization and transparency is compromised due to a reluctance to admit to unfavourable outcomes. The fickleness of the public support base for humanitarian endeavours encourages a tendency for exaggeration of the gravity of events in order to capture attention and discourages open discussion and debate within and between humanitarian organizations. Any such discussion regarding questionable practices or ineffective interventions, for example, can have implications for the whole industry and not just the organization in question (Terry 2002). The influence of these factors, and their potential to waylay the focus of humanitarian operations, creates further opportunity for conflict between the needs and goals of humanitarian organizations and their field staff, intensifying internal conflict (Small 1996, Lindenberg 1999). For example:

> When you report to donors you have to report that all targets were met. It would be useful for donors to know that it's more complex. They have to encourage more transparent reporting, but they don't ask about what could not be achieved. This translates down to an individual level where people set objectives for themselves that they will be able to put a spin on and say they have achieved.

Bureaucratic organizational structures

Many of the larger humanitarian organizations grew rapidly in the late twentieth century in response to a number of large-scale emergency operations, in particular during the 1990s. Many IGO1 and IGO2 staff spoke about the 'bureaucratic' feel of their organizations, implying that they were large, cumbersome, slow to respond and unnecessarily complicated in their processes.

Rapid change and increased competition in organizational environments means that the large bureaucratic structures of older-style organizations are no longer adaptive. The higher degree of competition, along with increased expectations for reporting and accountability, mean that organizations are required to adapt at a much higher speed. This leaves far less margin for error. However, ironically, an environment of rapid technological change and intense competition fosters the very anxieties that are likely to stimulate bureaucratic responses as a defence, placing these organizations at increased risk of being out of step and excessively preoccupied with self-organising and survival (Krantz 1998).

He spoke about how long it takes to get a new post created and questioned the notion of IGO1 being able to respond rapidly even in an emergency situation. In his experience, the response is too slow, even if the people get there rapidly, the resources take much longer and by the time they arrive, often the emergency is over.

Motivations and characteristics of aid workers

Both conscious and unconscious desires to effect reparation provide the underpinning drive to creative and caring endeavours such as humanitarian aid work (Roberts 1994). The pursuit of reparation is commonly expressed through such traits as the valuing of equity, a desire to challenge injustice and a high potential for idealism. These qualities bolster motivation and determination to work in difficult, volatile and even futile circumstances. They enable a strength of purpose and focus that allows these organizations and their staff to perform in some areas exceptionally well despite the many factors that undermine that performance.

Unconscious determinants of humanitarian idealism also, however, contribute to the development of defensive processes within institutions (Roberts 1994). For example, there is evidence that these personality traits may in fact also render humanitarian workers more vulnerable to stress and trauma. The turmoil and conflict inherent in the work environment of aid may ultimately be more damaging to those who have higher ideals, expectations and needs that the situation is able to fulfil (Walkup 1997(2), Barron 1999). The strengths of IGO1 and IGO2 staff with respect to their commitment also presented a vulnerability to exploitation by the culture of their organizations where their own health and wellbeing were placed at risk in the face of, for example, an acceptance of overwhelming and uncontained workloads and high levels of disruption to their personal lives and social supports. This high level of tolerance may also be seen to reduce incentive within humanitarian organizations to solve many of their structural and organizational problems, allowing a certain degree of complacency and dysfunction. The nature of the work, constraints in the external environment such as funding and resources, and a collective internal drive to do what needs to be done all contribute to the development of a culture where insufficient boundaries are placed around what people are reasonably expected (and expect of themselves) to do.

We are really balancing on the edge. It's difficult to solve it because people are so far stretched and there's nothing to lean on and no time and resources to spend or invest in resolving some of these issues.

In addition to seeking opportunities to 'make it better', the notion of 'saving lives', particularly within a situation of violence and conflict, can be experienced as exhilarating by some workers and a chance to prove their bravery, to the extent that they can feel 'listless without the excitement' (Vaux 2001: 72). Risk-taking behaviour has been found to be of considerable concern, both with regard to those who knowingly take risks and those who feel compelled by others to engage in high-risk activities against their better judgement (Macnair 1995). For example, 30 per cent of IGO2 respondents did not agree that they could choose not to travel to places where they felt unsafe.

The competitive nature of many aid workers may cloud their ability to respond accurately to the needs of beneficiaries, as they compete to prove their bravado and superior analysis. This competitiveness can tend to make it difficult for new workers to fit in and gain the support they particularly need early in their careers.

> It's something I call the 'Goma Club'. People would go. 'So what emergency experience have you had?' and suddenly your status was elevated if you'd been in Goma and if you hadn't been in Goma you were sort of ignored. It's a stressful situation anyway and on top of that you've got this thing of having to prove yourself rather than being given some credit for having something to offer.

Relationships with beneficiaries

There are a number of factors that lead many humanitarian workers, regardless at times of skill and experience, to step back from direct face-to-face work with beneficiaries and defend themselves against the people they are there to assist. Workers expressed a high level of frustration and despair regarding an acute and ongoing lack of resources. In addition, mixed and difficult feelings are evoked in response to poverty, vulnerability and adversity. The unconscious desire to see people as vulnerable in order to assuage feelings of guilt and compassion and to derive a sense of one's own goodness at helping can taint the altruism. Ironically, a reaction against the potential for weakness in the self may be found more often in humanitarian aid, where many workers also harbour a desire to demonstrate prowess and bravery.

> It's difficult for IGO1 to admit that they don't like dealing with beneficiaries. It's draining that you can't solve their problems and that they take a long time to tell their stories. We're not sufficiently in tune with them; we assume they're always the same. From an organizational perspective, there's not enough positive reinforcement of these skills.

As much as vulnerability and need may arouse conflicting emotions in those providing the care, it may also arouse anger, resentment and hostility in the recipients themselves at the situation they find themselves in. The anger they experience is very often directed towards those they have access to: workers at the field level. In some situations, workers have to protect themselves, either physically or emotionally, against the people they are there to protect. In addition, workers who hear reports of trauma, horror, human cruelty and extreme loss can be overwhelmed and they may begin to experience feelings of fear, pain and suffering similar to those of beneficiaries (Sexton, 1999: 2). The ability to tolerate such high degrees of stressful material requires support and skill, and people consistently reported that access to such support or relevant training is extremely limited.

> I wouldn't go to an emergency situation because I can't bear to see people die in front of us because of lack of resources. There is not much support for staff to deal with this.

Relationships between organization culture and stress

A number of studies have found the design and dynamics of workplaces to be more important than personal coping mechanisms in determining health or ill health (Karasek 1990; Gustavsen 1988; Menzies Lyth 1988). Collective coping mechanisms, including social defences discussed above, impact upon the organization and experience of work, often contributing to psychological strain (Menzies Lyth 1988). The means by which workers cope with stress is therefore influenced by collectively developed defence mechanisms and shared experience within particular organizational contexts.

Stress is a constant in humanitarian work, not unexpected or even in certain situations, intermittent. Without a supportive and containing system in place, activity can easily become driven by stress, suspicions between workers and factions become aroused, and anger and contempt get in the way of effective decision-making and colour attitudes towards local populations. Two INGO workers highlight the impact of inter-personal relationships in particular within the team:

> The greatest difficulty was the personal interactions with the other people you were working with, so you're living and working very closely with people. There's a real tension among the relationships. There are some really big personalities, and so living in that environment was horrible.

It doesn't matter how hard your work is, with the local people it's always rewarding, but it's your own people that can make your life just unbearable and that would be the only reason you'd think of resigning.

Incident-related stress

Of the IGO2 staff who said they had been at one or more times close to or in actual physical danger, only one-third agreed that they had been offered support promptly after a critical incident. One-quarter responded that being offered support after a critical incident was not applicable, thereby appearing to indicate that they did not regard having been in or close to physical danger as a critical incident. Of this group, between a third and a half reported one or more symptoms that might indicate some kind of ongoing stress reaction, such as persistent troubling thoughts, affected sleep, increased sensitivity or other changes. The results raise some questions as to the organization-wide understanding of the term 'critical incident' and the culture around offering and receiving support. For example, only a third of respondent supervisors agreed that they were clear regarding IGO2's policies for managing critical incidents and around half did not agree that they were clear about their role or were happy with their skills in relation to critical incident response.

With many respondents appearing not to regard being close to or in physical danger or involved in emotionally harrowing experiences as critical incidents, the question of bravado and risk-taking behaviour, as discussed above, is raised. While debriefing may not be the only or even always the most appropriate response following a critical incident or in response to a situation of cumulative stress, an irregular and unpredictable response by the organization appeared to contribute to stress levels:

> The tragedy in Baghdad had a significant adverse affect on me, and I did not and do not see any avenue within the organization to help me relieve the stress that has resulted.

> Debriefings by IGO2 should be mandatory. Currently they are a joke and there is no clear policy on where you debrief. Indeed it is pot luck as to whether you are offered a debrief or not.

In addition, cultural factors in this organization clearly impacted upon the amount of support workers perceived they had access to after crises or on a day-to-day basis:

It's difficult to talk to colleagues or supervisors because one never knows if these opinions/problems won't be used against them. Confidentiality or even discretion doesn't matter versus one's career.

In my field posts I have felt abandoned and unsupported by IGO2.

I feel the stigma of having been evacuated from a country because of 'stress-related' issues still lingers among some managers.

INGO workers also talked of the impact of organization culture upon the effectiveness of debriefing interventions:

You go to debrief at the overseas headquarters. They're not personal; they don't know you. There is a psychologist there, but it's going through the motions, you know? I give them exactly what they want to hear, when really it's not how I feel. Rather than cause a stir and actually tell it how it is and give it to them, because you'll get a black mark beside your name, I just play the game.

Organizational-related stress: administration and leadership

Administrative and human resource issues, just ahead of management issues, were identified in the IGO2 survey as the aspect of their work that most people found difficult to bear. Many of the responses and comments reflected a high level of frustration and dissatisfaction with the administrative support available, processes and policies, and culture around decision-making and action on such issues as recruitment and contracts. For example:

Most of my stress is caused by internal management issues (administration, HR, short-tasking, communication issues, un-reasonable workload, etc.) rather than external environmental issues.

Field experiences of the kind commonly considered as 'stressful', mostly in war zones and crisis areas, and mostly before coming to [headquarters], have affected me far less than what I had to experience in [headquarters] over the past two years.

The IGO2 survey revealed that while there was a generally positive response to questions regarding direct line supervisors, 'management issues' were rated the second-highest source of stress across all respondents, and fewer respondents agreed that they received sufficient guidance and support to do their job well or that they received sufficient recognition. There was a significantly more negative perception of the senior levels of management.

Most field-based IGO1 teams participating in the research shared similar structures, burdens and obstacles such as restricted funding and limited resources to meet the needs of their beneficiaries, and a number were also dealing with the impact of downsizing, for example. The teams that retained some sense of optimism and energy were the ones who reported feeling positive about their relationship with their managers. On the other hand, the teams who indicated a level of difficulty with their direct supervisors or local management also tended to be fragmented, less motivated, and one could argue, less functional or dynamic despite the presence of many capable workers.

> The way it's set up, it all depends on the [regional manager]. If you have a bad manager, it will colour every aspect of your life until they leave. If you have a good [regional manager] and supervisor it makes the difference.

There was not a strong feeling that leadership and management skills in relation to the management of people were valued generally in either IGO, despite the direct connection with the level of functioning of the teams. A desire to believe that the worthiness of the organization's goals and purpose is sufficient can cloud recognition of the part that human interactions play in the effectiveness and impact of outcomes. Many people are placed in management and leadership roles without any formal preparation and support, indicating a belief that management and leadership can be performed through the use of natural ability alone, without the need for additional learning of skills (Levine 2002). There was a perception among some that many managers were oriented towards criticism rather than positive reinforcement and that this was an approach favoured by the organization. Many also felt that their organization supported many punitive and even abusive managers, so that in some places people felt unsafe:

> There are still a lot of old-style managers who would prefer to terrorise staff.

> When staff are confronted by situations, they can forget their principles and become concerned with saving their skins. This has become part

of the culture; keep quiet around your supervisor because some are not open to dialogue.

This influenced where people wished to be posted and created an anxiety that the organization would not protect people from being posted with a negative or abusive manager.

If the behaviour and response of managers can significantly influence the resilience of workers (Barron 1999), it can be argued that field postings, where, for example, risk is higher, international staff are removed from their wider social supports and locally employed staff have insecure tenure, are some of the very situations where competence in leadership is of critical importance. Geographical isolation means that there are fewer opportunities for backup and alternative forms of support. At the field level, skilled managers are needed not only to respond to incidents, but to contain ongoing stress, to shield their teams from some of the wider politics and problematic dynamics and to foster a positive and productive work environment. There were many places in both organizations where this appeared to be the case. By contrast, in situations where relationships were poor, there was potential for a heightened impact of problems in the wider system. The additional demands these responsibilities place upon field-based managers can create a high degree of stress, and therefore the ability to manage the emotional demands of the role both for oneself and in relation to others is vital for the performance of the team as a whole. An INGO manager describes some of these demands:

> You're putting people through often some of the most intense experiences of their lives. They wanted to go to an exotic location and help people in a nice way, and they find themselves in the middle of a muddy, stinking Rwandan refugee camp with 200,000 people, some of whom were the perpetrators of unimaginable horrors. You do need to have a very good understanding or feel for team dynamics and how individuals work. I've been in evacuation situations where I've had to decide who stays and who goes. A lot of that is understanding where people are at and what their inner resources are and how they will cope with very difficult situations. You have to be patient, but you have to stick to your guns, you know, there are rules to be followed and you've got to know certain limits.

Intervention trends

While the provision of critical incident stress debriefing immediately after a significant incident is now reasonably common in international humanitarian organizations, other support systems responding to different types of stressors are less developed, and most organizations feel that these systems are inadequate (McCall 1999). Recruitment practices and the support, training and debriefing needs of staff have been emphasised in the literature as needing attention. However, a number of variables in humanitarian work, such as the loss of usual coping mechanisms and supports while placed in an unfamiliar and stressful environment, mean that it may be impossible to judge prior to deployment how well a person may cope once deployed. It is also questionable as to how possible it is to prepare people in advance for their experience in the field (McCall 1999; Macnair 1995; International Health Exchange and People in Aid 1997).

Withdrawal behaviours among employees, such as absenteeism and compensation claims, correlate highly with low morale; more so than with individual distress. For this reason, interventions that focus on improving morale tend to be more successful than those focusing on individual levels of distress. These interventions specifically include those that focus on improving the quality of leadership and people management. Conversely, traditional interventions such as stress management training, coping skills training programmes and occupational health and safety risk management approaches tend to be of less value at an organizational level and lead to far less impact on levels of absenteeism and wellbeing. Employee support services, such as counselling and debriefing, have also been found to be more effective in their impact upon morale than on individual psychological health, with their greatest benefit appearing to be in the demonstration of support and care of management (Cotton 2003). This INGO worker highlighted the impact on morale of similar types of interventions:

> They gave good briefing beforehand. You felt like you were looked after; people cared about that you were there, and they had taken care to select people they thought were adequate.

These findings would seem to argue against the value of relying upon individually focused strategies to solve the wider problems of morale, organizational functioning and culture. Recognition that both the problems and the solutions are more complex than just, for example, choosing the right people to start with, training them in how to cope and then providing them with psychological support when they become distressed, is essential before organizations can start to tackle what is really going on and how it might be ameliorated. 'It seems there is great comfort to be drawn in learning about, for example, selection and recruitment or identification of competencies or strategic planning as if these are all that are needed to get the best people in, to ensure they work well and that the organisation is on track and protected against surprises' (Raab 2000).

In response to the question, 'How aware is the organization of the stresses people experience?' this INGO worker highlighted the inadequacy of locating the solution to the problem solely within individuals:

> I don't think they're very aware at all. The organization has developed these approaches with debriefing and counselling and the centre at headquarters as being a response to HR policies, rather than there being a drive from senior management to actually look after their staff.

If one accepts the argument that organization culture and climate have a more significant impact upon occupational wellbeing than critical incidents, it becomes evident that these are the primary areas where interventions should be targeted. This is not to say that the other strategies are not important or of value, but more that they are insufficient on their own to sustain significant enough improvement, and therefore potentially contribute towards placing workers at greater risk when the greater underlying causes are not acknowledged. It is a far bolder task, and one that evokes far greater anxiety, for the leaders of an organization to recognise that 'the way we lead and the way we all do things around here, places our workers at risk', than to collude in the fantasy that it is possible to focus on technical or structured interventions to contain the unpredictable while avoiding acknowledgement of one's role in improving workplace health and outcomes.

Conclusion

It seems little wonder, given the complexity of the environment in which humanitarian organizations operate and the nature of what is at stake in the work, that problematic aspects of culture and social defences emerge, notwithstanding the high quality of many staff in the field. Organizational defences are unavoidable and are a part of every organization, but from a more integrated position some may be directed more creatively. Facing what is difficult is, in the end, the most effective way to free people up to get on with their core tasks, rather than allowing the 'undiscussables' to sap the energy of the organization from the inside.

Humanitarian organizations can be engaged in a constant struggle to hold their focus upon core organizational tasks while resisting the temptation to become sidetracked with tasks concerned more, for example, with self -perpetuation, bureaucratic 'organization' or pleasing donors. When this sidetracking occurs, worker job satisfaction tends to be supplanted by frustration and conflict, and people lose clarity regarding the reasons they are there. Alternatively, when energy is mobilized around a task and the task is meaningful and congruent, a great degree of satisfaction can be derived from working well and working well together.

The violence and trauma that humanitarian organizations work with on a regular basis cannot be ignored or dismissed as trivial. However, it is important to emphasise that the resilience of workers to manage the challenges they face in their external environment can be bolstered or undermined by the manner in which their organizations function. Workers are able to cope with the demands and stressors of working in violent settings more effectively if they are well supported and less troubled by the dynamics of their organization.

While there are many approaches that can and should be taken in addressing the problematic aspects of organization culture and climate, this chapter has emphasized that the most central factor in achieving a more functional position is the mobilization, strengthening and support of leadership. A realistic goal for leaders involved in a constant act of balancing conflicting tensions is to navigate a 'good enough' path through them. Some of the most effective aspects of leadership are 'dramatically ordinary stuff'; leaders who have the capacity to connect with both the people around them and with the task, facilitate realistic and open conversations about goals and processes, are known to advocate for their groups when necessary, and make effective links with the organization outside of their group (Binney 2003: 4).

The dynamics, attitudes and behaviour of the senior levels of management influence what happens at every other level, both consciously and unconsciously. Therefore it is critical that questions of leadership and authority are seen to be taken up at the highest levels. This would involve, for example, taking steps to improve cohesion among senior management groups and the visible engagement and role modelling by senior managers in open discussion of difficult organizational issues; learning, reflection and planning activities; drawing of clear and manageable boundaries around a task; and recognition of the importance of good people management skills at every level and the impact this has on the productivity and outcomes of the organization as a whole.

It is essential for leaders at every level to have the courage to face the more difficult issues with their teams, as this enables a freeing up to get on with the task. This might simply involve identifying and raising the one or two most pressing issues that need to be addressed in order for teams to move forward. Critical also is the development of a managerial culture that emphasizes day-to-day support of staff. The skills required to undertake such interventions need to be facilitated through a range of approaches, including not only training but also ongoing coaching opportunities, peer development and support, and the example and encouragement of senior leaders.

Development towards a position where, for example, challenging issues might be contained, linked and integrated rather than fragmented and split apart, can only occur through the example, bravery and guidance of leaders. An essential ingredient to achieving these aims is the will to do it – a commitment at all levels to working towards an organization that is determined to realise its potential through a recognition of the role that organizational culture, climate and dynamics play in the resilience of its workers and in the success of its outcomes.

References

Barron, R.A. (1999) 'Psychological Trauma and Relief Workers', in Leaning, J., Briggs, S. and Chen, L. (eds) *Humanitarian Crises: The Medical and Public Health Response*, Cambridge, MA: Harvard University Press.

Bierens de Haan, D.B., Van Beerendonk, H., Michel, N. and Mulli, J.-C. (2002) 'Le Programme de soutien psychologique des intervenants humanitaires du Comite International de la Croix-Rouge', *Revue Française de Psychiatre et de Psychologie Medicale*, 53, http://www.icrc.org/Web/fre/sitefre0.nsf/iwplist74/C2CE5D2 AB42D05A5C1256C750044F52C (accessed 13 July 2005).

Binney, G., Wilke, G. and Williams, C. (2003) *Leaders in Transition: the dramas of ordinary heroes*, Ashridge Consulting, www.ashridge.com/80256BC10040B3C1. nsf/0/A5105553CB8BB29480256DBF0037252F?Open (accessed 12 July 2005).

Cotton, P. and Hart, P. (2003) 'Occupational Wellbeing and Performance: A Review of Organizational Health Research', *Australian Psychologist*, 38(1).

Davidson, S. and Raynard, P. (2001) *Ahead of the Field: Pilot Agencies and the People in Aid Code 1997–2000*, Vol. 2002 People in Aid, www.reliefweb.int/rw/lib.nsf/ db900SID/LGEL-5SJGMR/$FILE/pia-ahead-2000.pdf?OpenElement(accessed 12 July 2005).

Eriksson, C.B., Vande Kemp, H., Gorsuch, R., Hoke, S. and Foy, D.W. (2001) 'Trauma Exposure and PTSD Symptoms in International Relief and Development Personnel', *Journal of Traumatic Stress*, 14(1), pp. 205–12.

Figley, C.R. (1995) 'Compassion Fatigue as Secondary Traumatic Stress Disorder: An Overview', in Figley, C.R. (ed.) *Compassion Fatigue: Coping With Secondary Traumatic Stress Disorder in Those Who Treat the Traumatized*, Vol.23, New York: Brunner-Routledge, pp. 1–20.

Gustavsen, B. (1988) 'Democratising occupational health: the Scandinavian experience of work reform', *International Journal of Health Services*, 18, pp. 675– 89.

Halton, W. (1994) 'Some unconscious aspects of organizational life: Contributions from psychoanalysis', in Obholzer, A. and Roberts, V.Z. (eds), *The Unconscious at Work: Individual and Organizational Stress in the Human Service*, London: Routledge.

Hinshelwood, R.D. and Skogstad, W. (2000) 'The Dynamics of Health Care Institutions', in Hinshelwood, R.D. and Skogstad, W. (eds), *Observing Organizations: Anxiety, Defence and Culture in Health Care*, London: Routledge.

International Health Exchange and People in Aid (1997) *The Human Face of Aid: A Study of Recruitment by International Relief and Development Organizations in the UK*, International Health Exchange and People in Aid, http://www.peopleinaid.org.uk/download/HUMAN%20FACE%20OF%20AID.pdf (accessed 12 July 2005).

Karasek, R. and Theorell, T. (1990) *Healthy Work: Stress, productivity and the reconstruction of working life*, New York: Basic Books.

Krantz, J. (1998) 'Anxiety & The New Order', in Klein, E., Gabelnick, F. and Herr, P. (eds), *Leadership in the 21st Century*, Madinson, CT: International Universities.

Levine, D.P. (2002) 'On Learning a Skill', *Socio-Analysis*, 4, pp. 87–97.

Lindenberg, M. (1999) 'Complex Emergencies and NGOs: The Example of CARE', in Leaning, J., Briggs, S. and Chen, L. (eds) *Humanitarian Crises: The Medical and Public Health Response*, Cambridge: Harvard University Press.

Macnair, R. (1995) *Room For Improvement: The Management and Support of Relief and Development Workers*, London: Overseas Development Institute, p. 101.

McCall, M. and Salama, P. (1999) 'Selection, training and support of relief workers: an occupational health issue', *British Medical Journal*, 318(7176), p. 113.

McDaniel, E.G. (1988) 'Psychological Response To Disaster', in Baskett, P. and Weller, R. (eds), *Medicine for Disasters*, London: John Wright.

Menzies Lyth, I.E.P. (1988) *Containing Anxiety in Institutions: Selected Essays*, London: Free Association Books.

Raab, N. (2000) *How Organisations Work (and Why They're Crazy)*, VICSERV Conference, Melbourne.

Raphael, B. and Wilson, J.P. (1994) 'When Disaster Strikes: Managing Emotional Reactions in Rescue Workers', in Wilson, J.P. and Lindy, J.D. (eds) *Countertransference in the Treatment of PTSD*, New York: Guildford.

Robbins, I. (1999) 'The psychological impact of working in emergencies and the role of debriefing', *Journal of Clinical Nursing*, 8(3), pp. 263–68.

Roberts, V.Z. (1994) 'The self-assigned impossible task', in Obholzer, A. and Roberts, V.Z. (eds), *The Unconscious at Work: Individual and Organizational Stress in the Human Services*, London: Routledge.

Schein, E.H. (1992) *Organization Culture and Leadership*, San Francisco: Jossey Bass.

Sexton, L. (1999) 'Vicarious traumatization of counsellors and effects on their workplaces' *British Journal of Guidance & Counselling*, 27(3), pp. 393–403.

Small, C. (1996) NGO *Management in Situations of Conflict*, Oxford: INTRAC, The International NGO Training and Research Centre, pp. 1–33.

Smith, B., Agger, I., Danieli, Y. and Weisaeth, L. (1996) 'Health Activities Across Traumatized Populations: Emotional Responses of International Humanitarian Aid Workers: The Contribution of Non-Governmental Organizations', in

Danieli, Y., Rodley, N.S. and Weisaeth, L. (eds), *International Responses to Traumatic Stress*, New York: Baywood Publishing.

Terry, F. (2002) *Condemned to repeat? The paradox of humanitarian action*, New York: Cornell University Press.

Vaux, T. (2001) *The Selfish Altruist: Relief Work in Famine and War*, London: Earthscan.

Walkup, R.M. (1997(2)) *Policy and Behaviour in Humanitarian Organizations: The Institutional Origins of Operational Dysfunction*, Doctoral Thesis, University of Florida.

Wright, S. (1994) '"Culture" in anthropology and organizational studies', in Wright, S. (ed.) *Anthropology of Organizations*, London: Routledge.

Terrorism: a New Type of Workplace Violence

Chapter 9

Organizational violence: a trigger for reactive terrorism

Vaughan Bowie

Introduction

This chapter examines terrorism as a new form of workplace violence that needs to be addressed in a comprehensive manner by organizations in the public, for-profit and not-for-profit sectors. Specifically this chapter looks at the inter-relationship between workplace violence and its possible role in fostering and triggering terrorist acts.

In this chapter the varying types of terrorism and the sources and triggers of such violence as indicated within the research literature will be outlined. We will then turn our attention to the ways in which organizational cultures and work practices may in themselves stimulate social and community conditions that provide breeding grounds for cultural, political and religious resentments. Such resentments in turn could then trigger reactive terrorist sentiments and action. The chapter will then examine the important but largely overlooked direct role that trans-national organizations, especially multi-nationals, may play in providing 'fertile ground' for terrorism to thrive and expand. The chapter concludes by outlining some strategies to identify and minimize such links between workplace violence and reactive terrorism.

Defining workplace violence and terrorism

In chapter 1 of this book a typology of workplace violence was outlined which included four key types of workplace violence:

- Type 1: External/Intrusive violence.
- Type 2: Consumer-related violence.
- Type 3: Relationship violence.
- Type 4: Organizational violence.

Each of these types could be a source of terrorist violence experienced within a work setting.

In the light of this typology the following definition of this phenomenon has been developed for this chapter. Workplace violence is a perceived or actual verbal abuse, emotional threat, physical attack or misuse of power upon an individual's person or property, or against a work group or organization by another individual, group or organization while undertaking work-related duties.

However, as Standing and Nicolini (1997) suggest, there is no perfect definition and this one would need to be contextualized and adapted to each workplace. Thus, such a contextualized definition of workplace violence would need to include at least the following aspects:

- Source: where is the violence coming from?
- Target: who is the violence aimed at?
- Perception of the act: the target(s) perceives it as a violent act.
- Impact: the act has some physical and/or emotional impact on the target(s).
- Work-related: the violence occurs while undertaking work-related duties.

An equally complex task is that of identifying and defining what comprises terrorism. Part of the problem in defining terrorism is that this term raises all sorts of emotions and it is indeed a contested concept (Smelser and Mitchell 2002). For those who are targets of such acts, the term immediately evokes images of hideous, irrational acts of violence committed by desperate, morally bankrupt individuals very different from themselves. On the other hand, terrorism is sometimes seen positively by those who directly or indirectly support its goals even though they may not agree with the methods used by such groups (Barkan and Snowden 2001).

Barkan (2001: 66) concludes that 'although there might not be one perfect definition of terrorism, these definitions and others like them underscore its essentially political nature, its use to provoke fear in the general population, and its use both by and against the state. Viewed dispassionately, terrorism is a violent tactic aimed at winning political objectives.' Barkan and Snowden (2001) go on to note that part of the reason for the difficulty in arriving at a comprehensive, overarching definition of terrorism may be that there are so many different types of such acts making one all-encompassing definition difficult to arrive at.

The Panel on Behavioral, Social and Institutional Issues (Smelser and Mitchell 2002: 1) came up with a working definition that 'includes the ingredients of (a) illegal use or threatened use of force or violence (b) with an intent to coerce societies or governments by inducing fear in their populations (c) typically with political and/or ideological motives and justifications and (d) an "extrasocietal" element, either "outside" society in the case of domestic terrorism or "foreign" in the case of international terrorism.' Such a comprehensive definition however immediately strikes at least one problem with the concept of the illegal use of force. Does this mean that state sponsored acts of force and violence such as genocide are 'acceptable' and not defined as terrorist acts? Also, most typologies of terrorism tend to include its purpose, perpetrators and supporters and its location (Hammell 2002). However, even the concept of a location for terrorist acts may be misleading with the increasing possibility of 'cyber terrorism' that can be committed simultaneously around the world through computer networks (Williams 2004).

Martin (2003: 32) identifies the following common features of many formal definitions of terrorism. These include:

- 'The use of illegal force

- Subnational actors

- Unconventional methods

- Political motives

- Attacks against "soft" civilian and passive military targets

- Act aimed at purposefully affecting an audience'

Such definitions might also include the sudden and unexpected nature of such acts.

Useful as these definitions are, they have some limitations and omissions and are based on what Martin calls traditional terrorism models. Also as indicated above, such definitions are very focused on terrorist groups rather than state-sponsored terrorism (Barkan and Snowden 2001). Such definitions may also omit or minimize the role of religious fundamentalism in triggering terrorist incidents.

A number of academics and commentators on terrorism have described a change from old or 'traditional' terrorism to 'new' terrorism. Such "traditional" terrorism, as characterized by Martin (2003), includes:

- Distinctly identifiable movements or organizations.

- The use of conventional, non-nuclear weapons.

- Specific grievances championing particular classes, causes or ethno-national groups.

- Selection of relatively small-scale, specific targets.

- Leftist ethno-nationalist motives.

- Left-wing ideological motives.

- Deliberate media manipulation and publicized incidents.

- Identifiable organizational structure and profile.

- Full-time professional operatives.

The emerging 'new terrorism' (Martin 2003) is characterized by:

- The development of loose cell-based stateless networks across the world.

- The potential for acquiring and use of weapons of mass destruction.

- Espoused motivations based on politically vague, religious or mystical causes.

- Links with organized crime and drug syndicates as a source of revenue.

- 'Asymmetrical' methods of conducting terrorist acts.

The main types of terrorism as identified in the research literature will be outlined below.

Types of terrorism

Broadly similar typologies of terrorism are repeatedly found in academic and policy analyses of such acts. Barkan and Snowden (2001) referring to the work of Gurr (1989) describe vigilante, insurgent, trans-national and state terrorism. Hoffman (1998) identifies ethno-nationalist/separatist, international, religious, and state-sponsored terrorism. Laqueur (1999) in the context of what he calls the 'new terrorism' describes far-rightist, religious state, 'exotic' and criminal terrorism. Other experts such as Martin (2003) identify forms of terrorism such as domestic terrorism, narco-terrorism, toxic terrorism, criminal terrorism and netwar terrorism. Williams (2004) identifies three main types of terrorism – ideological, religious and social – while excluding criminal terrorism as a 'true' form of terrorism.

For the purpose of this chapter Gurr's (1989) five key types of vigilante, insurgent, single-issue, separatist and revolutionary terrorism will provide a useful starting framework to which will be added other forms of terrorism – trans-national, state, religious and criminal – to give a more detailed overview. These additional types of terrorism are not totally distinct from those outlined by Gurr and may overlap with them in a number of ways. These nine types of terrorism are outlined below.

Vigilante terrorism. In this type of terrorism private individuals commit acts against other private citizens to express hatred or to resist social change. This type is the most common form of terrorism found throughout US history and is often omitted or downplayed in most terrorism typologies. An example of such acts are those committed by Klu Klux Klan members against Afro-Americans.

Insurgent terrorism occurs when private citizens commit terrorism against their government rather than private citizens, to win political goals. The Oklahoma bombings could fit into this type of terrorist act. Conceivably such acts could also be committed against non-government agencies including multi-nationals.

Single-issue terrorism is terrorism committed by an individual or small group in order to pressure the government (or organization) to change a specific policy. Examples of this could be bombings carried out by 'right to life' proponents.

Separatist terrorism aims to help an ethnic or religious group secede from a state. Basque separatists in Spain and the IRA in Northern Ireland are examples of this type of terrorism.

Social revolutionary terrorism aims to overthrow the government and bring about dramatic economic, political and social change.

Both vigilante and insurgent terrorism could also be grouped under the broader category of domestic terrorism.

The other four types of terrorism worth outlining in more detail are:

Trans-national terrorism. This occurs when terrorists living in one nation strike inside another nation. This is exemplified in the attacks of 11 September 2001 in the USA.

State terrorism. Sometimes called repressive terrorism, this type is used by a government to intimidate its own citizens. Barkan and Snowden (2001: 89) make the interesting observation that '[I]n the long run, in fact, state terrorism poses a much bigger threat – in the forms of death, injury, fear and misery – to the global community than does all other terrorism combined.'

Religious terrorism. There are some crucial differences between secular and religious terrorists. The non-religious, secular terrorists appeal to actual or potential supporters or those supposedly disadvantaged in some way to support their cause, while religious terrorists undertake such acts for no-one but themselves or in the name of a 'higher power'. Thus the limitation on secular terrorists not to alienate some actual or potential supporters doesn't apply to religious terrorists who feel justified in undertaking 'total war' (Martin 2003). Hoffman (1996) observes that in 1968 none of the major 11 active international terrorist groups could be classified as religious, but by 1996 nearly one-quarter of the approximately 50 major terrorist organizations had predominantly religious motivations and ideals.

Criminal terrorism is motivated by profit while criminal-political enterprises may use funds generated by crime to sustain their movement (e.g. the Taliban and Tamil Tigers). The UN (2002: 15) notes 'the links between terrorism and organized crime, including drug trafficking, money laundering, illicit trafficking of arms and corruption, which provide an environment that enables terrorist operations to expand.'

Each of these nine types of terrorism could directly impact upon a workplace from either an external source or internally. Such terrorist acts could arise within the workplace from those known to staff, such as colleagues, customers and clients, or from perpetrators outside the organization.

Further links between workplace violence and terrorism will be outlined below.

'Explaining' workplace violence and terrorism

Debate has raged over the centuries as to whether violent behaviour of both individual and collective types is irrational or a rational response to particular external circumstances or felt needs. The current debate around workplace violence is also informed and influenced by these historical perspectives as well as the personal and political worldviews of those who propound such theories.

Below we shall first examine the general individual, group and organizational 'explanations for violence' and then see how applicable such explanations are to workplace violence and terrorism in particular.

Individual explanations of workplace violence

At the individual level the research literature typologies of violence are generally divided into: intra-individual theories, social-psychological theories and sociocultural theories. Such individual explanations have also at times been used to explain group or collective violence and so it may be a rather arbitrary exercise to differentiate strictly between individual, group and organizational explanations of workplace violence.

These intra-individual, social-psychological and sociocultural theories can be used to help explain and understand workplace violence when committed by an individual in its various type 1–3 forms. Thus we could for example attempt to explain type 1 terrorist and protest violence as the result of an individual's genetic and experiential makeup.

Psychological perspective

From a psychological perspective, individuals who commit terrorist acts are seen as having psychological abnormalities or problems that predispose them to do so. This approach focuses on notions of the 'irrational person', the loner or disturbed individual. However, while terrorism is defined by its opponents as symptoms of a psychopathological mind, terrorism is seen as 'rational' by the person who commits it. Also, the available evidence has not found that most terrorists suffer from some type of psychopathology or 'have terrorist personalities'. Such explanations minimize or downplay the role of historical, political, economic, religious and various other structural conditions that underlie terrorism (Barkan and Snowden 2001).

Social-psychological perspective

Some attempts at bridging the gap between the psychological and structural explanations of terrorist violence use a social-psychological approach that connects the individual's psychological state to structural conditions (Moghaddam 2005). However useful as this social-psychological approach is it suffers from an inability to more fully explain why some people will partake in terrorist acts and others will not (Williams 2004).

Sociocultural perspective

A sociocultural perspective on terrorism examines such behaviours as an individual's rational responses to certain structural conditions such as oppression, unemployment, and religious and ethnic discrimination which they perceive as threatening their economic, political and social wellbeing (Barkan and Snowden 2001).

Group explanations of workplace violence

However, when such workplace violence is committed by groups or organizations these previous individualistic explanations need to be modified, expanded or new explanatory models developed. Let us now look at some key explanations of how violence can arise within the context of a group and how such interpretations can be applied to workplace violence.

Political process and resource mobilization theories

Scholars in the 1960s began to develop a more detailed understanding of collective behaviour that linked the views of the earlier 'irrationalists' to a new emphasis on the rational choice and political and high moral purpose of collective action. This new explanation of collective behaviour had several names, including political theory, political process theory, resource mobilization theory and political opportunity theory.

In such theories, collective action is seen as a 'natural' response of rational political actors to harsh social conditions. Collective action commences when peoples' resources such as money, time, and communication skills are mobilized by social movement leaders and when political and social conditions are changing in ways that aid such mobilization. Such action could include civil disobedience, protests, riots revolution and terrorism and other political behaviour. These theories emphasize the importance of mobilization, organization and resources while de-emphasizing the importance of psychological and social-psychological factors such as deprivation, grievances and discontent (Barkan and Snowden 2001).

Social constructionist perspective

More recently the resource mobilization perspective has given way to a social constructionist perspective. This perspective considers collective action as both rational and political, but it also reminds us of its various social-psychological dimensions (Barken and Snowden 2001). Key to the social constructionist perspective is the emphasis on how individuals decide to participate in collective action, including violence, and how they interpret the meanings that they attach to specific collective behaviour incidents.This approach highlights the importance of cultural aspects of collective behaviour that help mobilize their supporters. Such cultural and social aspects include religious and other belief systems that help construct collective identities that involve a shared understanding of how they define themselves and the goals that they are pursuing.

The ethnic competition model

Another possible explanation for collective violence including terrorism is the ethnic competition model, which could possibly be seen as a sub type of the social constructionist perspective. Barkan and Snowden (2001: 22) note that in this model, conflict results when groups compete for scarce resources. Such competition can increase when, for example, the economy takes a turn for the worse or immigration increases. Thus, when two or more ethnic groups living in the same nation or a smaller setting find themselves competing for jobs, housing and other resources, ethnic hostility and eventually conflict in the form of ethnic violence are likely to develop. They comment that such conflict will arise only if one or more of the ethnic groups perceive that the competition is unfair.

Martin (2003: 56), in drawing together aspects of the resource mobilization, social constructionist and ethnic competition perspectives, suggests that at the group level terrorism can emerge from social movements and/or from dramatic events in the lives of peoples or nations. Such two types of terrorism are not entirely independent and may be interconnected.

In the first instance terrorism can arise within an environment of political activism where a group aims to draw to the attention of the government or broader society its perceived grievances and bring about change (Williams 2004). Such movement may become more radicalized if the group becomes frustrated with the slowness of change or because of the violent reactions of its opponents. This radicalization may include the use of violence to achieve its goals. Examples of such movements are the anti-apartheid movement in South Africa or the IRA in Northern Ireland.

Terrorism can also grow out of traumatic events experienced by a people or a nation. Dramatic events that may also lead to terrorism occur when an individual, ethnic or religious group or a nation suffers from an event that has a major and lasting impact (Williams 2004). In some instances the children of victims of political violence may grow up violently opposing their perceived oppressors, as has occurred in the Palestinian intifada and 'ethnic cleansings' in the Balkans.

Responding to terrorism

Martin (2003) identifies two major responses to terrorism – those of counterterrorism and anti-terrorism – though the differences between these two are not always clear-cut. Counterterrorism involves the development of proactive policies that are specifically designed and implemented to eliminate terrorist environments and groups. Such counterterrorism policies have the ultimate goal of saving lives by proactively preventing or lessening the number of terrorist attacks. Anti-terrorism, sometimes referred to as offensive counterterrorism, is the use of offensive and defensive measures that seek to deter or prevent terrorist attacks (Williams 2004). Offensive strategies may include economic and diplomatic sanctions and pre-emptive military strikes, while defensive strategies typically include target hardening, enhanced security and other measures to make potential terrorist targets as secure as possible from attack.

Counterterrorism and anti-terrorism measures may range across a continuum from very passive non-reaction to highly active responses (Williams 2004). Such responses can be grouped into several policy options. Such options may include:

- Military force, including punitive and pre-emptive strikes.
- Intelligence gathering.
- Covert action, including misinformation, sabotage and assassinations.
- Increased security, including target hardening and profiling.
- Legal, repressive and conciliatory responses to terrorism.
- Diplomacy, sanctions and financial controls.
- Social and structural reform addressing underlying grievances and perceptions.
- Targeted and untargeted prevention strategies (Martin 2003).

The effectiveness of these various 'hard' and 'soft' responses to terrorism is often hard to measure. Offensive 'hard' strategies may in the short term 'eliminate' opposition but in the long term risk increasing the resolve of terrorists and stimulating support for their cause while doing little to address the religious, political, social and economic conditions at the root of some forms of terrorism. Terrorism response measures in democratic societies may also be a threat to civil liberties and lead to the unnecessary targeting and profiling of particular groups. 'Soft' response strategies based on social and structural reforms that address underlying grievances and perceptions leading to terrorism may not in the short term placate terrorists but in the long term may indeed bring about goals of reducing or resolving issues that trigger terrorism (Moghaddam 2005). 'However, such efforts are less likely to succeed when terrorist groups enjoy little public support and have goals unrelated to structural problems in their society' (Barkan and Snowden 2001: 88).

Almost all counterterrorism measures address only insurgent and trans-national terrorism while largely ignoring the vigilante and state varieties (Barkan and Snowden 2001). Thus, responding effectively to state-sponsored terrorism is extremely difficult if the government itself initiates this sort of violence, as it is unlikely to do anything about it. In some democracies it may be possible to dismiss such governments, while in other countries only revolution, peaceful or otherwise, may bring to an end state-sponsored terrorism.

Organizational violence and terrorism

At this juncture the chapter will not go on in detail and outline strategies that organizations can implement to prevent or minimize the impact of terrorism on the workplace, as such advice is readily available from other sources (Cohen 2002; Cavanagh 2003; Mankin and Perry 2004; Williams 2004). Instead, in the latter part of this chapter, based largely on the innovative work of McCarthy and Mayhew (2004), we will turn our attention to the ways in which organizational cultures and work practices may in themselves stimulate social and community conditions that provide breeding grounds for cultural, political and religious resentments. Such resentments in turn could trigger 'reactive' terrorist sentiments and action.

The focus on this particular link between workplace culture and management style and terrorism has been chosen as this is one area in which organizations themselves may be stimulants of terrorism rather than just passive targets of such actions. Thus workplaces may also have an important proactive role to play in reshaping their organizational philosophies and practices to minimize 'reactive' terrorism. Current anti-terrorism or counterterrorism measures largely do not seem to recognize or include strategies to prevent or minimize the potential for organizations to stimulate reactive terrorism. Attempts to introduce such measures would largely be seen as an unnecessary and unwarranted attempt to manipulate or control 'market forces'.

McCarthy and Mayhew (2004), in ground-breaking work on the

interaction between workplace violence and terrorism, make the intriguing observation that the spillage of bullying and violence from workplaces out into local communities may increase resentment and trigger further aggression, violence and terrorism that may mutate and 'blow back' onto workplaces. Thus there may be an important link between organizational cultures and practices that lead to workplace violence and the mutation of grievances into terrorist acts. Such organizational workplaces can be those of government agencies, not-for-profit aid, health and welfare organizations or faith-based agencies, as well as for-profit companies and multi-nationals.

In this case we are not examining agencies directly involved in warfare, anti-terrorism or counterterrorism measures. However, this difference is not always clear or distinct, given the long history of governments embedding their own security and counterterrorist operatives within 'legitimate' business and aid organizations or in the recruiting and training of staff of such agencies for covert activities. This picture may be further muddied where such organizations are sponsored overtly or covertly by national governments as a means of bringing about political, social, religious and economic change. As previously indicated, such state-sponsored terrorism is often the hardest to challenge and eradicate.

In a further development and application of the many previous explanations of individual and collective violence, McCarthy (2004a: 108) identifies global corporate behaviour as also key in triggering such reactive terrorism: 'Global corporations are key conduits for the transmission of systemic violence, identities, and economic, political and cultural forces that degrade and antagonize local cultures to the point they become seedbeds for terrorism. Attempts to impose alien styles of government or alternate belief systems on others, often in coalition with multi-nationals, may have a similar triggering effect'.

This transmission of systemic organizational violence leading to terrorism can occur in a number of ways. One stimulus to terrorism can be through the way in which organizations treat their staff, creating a climate of 'psycho-terror' (Leymann 1990) that may brutalize staff, who may in turn brutalize others or withdraw into anxiety, depression and post-traumatic stress disorder (PTSD). This brutalization may include increasing bullying and harassment of those less able to defend themselves or those who are identified as 'different', someone to fear or loathe as potential threat or terrorist. Such organizationally derived psycho-terror may also drive policies of mandatory detention of illegal refugees and asylum seekers, racial profiling, increasing xenophobia, the degrading of human rights and repressive legislation impacting on minority or 'suspect' individuals or groups (McCarthy and Mayhew 2004). This brutalization may cause members of such at-risk groups within or outside workplaces to respond in an aggressive and violent fashion, thereby further reinforcing the perspective that such groups need to be repressed, removed or destroyed. Thus a circular 'self-fulfilling prophecy' of repression and reaction may be created within an organization and its surrounding geographical communities and spheres of interest, possibly leading to mutation from resistance into global terrorist cells.

Alongside such direct brutalizing acts of psycho-terror, it is also conceivable that company policies and actions that create mass unemployment, major negative social change or environmental degradation in certain geographical areas may result in organizations and their employees facing terrorist acts, including sabotage, from people who have been directly harmed or disadvantaged by such company actions. Mining and oil exploration are examples of companies that have been targets of such violence. McCarthy (2004a: 80) notes that '[o]ne could reasonably conclude that corporations that fail to maintain corporate social and environmental responsibility in management practices and do not implement policies and procedures to prevent workplace bullying/ violence are likely to further the displacement, poverty and inequity in which terrorism takes root'. In a similar analysis Hearn and Parkin (2001: 126) note that '[g]lobal political economic developments and connections are not "without" violence and violation; they may involve slavery, indentured labour, child labour, trafficked labour and other exploitative practices and human rights violations.'

Some might say that if such trans-national organizations operate in an oppressive and degrading manner they should 'reap what they sow'. However, reactive terrorist responses may also impact on other organizations not directly involved in the perceived brutalizing acts. This is graphically illustrated in the increasing attacks on aid, health and peace-keeping agencies as documented by other authors within this book (see Wigley, Thomas). It is no longer possible for alienated groups to keep separate in their minds the quite different functions of multi-national businesses compared to those of aid, health and environmental groups. Also, further confusion may arise in the minds of oppressed groups when aid, health and welfare services are delivered by faith-based agencies of a different religious worldview to those who are receiving the aid. Such groups are now 'biting the hand that feeds them' when they think they can link the activities of supposedly benevolent organizations with an overall strategy of economic domination as well as social, economic and religious subjugation by the despised 'other'. This in turn may lead to such targeted aid and welfare organizations withdrawing from their core tasks, further disadvantaging and incensing their former recipient groups who again react in an even more destructive and embittered manner.

An example of this cycle is the recent withdrawal of Médecins sans Frontières from much of Afghanistan after the murder of a number of their workers was partially triggered by a rising concern for the safety of their staff that was being associated in the minds of militants with US militarism and belligerence. Aid agencies are perceived as less neutral and less independent, and staff will find it increasingly too difficult to work and will be increasingly targeted (The Lancet editorial 2001). Such a 'bread and bombs' approach by the Western military may irreparably damage the credibility and safety of aid workers and associated nationals. In another context, that of the recent tsunami disaster in Asia, there may be a danger that aid organizations from the US, Australia and their allies working in such areas may be seen as imposing alien ideas and cultures which in turn may eventually lead to acts of reactive terrorism by elements within these devastated communities.

Thus, inappropriate or oppressive organizational management techniques and business practices may help create a degraded and reactive societal, economic and political climate with pockets of terrorist resistance that attack the organizations and their representatives. This then can create a vicious cycle of repression, reaction and further repression both within the degraded culture and the host culture of the organization. Therefore, it is important to recognize the possible negative impact an organizational climate of bullying and abuse has not only upon staff but also on surrounding communities and cultures. Predominantly organizations that are targeted by terrorist groups see themselves as the 'innocent parties' who have been unfairly attacked in entirely unpredictable ways. However, such organizations may display gross ignorance and insensitivity to the family, cultural, political and religious sensibilities of the cultures and countries they are working within.

Even though such links between organizational culture and terrorism may at times seem tenuous, they need to be considered in the bottom-line calculations that large trans-national organizations must make alongside purely economic ones. Also, though this model seems to be most applicable in a global terrorism context, it could also easily be used to explain many types of internal local or country-based terrorist acts.

Breaking the nexus between organizations, workplace violence and terrorism

Some commentators (Ehrlich and Liu 2002; Hess 2003) have identified this link between the growth of capitalism and the spreading of its values through globalization and the sometimes violent reactions of those who feel their own values, religion, culture and economic wellbeing are under threat. However, what has not been so well recognized and examined, with some notable exceptions, is the role Western businesses and organizations may play in the spreading of these needs, aspirations and lifestyles as if they were either value-free or the only values worth considering (see Hearn and Parkin 2001; Singer 2002; Chua 2003; McCarthy and Mayhew 2004).

If, as has been demonstrated above, there may be at times a relationship between organizational cultures and practices and growing terrorism, what can be done to break or minimize this link? This nexus between organizational culture, values and practice and terrorism can be minimized or broken in a number of ways. Such strategies and responses may at times seem utopian or unrealistic. However, they need to be tried, as current strategies to combat this particular type of terrorism seem to be of limited effectiveness. Long-term structural prevention rather than operational, crisis prevention addressing this link between organizational culture and terrorism needs to be implemented. Such organizational strategies in the fight against terrorism need to show how such bodies themselves address issues of 'human rights, democratic capacity-building, and social and economic justice' (United Nations 2002: 13).

These strategies require responses at the local, national and international levels both within organizations as well as externally. These responses may be freely developed and instigated by organizational management themselves, imposed by shareholders and other stakeholders, suggested by international protocols and human rights bodies or mandated by law. Again, it would be naive to think that many multi-national organizations and businesses would voluntarily adopt such work practices and codes of conduct. In such cases it needs to be demonstrated to them that such non-oppressive organizational practices can indeed also be good for the 'financial bottom line', improve the organization's public image, or decrease costs in other areas such as security, staffing costs or mental health services (Zadek *et al.* 2003; United Nations 2003).

At another level it may also be important for organizations to be aware that their oppressive business practices may have a direct impact on other organizations from the same host or allied country. As mentioned above, aid workers' and peacekeepers' lives and security may be directly endangered by association in the minds of terrorists with other businesses from the same country operating in an exploitative or culturally insensitive manner.

Thus, various types and levels of 'carrots and sticks' will need to be used to ensure that workplace violence is minimized within organizations and that such violence does not spill across into their societal and business areas of influence.

At the local and national levels, the following statutory responses may help minimize workplace violence and bullying and reduce its spilling over into the associated communities (McCarthy (2004b):

- Public sector ethics acts.

- Dignity at work legislation.

- Common law.

- Trade practices legislation.

- Consumer protection legislation.

- Emergency services legislation.

- Whistle-blower protection legislation.

- Anti-discrimination/EEO legislation.

- Ombudsmen.

At the international level, there are a range tribunals, declarations, codes and programmes that may help decrease the impact of workplace violence and in turn mitigate reactive terrorism. These various regulatory safeguards do not generally have legal status within individual countries unless ratified by domestic legislation. A number of these key aggression and violence codes, regulations and programmes include:

- International Labour Organization (October 2003) Code of Practice on Workplace Violence in the Services Sector and Measures to Combat this Phenomenon.

- International Labour Organization (February 2003) Violence and Stress at Work in the Services Sectors.

- United Nations UN Action Against Terrorism (2004).

Williams (2004: 121–2) also in turn identifies 13 UN international anti-terrorism related conventions.

A recent attempt to grapple with some of the negative impacts that transnational business entities, in particular, may create in countries within which they operate is the United Nations Norms on the Responsibilities of Transnational Corporations and Other Business Enterprises with Regard to Human Rights. The norms note that 'transnational corporations and other business enterprises have … the capacity to cause harmful impacts on the human rights and lives of individuals through their core business practices and operations, including employment practices, environmental policies, relationships with suppliers and consumers, interactions with Governments and other activities.' (United Nations 2003: 1).

These UN norms require such trans-nationals not to be involved in or profit from violations of humanitarian law and other international crimes against humanity such war crimes, genocide, torture, forced disappearance, forced labour, hostage-taking or illegal executions. Such activities could also in extreme situations involve terrorist acts or create a climate in which such violations lead to retaliatory terrorism.

Under these norms such trans-national organizations are to be subject to periodic evaluation and verification by United Nations and other already existing international and national bodies or those yet to be established. Such a monitoring process needs to be clear and independent and also take into account input from all the key stakeholders. Furthermore, under these norms such businesses enterprises should conduct periodic internal evaluations concerning the impact of their own activities on cultural, political, religious, economic and human rights.

At the country and international level there are also a number of non-statutory strategies that could be implemented by employees, unions, shareholders, customers and organizations that may help decrease the impact of workplace violence and its spill-over into related communities, and in turn possibly mitigate reactive terrorism. Whitaker (2000) suggests that there are a number of ways to reduce the economic foundation of what he calls 'paraviolence industries'. Such businesses he contends can be influenced by boycotts in which people act together to express their disapproval through not using, buying or dealing with such industries. Such sanctions could also be put in place by other organizations, businesses or governments.

Such measures outlined in more detail by Whittaker (2000) and McCarthy and Mayhew (2004) include:

- Protests, boycotts, labour strikes.

- Stakeholder activism.

- Development of best practice guidelines for organizations.

- Triple bottom line accounting.

- Measuring performance against a sustainability index.

McCarthy and Mayhew suggest that further development and strengthening of this international web of statutory and non-statutory safeguards against workplace bullying and violence might be possible if they are linked with the global sustainability movement. This would require a critical number of international agencies, trans-national corporations (TNCs), non-government organizations (NGOs) and national governments to subscribe to indicators of sustainability aligned to defined international best practice for the prevention of workplace bullying/violence. Such an alignment would provide market, social and political benefits for all the key stakeholders as they follow international best practice in the recording, reporting and auditing of their organization's sustainability performance. Zadek *et al.* (2003) put forward as an example of such an alignment the concept of responsible competitiveness through corporate responsibility clusters.

Some of these measures may be instigated by the organizations themselves, while others may only come about through direct action by other key business stakeholders or concerned members of the public, locally as well as internationally. The increasing use of e-mails and the worldwide-web by activists and protestors has made it much easier and quicker to expose nefarious business practices and to rally support and public opinion against such actions.

There is also an important role for international advocacy groups such as Amnesty International and Human Rights Watch, for example, in exposing such paraviolence industries and their supporting stakeholders. Thus it is important that such groups continue to publicize the worst examples of state-sponsored violence while other international legal bodies continue to oppose such acts in a variety of ways. However, as previously indicated, such international responses have often proved quite ineffectual or lacked international consensus for action.

Required future action

McCarthy and Mayhew (2004) acknowledge that there is a need for an integration of workplace violence and bullying policies and initiatives across a wide range of agencies and organizations that are concerned with labour standards, human rights and justice, health and safety and security. They suggest that while the ILO Code of Practice on Workplace Violence in the Services Sector (2003) is a useful and strategic initiative it needs to be supported by the establishment of an international UN anti-violence/ workplace bullying action programme. Such a programme should also make clear the inter-relationship between workplace violence and bullying and reactive terrorist violence triggered by such actions spilling over into the associated communities.

McCarthy and Mayhew list in detail the many potential benefits that might accrue for international agencies, nation state governments, trans-national companies and NGOs from such a UN-backed anti-violence/ workplace bullying action programme. Some of the potential desired outcomes of such a workplace violence programme that they identify include that of helping to minimize what they call revenge terrorism. McCarthy and Mayhew believe that such a potential outcome from a UN-backed action programme could be aided by:

- The establishment of an international research forum on workplace violence to collect comparative international data on incidence and severity and study the inter-relationships between workplace bullying and violence and other oppressive behaviours, including terrorism.

- The development of internationally endorsed best practice guidelines for trans-national organizations that would establish procedures and practices to reduce workplace bullying and violence and to prevent it spilling over into their associated community in an oppressive and exploitative manner and in turn minimizing reactive terrorism, war and genocide.

- The development of global protocols for just and fair development, trade and finance with less powerful nations and communities in order to prevent systemic violence and major environmental degradation and action against them by large-scale capital-intensive projects or unfair trade practices.

Conclusion

This chapter has outlined the importance of the relationship between workplace violence and terrorism. Such a pathological symbiosis has the potential to trigger a cancer-like growth of reactive terrorism unless the nexus between these two can be further identified and broken. Building on the work of McCarthy and Mayhew and others, this chapter provides some strategies to identify and minimize this link and limit the blow-back of reactive terrorism onto peacekeeping, aid and welfare organizations as well as socially responsible trans-national organizations.

In the light of growing internationalism and globalization of markets alongside an increasing threat of terrorism, it is of crucial importance that multi-national and national companies and organizations are enabled to identify and minimize their activities that may trigger reactive terrorism.

References

Barkan, S.E. and Snowden, L.L. (2001) *Collective Violence*, Boston: Allyn and Bacon.

Cavanagh, T.E. (2003) *Corporate Security Management: Organization and Spending since 9/11*, The Conference Board Executive Summary.

Chua, A. (2003) *World on Fire: How Exporting Free Market Democracy Breeds Ethnic Hatred and Global Instability*, New York: Random House.

Cohen, D. (2002) *HR Implications of the Attack on America: One Year Later*, Alexandria, VA: Society for Human Resource Management.

Ehrlich, P.R. and Liu, J. (2002) 'Some Roots of Terrorism', *Population and Environment*, 24(2), pp. 183–92.

Gurr, T.R. (1989) 'Political Terrorism: Historical Antecedents and Contemporary Trends' in *Violence in America. Volume 2: Protest, Rebellion, Reform* (ed., Guer, T.R.), Newbury Park, CA: Sage Publications.

Hearn, J. and Parkin, W. (2001) *Gender, Sexuality and Violence in Organizations*, London: Sage Publications.

Hammel, E. (2001) 'Dimensions of Terrorism: Actors, Actions and Consequences', Appendix A in National Research Council *Terrorism: Perspectives from the Behavioral Sciences*. Panel on Behavioral, Social and Institutional Issues, Committee on Science and Technology for Countering Terrorism. Smelser, N. and Mitchell, F. (eds) Centre for Social and Economic Studies Division of Behavioral and Social Sciences and Education National Research Council of the National Academies, Washington, DC: National Academies Press.

Hess, H. (2003) 'Like Zealots and Romans: Terrorism and Empire in the 21st Century', *Crime, Law & Social Change*, 39: pp. 339–57.

Hoffman, B. (1998) *Inside Terrorism*, New York: Columbia University Press.

International Labour Organization, *Code of Practice on Workplace Violence in the Services Sector and Measures to Combat this Phenomenon* (October 2003) Geneva: International Labour Organization.

International Labour Organization, *Violence and Stress at Work in the Services Sector* (February 2003), An ILO Code of Practice Second Draft, Geneva: International Labour Organization.

The Lancet (2001) 'UN pleads for support for aid workers in Afghanistan after Taliban collapse', 24 November, v358, i9295, p. 17942001.

Lacqueur, W. (1977) *Terrorism*, London: Weidenfield and Nicolson.

Leymann, H. (1990) 'Mobbing and Psychological Terror at workplace', *Violence and Victims*, 5, pp. 119–1125.

Mankin, L.D. and Perry, R.W. (2004) *Commentary: Terrorism Challenges for Human Resource Management, Review of Public Personnel Administration*, London: Sage Publications.

Martin, G. (2003) *Understanding Terorrism Challenges, Perspectives and Issues*, London: Sage Publications.

McCarthy, P. and Mayhew, C. (2004) *Safeguarding the Organization Against Violence and Bullying: an International Perspective*, Hampshire UK: Palgrave Macmillan.

McCarthy, P. (2004a) Occupational Violence, Psycho-Terror and Terrorism', in McCarthy, P. and Mayhew, C. *Safeguarding the Organization Against Violence and Bullying: An International Perspective*, Hampshire UK: Palgrave Macmillan.

McCarthy, P. (2004b) 'Preventing Risk/Severity Spirals: A Cross-sectoral Approach', in McCarthy, P. and Mayhew, C. *Safeguarding the Organization Against Violence and Bullying: An International Perspective*. Hampshire UK: Palgrave Macmillan.

Moghaddam, F. (February–March 2005) 'The Staircase to Terrorism: A Psychological Exploration', *American Psychologist*, pp. 161-69.

Smelser, N. and Mitchell, F. (2002) *Terrorism: Perspectives from the Behavioral Sciences*. Panel on Behavioral, Social and Institutional Issues, Committee on Science and Technology for Countering Terrorism. Centre for Social and Economic Studies Division of Behavioral and Social Sciences and Education National Research Council of the National Academies, Washington, DC: National Academies Press.

Standing, H. and Nicolini, D. (1997) *Review of Workplace-Related Violence*, London: Health and Safety Executive, p. 6.

Singer, P. (2002) *One World: The Ethics of Globalization*, Melbourne: The Text Publishing Company.

United Nations General Assembly Security Council 2002 Report of the policy Working Group on the United Nations and Terrorism Annex A/57/273 S/2002/875, Geneva: United Nations.

United Nations 2003 Norms on the Responsibilities of Transnational Corporations and Other Business Enterprises with Regard to Human Rights, UN Doc. E/CN.4/Sub.2/2003/12/Rev.2.

http://www1.umn.edu/humanrts/links/norms-Aug2003.html

United Nations (2000) *UN Action Against Terrorism*, Geneva: United Nations.

Whitaker, L.C. (2000) *Understanding and Preventing Violence: The Psychology of Human Destructiveness*, Boca Raton, USA: CRC Press.

Williams, C. (2004) *Terrorism Explained: The Facts About Terrorism and Terrorist Groups*, Sydney, Australia: New Holland Publishers.

Zadek, S., Sabapathy, J., Dossing, H. and Swift T. (2003) *Responsible Competitiveness: Corporate Responsibility Clusters in the Action*. The Copenhagen Centre, European and Social Affairs DG of the European Commission Copenhagen (see www.copenhagencentre.org)

Preparing, training and supporting human service workers to respond to terrorist events

David F. Wee and Diane Myers

Introduction

The focus of this chapter is on human service workers who respond to terrorist events in the workplace. Most literature about responding to terrorist events focuses on first-line responders such as police, paramedics and firefighters involved in the immediate response to establish safety, extinguish fires, locate and treat the injured, recover the dead, establish and maintain the crime scene, and begin the investigation. Human service responders have a different focus of responsibilities: their job entails providing compassionate, humane and effective support services to both victims and first responders in the event. Human services may entail psychological first aid and crisis intervention, stress management, spiritual or pastoral care, and assessment and referral for a wide range of human needs in the aftermath. Human service responders may include human resource personnel, employee assistance and mental health professionals, clergy, occupational and other healthcare workers, social workers and occupational safety professionals. They may come from within the impacted organization, from responding government or private agencies, or from non-profit volunteer agencies. They may be trained (and in some cases, licensed) professionals or trained volunteers or peers.

Human service workers who respond to terrorist events in the workplace and provide support and services during the short-term to long-term recovery period can be affected through their work with victims. The terrorist events may be sudden and of short duration, or may be on-going terrorist events which occur over years and decades, as is the case of the Israeli/Palestinian conflict and in Northern Ireland.

A human service response to terrorist events, both large-scale and smaller-scale, for both Workplace Violence Typology (see Bowie, Fisher and Cooper, Chapter 1) Type 1 (external/internal violence) and Type 2 (consumer-related violence), requires preparedness, training and support. These three prerequisites are necessary to provide knowledge, experience and strategies for human service workers to respond to workplace violence.

As noted by the Institute of Medicine (2003), and Ursano, Vineburg and Fullerton in this volume, many human service responders lack preparedness and training in the psychological impacts of terrorism and the basic principles of disaster mental health. Without such training, human service responders are at risk of being ineffective in their efforts to help promote effective disaster coping and to prevent maladaptive coping in those impacted. Likewise, they are at high risk themselves for secondary traumatization, compassion fatigue and burnout reactions that can compromise their own psychological and physical health and wellbeing. Secondary traumatic stress (used interchangeably with the term compassion fatigue) is defined as 'the natural consequent behaviours and emotions resulting from knowing about a traumatizing event experienced by a significant other – stress resulting from helping or wanting to help a traumatized or suffering person' (Figley 1993). Likewise, burnout is also a risk factor for human service responders to workplace violence and terrorism. Burnout can be defined as a gradual and progressive process that features physical and emotional exhaustion, depersonalization, reduced feelings of personal achievement, and work-related and inter-personal symptoms.

Human service workers and mental health professionals treating victims of terrorism can be affected by their work. Working with victims of terrorism which spans many years, as in the case of the Israel-Palestinian conflict, multiple decades as in Northern Ireland, and in other areas of the world where there are ongoing terrorist events can affect helpers' personal lives, professional values and work relationships (Ramon 2004), and the therapy they do with clients (Rice and Kapur 2002). Reactions to ongoing terrorism and violent conflict can result in worker anger and anxiety, and can negatively influence workers' feelings of safety, especially when working in the field (Lindsey 2004). The inter-personal nature of terrorism, when the conflict is between groups, can lead to increased stress and strain and can lead to increased negative impacts on the workers (Eidelson, D'Alession and Eidelson 2003; Gibson and Iwaniec 2003). Increased somatic and physical complaints have been found among disaster mental health workers providing crisis counselling to victims of terrorism (Moore 2004). Holmqvist and Anderson found psychotherapists who worked with traumatized survivors of political torture experienced significantly different reactions from therapists who didn't work with survivors of political torture. The broader causes of violent conflict and terrorism can lead the professional to experience hopelessness and helplessness when considering their desire and efforts to change the conditions that cause the violent conflict and terrorism (Ramon 2004).

Riba and Reches (2002) studied the impact upon Emergency Room (ER) nurses of two years of terrorist attacks on the civilian population of Israel. The nurses identified numerous hardships, great anxiety, as well as a strong sense of professional fulfilment from caring for victims of multi-casualty terrorism. The authors described how terrorism against a civilian population 'stirs up profound identification with each and every victim and presents a special challenge for the professional caregivers' (p. 2). Although caring for patients of terrorist attacks produced anxiety for the nurses, it also produced rewards. One nurse stated, 'To have reached your peak level of performance, given your all, done all you are capable of doing, and done so in the context of closely knit teamwork ... and out of a sense of empathy with the victims brings a feeling of deepest satisfaction' (p. 6). Nonetheless, the nurses clearly experienced symptoms of post-traumatic stress from their work: intense memories, guilt over patient deaths, fears of professional inadequacy, sleep disturbance and nightmares, hyperactivity, and loss of a sense of safety in the world. The authors emphasize the importance of providing emotional support, formal and informal debriefing, and stress management training for nurses.

Clearly more research is needed on the short- to long-term impact on human service workers and mental health professionals working with victims of terrorism and ongoing terrorist events. Study is needed to identify the personal, psychological, social, work and health impacts of providing services to victims of terror. The effects of responding to single terrorist events and ongoing terrorist events need to be better understood not only from the standpoint of negative impacts, such as compassion fatigue and burnout, but also as sources of compassion satisfaction. More needs to be learned about human service workers' resilience, and the benefits they experience while helping other humans' recovery from workplace violence and terrorism.

Disaster mental health as a foundation

Experience and research in the field of disaster mental health provide an important knowledge base for understanding the risks for human service workers responding to workplace violence or terrorism. The psychological impact of disaster work on emergency service personnel and disaster workers in general has been examined by a number of investigators (Durham, McCammon and Allison, Jr. 1985; Hartsough and Myers 1985; Lanning and Fannin 1988; McFarlane 1988; Miles, Demi and Mostyn-Aker 1984; Mitchell 1986; Moran and Britton 1994; Robinson 1989; Taylor and Frazer 1982; Wee 1994a; Wraith and Gordon 1988). The findings clearly indicate that disaster response can cause psychological effects in the worker and influence those closest to them.

Stresses for disaster recovery workers in *long-term assignments* (i.e. more than several days) have been studied among American Red Cross and Federal Emergency Management Agency (FEMA) workers. Rosensweig and Vaslow (1992) surveyed 500 FEMA employees, and the resulting report made specific recommendations for stress reduction for FEMA workers. Myers (1992, 1993a, 1993b, 1994a, 1994b) and Myers and Zunin (1993a, 1993b, 1994a, 1994b) incorporated many of those recommendations into the stress management programmes they developed and directed for FEMA workers. Hartsough and Myers (1985) described the typical phases involved in response to disaster, and the stressors inherent in each phase for the workers, including the 'letdown' involved after long-term response to disaster. The Center for Mental Health Services (CMHS) and FEMA have developed many publications and training materials on management of worker stress response to disasters (Department of Health and Human Services [DHHS] 1988a; DHHS 1988b; FEMA 1987a; FEMA 1987b). Armstrong *et al.* (1991) described stressors experienced by Red Cross relief personnel working in the two-month period following the Loma Prieta earthquake, and described a multiple stressor-debriefing model they developed for use in exit debriefings for personnel.

Figley (1995) provided a ground-breaking exploration of crisis workers, trauma counsellors, nurses, physicians and other caregivers who become victims themselves of secondary traumatic stress disorder (STS) or 'compassion fatigue' in the process of assisting trauma victims.

Studies of disaster *mental health* workers have identified stress reactions and patterns of mental and physical distress. While the disaster mental health workers can help others to recover, they can also be affected by the pain and suffering they share with the survivors they attempt to help (Myers and Wee 2002, 2004; Wee and Myers 1997). A very small number of studies has further narrowed the focus of research to examine the psychological impacts of providing mental health counselling in the specialized context of large-scale response to disasters or workplace violence (Bartone, Ursano, Wright and Ingraham 1989; Berah, Jones and Valent 1984; Frederick 1977; Hodgkinson and Shepherd 1994; Raphael, Singh, Bradbury and Lambert 1984; Wee and Myers 1997; Winget and Umbenhauer 1982). A study of Critical Incident Stress Management team members found that this group of mental health professionals and emergency service peers can also be affected by compassion fatigue and burnout (Wee and Myers 2003). These studies recommend that this specialized group of disaster crisis intervention workers pay special attention to their vulnerability to stress and post-trauma sequelae, lest they become 'victims-by-proxy'.

The psychological impact on human service workers providing assistance to victims of terrorism is illustrated in the following study of crisis counsellors following the bombing of the Alfred P. Murrah Federal Building in Oklahoma City in 1995. The study of counsellors working in Project Heartland, the federally funded crisis counselling programme following the bombing, was conducted and described by Wee and Myers (2002) and Myers and Wee (2004).

1. Counsellors were psychologically impacted by their work whether or not they personally experienced the bomb blast.

   - Many of the respondents (61.8 per cent, n = 21) reported that they believed that someone they knew might die as a result of the bombing.

   - 64.7 per cent of the counsellors exhibited some degree of severity for post-traumatic stress disorder, as measured by the Frederick Reaction Index (Frederick 1988).

   - 44.1 per cent of counsellors exhibited 'caseness' on the SCL-90-R Global Severity Index score. Caseness refers to the subjects who are considered to be at risk or a positive case for a psychiatric disorder (Derogatis 1994).

   - 73.5 per cent of counsellors were rated as being at moderate risk or greater for compassion fatigue: moderate risk (23.5 per cent), high risk (29.4 per cent) or extremely high risk (20.6 per cent), as measured by the Compassion Fatigue Self Test for Psychotherapists (Figley 1995).

   - 76.5 per cent of counsellors were rated as being at moderate risk or greater for burnout: moderate risk (35.3 per cent), high risk (26.5 per cent) or extremely high risk (14.7 per cent), using the same Compassion Fatigue Self Test.

- Over half (52.9 per cent) of the counsellors evaluated their crisis counsellor disaster roles as more stressful than other jobs they had experienced.

2. Longer duration of work providing counselling services to the workplace terrorism victims was significantly related to higher mean distress scores.

3. Certain categories of counsellors had levels of distress higher than their co-workers: administrators of the counselling program; males; and ethnic groups other than Caucasian.

Moore (2004) studied a sample of disaster mental health workers 15 months after the Oklahoma City bombing and found a significant relationship between somatic complaints and compassion fatigue and degree of disorder for post-traumatic stress disorder. While the group means for degree of disorder for post-traumatic stress disorder declined from the ninth month to the fifteenth month measurement, the group means for compassion fatigue were not significantly different.

Flanagan (2002) reported that despite efforts to take care of Project Heartlands' 70 mental health staff members, the long-term mental health response to the Oklahoma City bombing took its toll with physical health problems as well as mental health sequelae. All six mental health professionals who were involved with Project Heartland from inception to closing of the programme experienced chronic health problems, among them lupus, multiple sclerosis, a brain tumour, heart problems, and symptoms involving balance which have no firm diagnosis.

The findings of these studies suggest that the nature of the Alfred P. Murrah Federal Building bombing as a terrorist act, the length of time providing crisis counselling, and certain categories of crisis counsellor job duties during the recovery were factors related to high compassion fatigue and burnout scores. The nature of the crisis counsellor role may put the crisis counsellor at greater risk for compassion fatigue and burnout. The empathic engagement of the victims of terrorism by the crisis counsellor providing long-term care may contribute to the crisis counsellor's psychological vulnerability to secondary traumatic stress reactions and emotional exhaustion. *This severity of stress among the crisis counsellors in these studies is higher than the distress levels found in almost all other groups of emergency and rescue workers studied in the last 20 years.*

The levels of stress and distress of the crisis counsellors should in no way be interpreted as judgement or criticism of their efforts to ease human suffering. Rather, the risk for compassion fatigue and burnout might be viewed as evidence of the extraordinary empathy, sympathy, understanding and energy devoted to caring for the children, mothers, fathers, sisters, brothers, families, neighbours, emergency service workers and fellow human beings struck by this catastrophic infliction of workplace violence.

Additional knowledge of secondary traumatic stress and compassion fatigue can be gleaned from Flannery's research and writings about the Assaulted Staff Action Program (ASAP). The programme provides crisis intervention and support services in the aftermath of assaults and other critical incidents at psychiatric facilities. Flannery found that his intervention team members at times experienced psychological reactions, such as intrusive memories of prior events, that had the potential to impair team member effectiveness (Flannery 1998). He emphasised the importance of ASAP team leaders and members monitoring all team members for the possibility of this occurrence.

These results strongly suggest that serious attention needs to be paid to developing effective stress management and prevention programmes for these at-risk workers. Human service workers can experience a 'double dose' of both direct exposure to the violence themselves as well as indirect exposure to the violence in the process of supporting the victims (Bowie 2002). Managers and supervisors have the responsibility of assessing the possibility of the 'double dose' experience occurring in human service staff and to take action to manage and prevent it (Bowie 2002).

The remainder of the chapter will provide guidance for management and for human service teams responsible for providing a human service response to workplace violence and terrorist events. It will discuss *preparing, training and supporting* human service workers, with a focus on preventing compassion fatigue and burnout in the human service workers themselves.

Preparing organizations and human service workers

Organizational commitment

Preparing human service workers for Type 1 and Type 2 Workplace Violence Typologies requires organizational commitment and preparation. The organizational mission must explicitly include commitment of the organization's resources for planning, preparing, financing, staffing, training, and exercising response capacity. The organization must recognize the psychological impact of workplace violence and commit to providing the policies and procedures for mitigating both the primary traumatic reactions and secondary traumatic reactions, or compassion fatigue. In the United States, numerous training institutions prepare workplaces and personnel for the impact of terrorism. Many of the training programmes are included in the Federal Emergency Management Agency (FEMA) *Compendium of Federal Terrorism Training* (2004). In many states, training is also provided through state and county Offices of Emergency Services. However, from the standpoint of addressing the *mental health* and *human service* needs of workers affected by workplace terrorism, very few of these government courses address such issues. In a study conducted by Myers in 2001, it was found that only four out of 94 federal courses (4.2 per cent) preparing personnel in the United States to respond to terrorism addressed the psychological needs of the responders or citizens. By 2004, the number of courses available had expanded to 294. However, the percentage addressing mental health, psychological or stress management issues had dropped, with only five out of 294 courses (1.7 per cent) including those topics in the course description, agenda or objectives (Myers 2004). Therefore, managers and human service teams will need to consult research and publications such as those included in this book for guidance on these topics.

Organizational mission statement: 'Good workplace safety is good business practice'

The organization's mission must include preparing the organization and the human service workers to respond to workplace violence and terrorism. The organization's mission statement must reflect an understanding that workplace safety practices and 'state of the art' response to workplace mental health and welfare issues following violence and terrorism is a good business practice that protects and maintains human resources and continuity of business.

Coupled with the traumatic effects of workplace violence on individual personnel, there can be predictable effects on the functioning of the work unit if the psychological sequelae are not dealt with appropriately (Myers and Wolfe 1996). A study of violence in the California state hospital system (Forest, Woodruff and Bloom 1991) identified a significant number of negative work unit effects when incidents of violence were not followed by appropriate human service/mental health interventions. The effects included lowered morale; lowered productivity; staff turnover and resulting costs; stress disability claims and associated treatment costs; litigation against the workplace; 'splitting' of staff and lack of unity; feelings of anger, devaluation, frustration, and helplessness; increased tensions; rumours; opinions that the work site is unsafe; demands for better security; anger and blame towards the organization; feeling unsupported by management; exacerbation of pre-existing problems and tensions; increased use of sick/vacation time; grievances; and demands for investigation of the incident. To avoid these problems in the aftermath of workplace violence and terrorism, an organizational mission statement that includes workplace safety and human service response to violence makes good business sense.

The Human Resources department may be tasked with the responsibility of developing policies and procedures for planning, preparing and supporting human service workers who respond to workplace violence. Examples of policies include the development of a workplace violence response plan, which describes the organization, roles, responsibilities and activities that will be implemented in response to workplace violence. The plan should also differentiate the scale of workplace violence response that is required for Type 1 and Type 2 Violence Typologies. A critical aspect of the workplace violence plan is the acknowledgement that the workforce is at risk of psychological reactions to workplace violence, and the human service workers are also at risk for compassion fatigue. The workplace violence response plan would include procedures for supporting the human service workers responding to the violence. Training human service workers to recognize, intervene in and manage their stress response should be done in advance.

Training human service workers about the organization's responsibilities, policies, procedures, interventions and support following workplace violence should be done yearly, and more frequently in high-risk workplaces.

Working as a team

Social support is known to be a source of significant psychological benefit for trauma survivors (Keane, Scott, Chavoya, Lamparski and Fairbank 1985; Solomon 1986). Building a *team approach* to human service work can help to prevent and also intervene in compassion fatigue for the workers (Munroe, Shay, Fisher, Makary, Rapperport and Zimering 1995). Stress management consultants (Hartsough and Myers 1985; Myers 1989a, 1989b, 1994b; NIMH 1987a, 1987b) have long emphasized the importance of working in a 'buddy system' in response to disaster as well as workplace violence, utilizing teams of at least two workers to ensure that staff can serve as a check-and-balance for each other and monitor the other's stress level while providing support and encouragement (Holmqvist and Anderson 2003).

Training human service workers to respond to workplace terrorism

The human service workers in work sites must have appropriate training to respond to workplace violence and terrorism and manage stress reactions of the personnel. Training must be based on screening and selection of human service workers that are most likely to be able to carry out these responsibilities. In addition, both management and the *entire workforce* require training about the workplace safety plan, response plan, and human service roles and responsibilities in the aftermath.

Training human service workers for their roles

Human service workers in any type of workplace must have initial and ongoing specialized training in responding to workplace violence. First, it is essential that colleges, graduate and professional schools of mental health, human services, social work, psychiatry, psychology and psychiatric nursing include coursework and supervised practice in the field of workplace violence, disaster, terrorism, trauma assessment and treatment. In addition, conferences, workshops and other continuing education forums are necessary both to maintain and update knowledge and skills (Myers and Wee 2004).

Human service worker teams may include health and mental health professionals such as those listed above, and may also include 'peers' chosen from the workplace environment and trained to provide crisis intervention, psychological first aid and supportive interventions to workplace personnel affected by terrorist events. Training for human service workers to respond to workplace violence and terrorism should include training objectives and training content that cover the following:

- The workplace safety plan and roles and responsibilities of personnel.

- The role and objectives of the human service crisis response team.

- Appropriate organizational interventions including **needs assessment; consultation; outreach** in the workplace; **defusing** of individuals and **debriefing** of carefully screened groups, as needed; **education** about post-trauma reactions, coping strategies and resources; and **crisis intervention, crisis counselling,** and referral for additional treatment and resources as needed. This model of intervention, developed by Myers and Wee (2004), is called the CODE-C service delivery model.

Training human service workers for self-care, stress management and prevention of compassion fatigue

An important component of human service worker training involves education about potential compassion fatigue, burnout, stress management and self-care (Dutton and Rubinstein 1995). Stress management training developed by Myers (1989a, 1989b, 1997, 1992, 1993a, 1994a), Myers and Zunin (1993a, 1993b, 1994a, 1994b) and Wee (1994b) for mental health and other human service workers in numerous disasters has relevance to response to workplace violence and terrorism, and includes the following stress management topics (Myers and Wee 2004):

- Phases of response to workplace violence.

- Factors that influence human service workers' stress reactions (factors related to the worker, the role, the setting, the community and the terrorist event itself).

- Sources of stress for human service workers.

- Stressors in specific work environments.

- Personal coping strategies for human service workers before, during and after the response to workplace violence assignment.

- Stress management techniques, including but not limited to:
  - Stress inventory
  - Deep breathing techniques
  - Stretching
  - Cognitive techniques
  - Relaxation
  - Meditation
  - Imagination
  - Humour
  - Verbal expression, discussion, ventilation, and catharsis
  - Creative expression (writing, dance, music)
  - Time management
  - Conflict resolution
  - Social support.

- Resistance and resiliency-building and 'lifestyle': work schedule, rest, nutrition, exercise, social support, relaxation and recreation.

Supporting human service workers responding to workplace violence

Before undertaking a workplace violence assignment, human personnel should be *oriented and briefed* as thoroughly as possible about what they will encounter in their assignment location and role. This forewarning can help personnel to anticipate and to prepare emotionally for what they may experience (Hartsough and Myers 1985; Myers 1994b). It also provides them with concrete information that will be essential to them in their work and crucial to their wellbeing and safety. During ongoing assignments, if work sites, roles or responsibilities change, briefing the worker on the new situation can reduce anxiety and ease the transition into the new assignment.

During the immediate impact phase of the response to workplace violence, workers usually respond with enthusiasm and often heroism to the immediate needs of the situation. It is the rule, rather than the exception, that human service workers tend to overextend themselves in their efforts. Human service workers responding to workplace violence are usually not the best judges of their level of functioning, and usually underestimate the effects of stress and fatigue on their health and performance. Thus, *good on-scene supervision* from the team leader is helpful. The following suggestions may be helpful to supervisors in dealing with compassion stress among human service workers (Myers 1994b):

- Remember that early identification and intervention with stress reactions are the keys to preventing compassion fatigue. Review stress symptoms with workers before they go into the field. Provide handouts for workers regarding stress management and self-care.

- Assess workers' appearance and level of functioning regularly. It is not uncommon for workers to deny their own levels of stress and fatigue. For example, they may say they are doing 'fine', but may be exhibiting multiple stress symptoms and appear very fatigued.

- Try to rotate workers among low-stress, moderate-stress and high-stress tasks. Limit workers' time in high-stress assignments (such as working with families identifying the deceased at the morgue) to an hour or so at a time, if possible. Provide breaks and personal support to staff in such positions.

- If possible, limit the length of shifts to 12 hours *maximum*. A 12-hour shift should be followed by 12 hours off duty.

- Ask workers to take breaks if effectiveness is diminishing; order them to do so if necessary. Point out that the worker's ability to function is diminishing due to fatigue, and that they are needed functioning at full potential to help with the operation. Allow the worker to return to work if he/she rests and functioning improves. On breaks, try to provide workers with the following: bathroom facilities; a place to sit or lie down away from the scene; quiet time alone; food and beverages; and an opportunity to talk with a supervisor or co-workers, if they wish.

The importance of supervision continues and magnifies as staff move into long-term recovery work with the affected organization. Cerney (1995) notes that much secondary trauma can be avoided or its effects ameliorated if human service workers use regular supervision or consultation. Within the process of supervision, blind spots can be detected, overidentification can be corrected, alternative intervention approaches can be discussed and evaluated, and, especially important in prevention of compassion fatigue, the workers' own overextension or overinvolvement can be identified and understood. Pearlman and MacIan (1995) emphasize the special importance of good supervision for those workers with a personal trauma history and those who are newer to the human service field. It is important to continue to monitor the needs of those human service worker staff who are themselves survivors of the workplace violence. Appropriate supervision, consultation, and support can help to ensure that they do not become overwhelmed, and that their personal needs and professional roles do not become blurred. Supervision should include not only clinical guidance and oversight. It must also ensure that interventions and supportive approaches are appropriate to the phase of workplace violence recovery, are appropriate to the goals and objectives of the human service worker programme, and are culturally and ethnically fitting.

In response to workplace violence and terrorism, administrative staff should consider bringing in outside *consultants* specifically to provide stress management services and education to human service workers (Varblow 1994; Wee and Myers 2002). Consultants with prior experience in workplace violence and other mental health projects can offer refreshing insights and concrete ideas that can assist staff in reaching their goals. More importantly, consultants can suggest approaches to stress management and compassion fatigue prevention have been used elsewhere in the field and have proved to be helpful.

Hand in hand with the importance of good supervision is the necessity for *continuing education and training* throughout the duration of the response to workplace violence by human service workers. Continuing education and training provide rewards for staff that have tangible positive effects on morale (Myers 1994b). Topics for continuing education will be identified as new issues emerge while the human service programme responds to workplace needs. Providing training on these emerging topics will help increase the knowledge and skills of the workers.

In some circumstances, *personal psychotherapy* can be important in preventing or intervening with compassion fatigue in human service worker staff. Dutton and Rubinstein (1995) point out that trauma workers with personal histories of trauma may need to pay deliberate personal attention to their own healing process in order to manage most effectively the difficult task of coping with their own trauma reactions. Pearlman and Saakvitne (1995) emphasize that for some human workers, psychotherapy can provide a regular opportunity to focus on oneself, one's own needs, and the origins of one's personal responses to the work.

Group therapy and support groups can also be of help to human service workers, providing a safe space both for healing and for exploring the interaction of a worker's past with his or her current work with survivor clients (Pearlman and Saakvitne 1995). Groups for human service workers are particularly effective in dealing with the unique aspects of response to workplace violence.

Human service worker strategies for self-care

Many publications offer suggestions about human service worker self-care during response to a traumatic event (Hartsough and Myers 1985; Myers 1989a, 1989b, 1994b; Myers and Wee 2004; National Institute of Mental Health 1987a, 1987b; Wee 1994b). Some suggestions for workers include:

1. Request a briefing at the beginning of each shift. This will update workers on what has happened since your last shift, and prepare you for what you may encounter during your shift.

2. Develop a 'buddy' system with a co-worker and keep an eye on each other's functioning, fatigue, needs and stress symptoms. Tell the buddy how to recognize when you are getting stressed and agree to take a break when he/she suggests it.

3. Encourage and support co-workers. Listen to each other's feelings. Don't take anger too personally. Hold criticism unless it's essential. Share a snack or something to drink.

4. Try to get some activity and exercise. Using the stairs instead of the elevator can provide exercise during a busy workday. Gently stretch out muscles that are tense.

5. Eat regularly. If not hungry, eat frequently, in small quantities. Try to avoid excessive sugar, fats and caffeine. Drink plenty of liquids.

6. Humour can break the tension and provide relief. Use it with care, however. People are highly suggestible in response to workplace violence situations, and survivors or co-workers can take things personally and be hurt if they feel they are the brunt of humour.

7. Give yourself positive mental messages, such as 'I'm doing fine' and 'I'm using the skills I've been trained to use.'

8. Take deep breaths, hold them, and then blow out forcefully. This reduces tension.

9. Take breaks if effectiveness is diminishing, or if asked to do so by your supervisor. At minimum, take a break every four hours.

10. Use a notebook to remember important things. This will help compensate for the memory problems that are common in stressful situations.

11. Try to keep noise to a minimum in the work site. Remind others to do the same.

12. Try to avoid interrupting co-workers when they are in the middle of a task.

13. Defuse at the end of each shift by taking a few minutes to talk with co-workers about your day.

14. When off duty, enjoy some recreation that takes your mind off the response to workplace violence. Draw on supports that nurture you. This may include friends, meditation, reading or religion.

15. Treat yourself to a nice meal, music, a massage, or take a long bath during time off.

16. Give yourself permission to spend time alone after work. However, don't totally withdraw from social interaction.

17. Get adequate sleep. Learn relaxation techniques that can help you fall asleep.

18. On long workplace violence assignments, attend periodic debriefing or worker support groups to talk about the emotional impact of the job. Use stress management programmes if they are available. If such programmes are not offered, try to get them organized.

19. If you are on a workplace violence assignment away from home, remember the following:

    • Bring familiar foods and snacks from home that not may not be available on your workplace violence assignment.

- Make new friends. Let off steam with co-workers.
- Find local recreation opportunities and make use of them.
- Remember things that were relaxing at home and try to do them now.
- Stay in touch with people at home. Write, e-mail or call often.
- Avoid excessive use of alcohol and caffeine.
- Keep a journal.

Much has been learned from the field of disaster mental health about the period of readjustment that disaster workers experience at the *end of their disaster assignment.* Extrapolating from the field of disaster to the topic of human service workers' response to workplace violence, it is important to plan for the end of the workers' assignment or the closure of the human service recovery programme. This includes programme closure activities, critique of the recovery project, group debriefing of staff, follow-up, and recognition of staff. There is a certain amount of work to be done in ending.

Disaster workers usually experience a mixture of emotions at the end of the work: relief that it is over, and sadness and guilt at leaving it behind. In addition, there is often a sense of 'letdown' and some difficulty in transitioning back into regular job and family responsibilities.

Human service workers who have spent weeks or months supporting victims of workplace violence or terrorism can be helped to anticipate these mixed emotions through education and training. Topics of training can include common reactions and coping strategies that can help with the transition.

A critique of the workplace violence response can be helpful to staff by bringing cognitive closure to the human service workers. A critique is a critical evaluation of the project, its difficulties and its successes. It is different and separate from a debriefing, which attends to the psychological and emotional impact of the work on personnel. A critique can result in constructive input and changes to the workplace violence plan, policies and procedures to improve human service response to the next situation (Myers 1994b). A critique can also help staff to take pride and feel a sense of ownership in the work. It helps them to see the positive effect of their efforts in the response to workplace violence.

A formal stress debriefing to address the emotional and psychological impact that the response to workplace violence assignment has had on workers can help them to process the personal impact of the work. Follow-up and support services, following a multi-component model of care such as Critical Incident Stress Management (CISM), is important.

Recent questions have been raised in the field of traumatology about the efficacy of 'debriefing' in preventing post-traumatic stress disorder.

The purpose of a post-assignment stress debriefing is not 'clinical' in nature. It is not psychotherapy. Rather, it is a psycho-educational forum to allow human service workers to discuss the work they have done, their personal reactions to the work, find meaning in their work, and deal with any lingering stress or emotional issues by utilizing effective coping techniques or through referral to additional resources. Myers and Wee (2004) present a thorough discussion and review of the research and literature on this debriefing, concluding that Critical Incident Stress Management or a similar comprehensive, multi-component system of care provides tangible, practical and valuable support to human service workers responding to disaster, violence and terrorism.

McCammon and Allison outline the conceptual components of a variety of post-trauma debriefing models (1995). Important to all of the models is the empathy, understanding, and peer support generated when the debriefing is conducted for a group of people who have worked together. It allows human service workers to identify and talk about the feelings associated with the workplace violence assignment, provides 'normalization' of their responses, and lends peer support as the project comes to a close. Debriefing serves an educational purpose, informing workers of the common stress and grief reactions and transition issues to expect when the project is over. Resources to assist them with transitional issues, compassion fatigue or STS in the aftermath of their assignment should be discussed.

The multiple stressor debriefing model developed by Armstrong, O'Callahan and Marmar (1991) and the disaster worker debriefing model developed by Myers and Zunin (1994b) also work well for the purpose of intermittent stress management and exit debriefing following workplace violence response (Myers and Wee 2004). Both of these models, while based on the prototype of Mitchell's Critical Incident Stress Debriefing model, include the added dimension of encouraging participants to discuss any of a large number of incidents that they might have experienced in the weeks or months of their workplace violence work. In both models, questions are framed to encourage discussion of incidents that were 'challenging' or 'difficult', with participants discussing the events themselves as well as any thoughts, feelings, stress reactions and coping approaches associated with the event (Myers and Wee 2004).

To facilitate the ending of crisis counselling projects in natural disasters, Myers developed a structured small-group exercise that can be done within the context of a debriefing or as a separate activity (Myers and Wee 2002). In small groups, staff discuss the following questions:

1. How has this human service worker assignment been different from other jobs you have had?

2. What have been the most challenging aspects of the work?

3. What have been the special rewards of the work?

4. How have you been changed by the work? What are some things you will be taking with you from this job?

5. Describe a meaningful, profound or touching incident that happened to you during your work.

6. What do you anticipate your transition will be like as you leave the response to workplace violence project and move on? What will help you with this transition?

Recognition of the efforts and accomplishments of human service workers will assist in bringing closure to their response to the workplace violence experience and in validating the value of their work. A plaque or a letter of appreciation have much meaning for personnel. Those outside the field of workplace violence response may not recognize the risks inherent in psychological trauma intervention. However, human service workers who respond to workplace violence routinely place themselves in positions of risk for compassion fatigue and STS in order to assist the impacted workplace in its recovery, and a word of recognition goes a long way.

Knowing what we know about the risks of compassion fatigue for trauma intervention workers, it is important to provide *follow-up* to human service workers after the completion of their workplace violence assignments. Human service team leaders should develop follow-up protocols and resources for staff experiencing compassion fatigue or STS in the aftermath of their work assignment. While resources for any problems that develop or continue from their human service work should be discussed during worker debriefing, a formalized follow-up in the form of a questionnaire or stress assessment may also be considered. Professional/Quality of Life: Compassion Satisfaction and Fatigue Subscales (Stamm 2002) or a PTSD assessment scale can be used at the end of the assignment and at periodic intervals in the first year following disaster work. If the same tests were also used to evaluate worker stress pre-disaster, they will provide a useful analysis of the impact of the work. Assessments can indicate the need for additional debriefing, support or psychotherapy to treat any compassion fatigue or STS resulting from the assignment. Support and treatment services should be offered as a matter of course to workers whose test results indicate a significant level of distress.

Summary

Human service responders following workplace violence, terrorism and areas with ongoing terrorism, have a job that entails providing compassionate, humane and effective support services both to victims and first responders in the event. Human services may entail psychological first aid and crisis intervention, stress management, spiritual or pastoral care services, and assessment and referral for a wide range of human needs in the aftermath. In the process, human service workers place themselves at risk for secondary traumatization, compassion fatigue and burnout in the course of their work. The concepts and strategies presented in this chapter are intended to assist organizations in preparing, training and supporting these human service workers in the course of their challenging and important work.

References

Armstrong, K., O'Callahan, W.T. and Marmar, C.R. (1991) 'Debriefing Red Cross disaster personnel: The multiple stressor debriefing model', *Journal of Traumatic Stress*, 4, pp. 581–93.

Bartone, P., Ursano, R., Wright, K. and Ingraham, L. (1989) 'Impact of a military air disaster', *Journal of Nervous and Mental Disease*, 177, 317–28.

Berah, E., Jones, H. and Valent, P. (1984) 'The experience of a mental health team involved in the early phase of a disaster', *Australia and New Zealand Journal of Psychiatry*, 18, 354–8.

Bowie, V. (2002) 'Defining violence at work: a new typology', in M. Gill, B. Fisher and V. Bowie (eds), *Violence at work: causes, patterns, and prevention*, Cullompton, Devon: Willan.

Cerney, M.S. (1995) 'Treating the "heroic treaters"', in C.R. Figley (ed.), *Compassion fatigue: Coping with secondary traumatic stress disorder in those who treat the traumatized*, New York: Brunner/Mazel.

Department of Health and Human Services (1988a) *Prevention and control of stress among emergency workers: A pamphlet for team managers* (DHHS Publication No. ADM 88-1496), Washington, DC: US Government Printing Office.

Department of Health and Human Services (1988b) *Prevention and control of stress among emergency workers: A pamphlet for workers* (DHHS Publication No. ADM 88-1497), Washington, DC: US Government Printing Office.

Derogatis, L. (1994) *SCL-90-R Administration, Coding, and Procedures Manual*. Minneapolis: National Computer Systems, Inc.

Durham, T.W., McCammon, S.L. and Allison, Jr., E.J. (1985) 'The psychological impact of disaster on rescue personnel, *Annals of Emergency Medicine*, 14(7), 664–8.

Dutton, M.A. and Rubinstein, F.L. (1995) 'Working with people with PTSD: Research implications', in C.R. Figley (ed.), *Compassion fatigue: Coping with secondary traumatic stress disorder in those who treat the traumatized.* New York: Brunner/Mazel.

Eidelson, R.J., D'Alession, G.R. and Eidelson, J.L. (2003) 'The impact of September 11 on Psychologists', *Professional Psychology: Research and Practice,* 34(2), pp. 144–50.

Federal Emergency Management Agency (1987a) *FEMA workers can be affected by disasters* (Brochure L-156), Washington, DC: Federal Emergency Management Agency and National Institute of Mental Health.

Federal Emergency Management Agency. (1987b). *Returning home after the disaster: An information pamphlet for FEMA disaster workers* (Brochure l–157), Washington, DC: Federal Emergency Management Agency and National Institute of Mental Health.

Federal Emergency Management Agency (2004) *Compendium of federal terrorism training for state and local audiences.* Retrieved July 25, 2004 from: http://www.fema.gov/compendium/index.jsp

Figley, C.R. (Feburary 1993) 'Compassion stress and the family therapist', *Family Therapy News,* pp. 1–8.

Figley, C.R. (ed.) (1995) *Compassion fatigue: Coping with secondary traumatic stress disorder in those who treat the traumatized,* New York: Brunner/Mazel.

Flanagan, S. (Spring 2002) 'Responding to terrorism: Public mental health systems move to forefront', *National Technical Assistance Center for State Mental Health Planning Networks,* 1–5.

Flannery, Jr. R.B. (1998) *The assaulted staff action program: Coping with the psychological aftermath of violence.* Ellicott City, MD: Chevron Publishing Corp.

Forest, D.J., Woodruff, C. and Bloom, V. (1991) *Crisis response team (CRT): The model.* Paper presented at the Forensic Mental Health Association, 15th Annual Conference, Asilomar, CA.

Frederick, C.J. (1977) 'Current thinking about crisis or psychological interventions in United States disasters', *Mass Emergencies,* 2, 43–9.

Frederick, C.J. (1988) *Frederick Reaction Index (Form A).* Unpublished manuscript.

Gibson, M. and Iwaniec, D. (2003) 'An empirical study into the psychosocial reactions of staff working as helpers to those affected in the aftermath of two traumatic incidents', *British Journal of Social Work,* 33, pp. 851–70.

Hartsough, D.M. and Myers, D.G. (1985) *Disaster work and mental health: prevention and control of stress among workers.* (DHHS Publication No. ADM 85-1422). Rockville, MD: National Institute of Mental Health.

Hodgkinson, P.E. and Shepherd, M.A. (1994) 'The impact of disaster support work', *Journal of Traumatic Stress,* 7, 587–600.

Holmqvist, R. and Anderson, K. (2003) 'Therapists' reactions to treatment of survivors of political torture', *Professional Psychology: Research and Practice,* 34(3), pp. 294–300.

Institute of Medicine of the National Academies (2003) *Preparing for the psychological consequences of terrorism: A public health strategy,* Washington, DC: The National Academies Press.

Keane, T.M., Scott, W.O., Chavoya, G.A., Lamparski, D.M. and Fairbank, J.A. (1985) 'Social support in Vietnam veterans with post-traumatic stress disorder:

A comparative analysis', *Journal of Consulting and Clinical Psychology*, 53, 95–102.

Lanning, J.K.S. and Fannin, R.A. (August/September/October 1988) 'It's not over yet', *Chief Fire Executive*, 40(44), 58–62.

Lindsay, J. (2004) 'An exploration of the experiences of Palestinian practitioners working during the second Intifada'. Unpublished conference presentation at the Global Conference on Social Work, Adelaide, October 2004.

McCammon, S.L. and Allison, E.J. (1995) 'Debriefing and treating emergency workers', in C.R. Figley (ed.), *Compassion fatigue: Coping with secondary traumatic stress disorder in those who treat the traumatized*, New York: Brunner/Mazel.

McFarlane, A.C. (1988) 'The longitudinal course of post traumatic morbidity. The range of outcomes and their predictors', *Journal of Nervous and Mental Disease*, 176(1), 30–9.

Miles, M.S., Demi, A.S. and Mostyn-Aker, P. (1984) 'Rescue workers' reactions following the Hyatt Hotel Disaster', *Death Education*, 8, 315–31.

Mitchell, J.T. (September/October, 1986) 'Critical incident stress management', *Response*, pp. 24–5.

Moore, A.F. (2004) *Compassion fatigue, somatization, and trauma history: A study of disaster mental health professionals after the Oklahoma bombing*. Unpublished doctoral dissertation. Alliant International University, San Francisco, CA.

Moran, C. and Britton, N.R. (1994) 'Emergency Work Experience and Reactions to Traumatic Incidents', *Journal of Traumatic Stress*, 7(4).

Munroe, J.F., Shay, J., Fisher, L., Makary, C., Rapperport, K. and Zimering, R. (1995) 'Preventing Compassion fatigue: A team treatment model', in C.R. Figley (ed.), *Compassion fatigue: Coping with secondary traumatic stress disorder in those who treat the traumatized*, New York: Brunner/Mazel.

Myers, D. (1989a) *Training manual: Disaster mental health*. Sacramento, CA: California Department of Mental Health.

Myers, D. (1989b – 1997) Unpublished training materials.

Myers, D. (1992) *Hurricane Andrew disaster field office stress management program after action report*, Miami, FL: Federal Emergency Management Agency.

Myers, D. (1993a) *Disaster worker stress management: Planning and training issues*. Washington, DC: Federal Emergency Management Agency and Center for Mental Health Services.

Myers, D. (1993b) *After Action Report, 1993 California Winter Storms*. Washington, DC: Federal Emergency Management Agency.

Myers, D. (1994a) *A stress management program for FEMA disaster workers: Program description, operational guidelines, and training plan*. Washington, DC: Federal Emergency Management Agency and Center for Mental Health Services.

Myers, D. (1994b) *Disaster response and recovery: A handbook for mental health professionals*, Rockville, MD: Center for Mental Health Services.

Myers, D. (2001) 'Weapons of mass destruction and terrorism: Mental health consequences and implications for planning and training', *The ripple effect from ground zero: Coping with mental health needs in time of tragedy and terror*, New York: American Red Cross.

Myers, D. (2004) *A review of the compendium of federal terrorism training for state and local audiences: A search for content on mental health and stress management topics.* Unpublished raw data.

Myers, D. and Wee, D.F. (2004) *Disaster mental health services: A primer for practitioners*, New York: Brunner-Routledge.

Myers, D. and Wee, D. (2002) 'Strategies for managing disaster mental health worker stress', in Figley, C.R. (ed.) *Treating compassion fatigue*, New York: Brunner-Routledge.

Myers, D. and Wolfe, D. (1996) 'Critical Incident Stress Debriefing After Workplace Violence', in *The Complete Workplace Violence Prevention Manual*, Costa Mesa, CA: James Publishing Co.

Myers, D. and Zunin, L.M. (1993a) *After action report: 1993 Florida winter storms disaster field office stress management program*, Tampa, FL: Federal Emergency Management Agency.

Myers, D. and Zunin, L.M. (1993b) *After action report: 1993 Midwest Floods Stress Management Program*, Kansas City, MO: Federal Emergency Management Agency.

Myers, D. and Zunin, L.M. (1994a) *Stress management program after action report: 1994 Northridge Earthquake*, Pasadena, CA: Federal Emergency Management Agency and California Governor's Office of Emergency Services.

Myers, D. and Zunin, L.M. (1994b) *Stress management program for disaster workers: A national cadre of stress management personnel: Training manual*, Atlanta, GA: Federal Emergency Management Agency.

National Institute of Mental Health (1987a) *Prevention and control of stress among emergency workers: A pamphlet for manager*, Rockville, MD.

National Institute of Mental Health (1987b) *Prevention and control of stress among emergency workers: A pamphlet for workers*, Rockville, MD.

Pearlman, L.A. and MacIan, P.S. (1995) 'Vicarious traumatization: An empirical study of the effects of trauma work on trauma therapists', *Professional Psychology: Research and Practice*, 26, 558–65.

Pearlman, L.A. and Saakvitne, K.W. (1995) 'Treating therapists with vicarious traumatization and secondary traumatic stress disorders', In C.R. Figley (ed.), *Compassion fatigue: Coping with secondary traumatic stress disorder in those who treat the traumatized*, New York: Brunner/Mazel.

Ramon, S. (2004) 'The impact of the 2nd Intifada on Israeli Arab and Jewish Social Workers', *European Journal of Social Worker*, 7(3), pp. 285–303.

Raphael, B., Singh B., Bradbury, B. and Lambert, F. (1984) 'Who helps the helpers? The effects of a disaster on the rescue workers', *Omega*, 14, 9–20.

Riba, S. and Reches, R. (30 September 2002) 'When terror is routine: How Israeli nurses cope with multi-casualty terror', *2002 Online Journal of Issues in Nursing.* Retrieved October 2002 from:
http://nursingworld.org/ojin/topic19/tpc19_5.htm

Rice, C.A. and Kapur, R. (2002) 'The impact of the "Troubles" on therapy groups in Northern Ireland', *Group*, 26(3), pp. 247–64.

Robinson, R. (Spring 1989) 'Critical incident stress and psychological debriefing in emergency services', *Social Biology Resources Center Review*, 3(3) pp. 1–4.

Rosenschweig, M.A. and Vaslow, P.K. (1992) *Recommendations for reduction of stress among FEMA disaster workers*, Rockville, MD: National Institute of Mental Health.

Solomon, S. (1986) 'Mobilizing social support networks in times of disaster', in C. Figley (ed.), *Trauma and its wake, Volume II: Traumatic stress theory, research, and intervention*, New York: Brunner/Mazel.

Stamm, B.H. (2002) 'Measuring compassion satisfaction as well as fatigue: developmental history of the compassion fatigue and satisfaction test', in C.R. Figley (ed.) 107–119, *Treating Compassion Fatigue*, New York: Brunner/Mazel.

Taylor, A.J.W. and Frazer, A.G. (December 1982) 'The stress of post-disaster body handling and victim identification work', *Journal of Human Stress*, 8(12), 4–12.

Varblow, P. (1994) 'Stress management', in *Project Rebound, 2nd Quarterly Report*, Los Angeles, CA: Los Angeles County Department of Mental Health.

Wee, D.F. (1994a) 'Disasters: Impact on the law enforcement family.' in J.T. Reese and E. Scrivner (eds), *Law Enforcement Family: Issues and Answers*, Washington, DC: US Department of Justice, Federal Bureau of Investigation.

Wee, D. (1994b) *Disaster training for crisis counselors*. Unpublished training materials.

Wee, D. and Myers, D. (1997) 'Disaster mental health: Impact on workers', In K. Johnson, *Trauma in the lives of children*, Alameda, CA: Hunter House Press.

Wee, D. and Myers, D. (2002) 'Stress response of mental health workers following disaster: The Oklahoma City bombing', in C.R. Figley (ed.), *Treating compassion fatigue*, New York: Brunner/Mazel.

Wee, D. and Myers, D. (2003) 'Compassion satisfaction and fatigue in critical incident stress management', *International Journal of Emergency Mental Health*, 5(1), pp. 33–7.

Winget. C.N. and Umbenhauer, S.L. (1982) 'Disaster planning: The mental health worker as "victim-by-proxy"' *Journal of Health and Human Resources Administration*, 4, 363–73.

Wraith, R. and Gordon, R. (1988) *Workers' Responses to Disaster*, Melbourne, Australia: Department of Child and Family Psychiatry, Melbourne Royal Children's Hospital.

Note: Government publications referenced in this chapter are in the public domain and are not copyrighted. They may be reproduced or copied without permission from the government agency or from the authors. Citation of the author and source is requested.

Chapter 11

Workplace preparedness and resiliency: an integrated response to terrorism

Nancy T. Vineburgh, Robert J. Ursano and Carol S. Fullerton

Introduction: workplace as target of terrorism

The unspeakable images of innocent employees and visitors leaping to their deaths from the World Trade Center Towers on the morning of 11 September 2001 gave new meaning to terrorism as the most extreme form of violence affecting the workplace. Horrific as were those events, it is their images, real-time and lingering, that constitute the primary goal of terrorism: to destabilize trust in public institutions, to change peoples' beliefs, sense of safety and behaviours (Holloway *et al.* 1997). Of all institutions, these effects are especially deleterious in the workplace. Disrupting the workplace disrupts the economic, intellectual and social capital of a nation, as well as the routines and health of its citizens, their families and communities.

In the United States, the workplace has been the identified target of terrorism. The events of 9/11, the anthrax attacks of 2001, the 1995 Oklahoma City bombing of a federal office building, and the 1993 World Trade Center explosions underscore this reality. Because most acts of terrorism in the US have occurred where and when people work, and because corporations and the workplace are identified as high-value targets of international terrorism, it is essential that interventions for preparedness, response and recovery occur in occupational settings (Ursano *et al.* 2004a; Vineburgh 2004).

While workplaces differ in size, industry and employee populations, the human impact of terrorism is predictable, expectable and requires organization-wide preparedness that includes both general and worksite-specific interventions. Responsibilities for employee health and productivity also vary within corporations, but these functions (human resources, employee assistance programmes, security and facilities, medical, occupational health, wellness and worklife) play an essential role in equipping workers and organizations to prepare for and respond to the threat and/or actuality of terrorism.

On the morning of 9/11, corporate leadership from diverse industries shared similar reactions and set similar priorities (Greenberg 2002; Argenti 2002), best expressed by Ray O'Rourke, managing director for global corporate affairs at Morgan Stanley. 'We knew within the first day that, even though we are a financial services company, we didn't have a financial crisis on our hands; we had a human crisis. After that point, everything was focused on our people. (Argenti 2002).

The events of 9/11 and the anthrax attacks that followed dramatically reinforced in the minds of employers the importance of the human continuity of organizations and the functions that foster that continuity (Coutu and Hyman 2002; Greenberg 2002; Mankin and Perry 2004). Similarly, many workplace providers who rose to the occasion during and following these events saw in their expanded role as disaster responder a new calling for a new future – protecting the workplace from terrorism (Monaghan 2003; Mankin and Perry 2004).

This chapter addresses the new role that workplace health professionals can play in consequence management for terrorism. In mapping such a role, it is important to acknowledge that a number of barriers to preparedness may exist within any one workplace. These include: 1) corporate focus on operational rather than human continuity (Mankin and Perry 2004; Ursano *et al.* 2004a; Ursano and Vineburgh 2004a); 2) corporate silos that prevent the collaboration and coordination essential to facilitating employee preparedness (Vineburgh 2004; Ursano *et al.* 2004a; Ursano and Vineburgh 2004b); 3) employer and employee resistance to engage in preparedness activities; 4) needs for professional training of workplace health providers in disaster mental health (Institute of Medicine [IOM], 2003a); 5) absence of a common language to communicate the conceptual and practical implications of disaster behavioural and mental health, and the central role of behaviour in preparedness and response (Holloway and Waldrep 2004). This chapter will address the first three, organizational barriers and provide some basic principles of disaster mental health that should be part of a disaster response training curriculum for workplace professionals tasked with this responsibility.

To surmount these barriers, we introduce an Integrated Workplace

Table 11.1 Integrated workplace resiliency model: role of workplace health and productivity professional

		Behavioural	Psychological	Resiliency
Educate	Event	•Senior management: need for/assemble integrated corporate response model/ team •Workforce: disaster behaviours, i.e. evacuation, shelter-in-place, family communication plans	•Incorporate disaster health promotion into existing campaigns for depression, alcohol, anxiety	•Shared values •Social cohesion
Communicate	Pre-event	•Grief leadership •Promote/partner/stay on corporate risk communication message •Integrate message into existing EAP resources (e.g. employee helpline, website, etc.)	•Provide psychological first aid to employees/ families •Deploy resources off-site/family centres •Promote personal care: eat, sleep, exercise, resume schedule	•Corporate continuity •Social capital/ human focus
Evaluate	Post-event	•Conduct health promotion of behaviour risks: increased smoking, alcohol, drugs, family violence	•Health promotion about normal distress; more serious reactions requiring evaluation •Assess/evaluate over time problems requiring treatment •Attention/ outreach vulnerable populations	•Expected outcome •Need for human resources response to disaster fallout •Opening of fault lines: race, ethnicity, perceived differences in medical treatment

Resiliency Model (see Table 11.1). This approach is both a strategy for moving organizations in the direction of terrorism planning, and a health promotion vehicle to educate leadership, management and employees about disaster preparedness. With an aim to establishing an integral and integrated role for the workplace health and productivity professional in this process and practice, we advance a framework derived from a public health model that views terrorism as a threat to the health of an *entire* nation. Employers and workplace health and productivity professionals can play an important role in protecting the health of their organization and its people, but also the health of their communities and their country.

It is hoped that the concepts and strategies outlined in this chapter will have applicability internationally, as well as across various workplaces and industries. Given the number of multi-national corporations, collaborative efforts are essential to prevent, mitigate and recover from the global impact of terrorism and its effects on the workplace.

Workplace: a new setting to prepare and advance population health

The report, *Preparing for the Psychological Consequences of Terrorism: A Public Health Strategy*, from the Institute of Medicine of the National Academy of Sciences (NAS) of the United States (IOM 2003a) has recognized the workplace as a new setting for terrorism preparedness, and workplace health providers as important partners in this process. The context of this report and its recommendations are significant for developing the human component of a workplace preparedness strategy for terrorism.

In 2002, NAS, a private, non-profit American society that brings together subject matter experts to advise our federal government on scientific and technical matters, convened a group of disaster mental health experts to address the unprecedented psychological effects of 9/11. While not the first terrorism on American soil, the events of 9/11 were the first to have such a profound and pervasive impact on the nation (Silver *et al.* 2002; Vlahov *et al.* 2002, Stein *et al.* 2003). Among those Americans (16 per cent) who experienced persistent stress two months after 9/11, this distress disrupted their work (65 per cent reported accomplishing less), their social life (24 per cent avoided public places) and led to increased health risks (38 per cent using alcohol, medication or other drugs to relax, sleep and reduce terrorism-related worries) (Stein *et al.*).

The convened expert Committee on Responding to the Psychological Consequences of Terrorism recommended adopting a unifying public health strategy that reflects and incorporates the mental health implications of terrorism. Likening terrorism and the fear it propagates to a disease transmission model, this proposed public health strategy focuses on health promotion (raising awareness of the risk) and prevention (interventions to mitigate the risk) in addition to treatment, and conceptualizes interventions for the pre-event, event and post-event phases of the terrorist event. A primary objective of a public health approach (in this case, one designed to manage the psychological and behavioural impact of terrorism) is to protect and enhance 'population health', a term that refers to the overall health of a community, an organization or group, rather than of an individual (IOM 2003b). Examples of population health interventions are seat belts to modify the risk of automobile accidents and fluoride in drinking water to modify the risk of tooth decay. Workplace preparedness for terrorism is a population health intervention to prevent and/or modify the risk of injury and morbidity from exposure to terrorism, a disaster that has far-reaching effects on an entire population.

Employers are important population health partners (IOM 2003b) with resources and established relationships that can foster preparedness (IOM 2003a). Workplace health and productivity professionals (employee assistance professionals (EAPs), corporate medical directors, occupational health, wellness and worklife professionals) are ideally positioned for an important role in disaster response because their work encompasses prevention, health promotion and treatment, the three elements of a public health approach. Many workplace health and productivity professionals provide employee health prevention and promotion activities on a day-to-day basis in the form of educational outreach, health campaigns and mental health services including evaluation, referral and/or treatment. These services often benefit employee families. However, workplace professionals lack training in disaster mental health. With training, workplace health and mental health providers, many of which reside in the private sector, could make a significant contribution in the delivery of disaster-related interventions pre-event, event and post-event (IOM 2003a; Ursano, Fullerton and Norwood 2003). In the United States this is particularly important because the federal response to disaster is geared to the local immediate needs, which does not address pre-event preparedness nor the widespread and often prolonged psychological and behavioural effects caused by exposure to terrorism.

Disaster mental health: understanding the psychological and behavioural consequences of terrorism

Disaster mental health encompasses both psychological and behavioural issues related to trauma exposure or its threat. Disasters are either naturally occurring (earthquakes, hurricanes, floods) or human-made (industrial and environmental accidents, terrorism, bioterrorism). Terrorism, a subset of human-made disasters, carries a potentially greater mental health impact than other disasters because of its malicious intent that can generate a sense of disbelief and anger, lack of control and altered sense of safety in populations close to, and far from, the actual proximity of the event (IOM 2003a). Psychological and behavioural implications of terrorism encompass the *pre-event* stage in terms of *attitudes* and *activities* towards preparedness that can facilitate or thwart it; the *immediate* responses of affected individuals and organizations; and the *longer-term* effects ranging from distress to psychiatric illness and altered and risky health behaviours, which can be transitory or prolonged.

Pre-event behavioural issues that are workplace specific include employer and employee *attitudes* about preparing for terrorism. Several US studies indicate that despite the public's belief there will be more terrorism, the public is generally not knowledgeable about preparedness within their own workplace (National Center for Disaster Preparedness 2003). One national survey found only 36 per cent of citizens familiar with emergency plans in their workplace, yet citizens reported interest in having their workplace update their plans and practice drills (Council for Excellence in Government 2004). Another national study found that nearly half of US workers felt their employer was not prepared for a terrorist attack; of those, 9 per cent said it did not matter because they believed their company would never be affected (Comp Psych Survey 2004).

Immediate responses to disasters and terrorism involve a term and concept, 'disaster behaviour', that may be unfamiliar, but can be extremely useful in communicating the value of preparedness to employers, management and employees. Renowned Norwegian disaster psychiatrist Lars Weisaeth (1989) used the term to describe behaviours in the face of disaster, such as spontaneous reactions like fear and panic, or planned reactions such as evacuation, shelter-in-place and quarantine. These reactions are of critical importance in the workplace (Hall *et al.* 2003; Ursano and Norwood 2003). During the 1993 World Trade Center explosion, 32 per cent of individuals had not begun to evacuate by over one hour, 30 per cent decided *not* to evacuate and only 36 per cent had participated in a *previous* emergency evacuation (Aguirre *et al.* 1998). Importantly, large groups (greater than 20 people) took 6.7 minutes longer to initiate evacuation, a timeframe of life or death in many disasters. In addition, the higher the location, the greater the delay in initiating evacuation, and the more people were known to one another, the longer the group took to initiate evacuation (Aguirre *et al.*, 1998).

Longer-term psychological and behavioural issues, which are among the most prevalent and costly consequences of terrorism, include its effects on people's expectations of the future, on their economic and social behaviours including their sense of safety, and for some their mental health in the form of distress, psychiatric illness and altered behavioural health risks (Ursano *et al.* 2004b). Individuals exposed to trauma have been found to increase their use of alcohol, tobacco and other drugs, especially those with pre-existing alcohol abuse or other psychiatric difficulties (Galea, Ahern, Resnick *et al.* 2002; North, Nixon, Shariat *et al.*1999; Pfefferbaum and Doughty 2001; Ursano *et al.* 2003; Vlahov, Galea, Resnick *et al.* 2002). People who are exposed to terrorism and disaster are at increased risk for post-traumatic stress disorder as well as depression, generalized anxiety disorder and panic disorder and increased substance use (Fullerton *et al.* 2003; North *et al.* 1999; North, Tivis, McMillen *et al.* 2002). These behaviours and disorders can be costly in the workplace in terms of safety, productivity and morale, all factors that affect the health and productivity of a corporation.

Resiliency: the expected outcome of disaster

It is important to recognize that resiliency, the ability of most people to recover and return to normal life, is the documented and therefore expected outcome in all studies of disaster (see e.g. North 2003; Ursano 2002; Ursano *et al.* 2003). Resiliency is a growing topic of interest in mental health and mental health promotion (American Psychological Association Help Center 2004; Vineburgh 2004). Resiliency is also a growing topic of interest in the workplace as it bridges the health and continuity of the organization and its people (Coutu 2002; Vineburgh 2004). There is an interest among employee assistance programmes (EAP) such as Chevron/Texaco (Blair Consulting Group 2003) and Dupont, as well as EAP professional associations such as the Employee Assistance Society of North America (EASNA) whose 2004 annual conference theme was 'Resiliency in the World of Work', to use resiliency as a health promotion vehicle and way to integrate mental health into other productivity functions and outcomes. A workplace strategy that reframes disaster preparedness as a means of fostering organizational and employee resiliency can be an effective way to communicate about and motivate preparedness (Vineburgh 2004).

New roles and collaboration for terrorism response

The events of 9/11 gave rise to new roles and collaborations among many workplace health and productivity professionals that must be further developed and sustained to achieve organizational and employee preparedness. The role and relationship between employee assistance and human resources in response to terrorism provides an interesting example of new and needed collaborations.

Employee assistance programmes and providers deal with a broad range of psychological and behavioural disorders. In the United States, workplace mental health programmes began after World War II to address problem drinking in the workplace, expanding in the 1970s and 80s to encompass the emotional health and distress of employees. Most EAP programmes were 'internal', featuring mental health counsellors as employees working within the corporation. With the advent of managed care in the 1980s, behavioural health carve-outs (private companies that offer mental health benefits and services) began offering EAP services, and many corporations chose to outsource their mental health and substance abuse assessment and treatment to these large networks. Such programmes are referred to as 'external EAP' programmes. Some companies have both 'internal' and 'external' EAPs, called a mixed model.

Although EAP programmes vary, most conduct employee health promotion and education activities, mental health assessment and referral, and sometimes treatment including alcohol and drug or mental health counselling. Many EAPs in the United States also conduct national mental health awareness programmes like National Depression Screening Day and National Alcohol Screening Day, and offer confidential and interactive screening resources (employee helplines and online programmes) that encourage self-identification and help-seeking for depression, anxiety, post-traumatic stress disorder and alcohol problems ranging from risky drinking to alcohol dependence (Raskin and Williams 2003). The majority of American employers offer EAP services (Roman and Blum 2002), as do a growing number of employers worldwide (Masi 2000; Reddy 2003).

To manage the human consequences of 9/11, EAPs worked hand-in-hand with human resource departments whose staff were present at off-site family assistance centres addressing the needs, immediate and long-term, of victims' families, including benefits and services (Greenberg 2002). Despite the leadership role of human resources during and after 9/11, and despite major workplace terrorist events (the 1993 World Trade Center attack and the Oklahoma City bombing), no articles addressing employee consequences of terrorism were published in human resource journals between January 2001 and March 2003 (Mankin and Perry 2004). Human resource departments are a logical locus for terrorism preparedness because most employee health and benefits activities reside in human resources, including EAP programmes that provide direct psychological services.

The partnership between human resources and employee assistance can also address the interface between work and family by encouraging the creation of family communication plans, an essential aspect of preparedness for terrorism. The workplace is an excellent place to encourage families to have family/work and family communications plans, and to be knowledgeable about disaster policies and plans in settings where their children and loved ones reside when not at home, such as schools, day care and elder care communities.

Human resources and employee assistance can be formidable partners in equipping organizations and workers for the impact of terrorism. Because most EAP programmes (internal and external) report to their corporation's human resources department, it is incumbent upon human resources to seek organizational buy-in for disaster preparedness planning, especially around terrorism; to advocate for the integration of a human continuity focus; and to include their organization's employee assistance and/or related occupational health, worklife and medical services in the process and planning. Presently, many human resource departments have been reluctant to collaborate with their employee assistance programmes or bring the human focus of disaster response into alignment with operational planning. The reasons for this resistance are certainly complex.

Workplace barriers and opportunities for organizational and employee preparedness

Of the five barriers to preparedness listed in the introduction to this chapter, there are three organizational barriers that workplace professionals may more commonly encounter in the process of equipping organizations and workers to deal with the impact of terrorism. They are are: 1) the tendency of corporations to focus on business or operational versus human continuity; 2) a silo effect preventing collaboration between functions that can facilitate employee preparedness; and 3) employer and employee emotions ranging from complacency to fear regarding preparedness activities.

Corporations commonly view their strength and hence their preparedness needs around the physical and cyber security of their organizations (Mankin and Perry 2004; Cavanagh 2003). Several studies have found that less than 50 per cent of US corporations surveyed had any disaster plans in place, and for those that did, the focus was on natural disasters (hurricane, flood, fires) or safety issues related to industrial accidents as opposed to terrorism planning and its impact on employees (Mankin and Perry 2004).

Corporate continuity can be viewed as consisting of '3 Rs': redundancy, reliability and resiliency (Ursano *et al.* 2004a). Redundancy refers to a corporation's physical back-up as in alternate sites and bench strength in terms of leadership roles. Reliability refers to a corporation's hardware as in its IT systems and operations. Resiliency represents the human capital of the organization – its people. In the United States, many corporate leaders as a result of 9/11 recognized that their first priority in the face of disaster is their organization's people, who are also the most resilient element (Greenberg 2002; Argenti 2002; Coutu and Hyman 2002).

The second major barrier to workplace preparedness is the effect of corporate silos preventing important collaborations for employee preparedness. Corporate security is an excellent example of this silo effect. The traditional role of corporate security in the United States has been operational – guarding the perimeter. At a national conference of senior-level security professionals, there was an expressed interest in expanding their security role to encompass employee preparedness for terrorism (The Conference Board 2003). These professionals wanted a more human role in protecting employees and were seeking creative ways to collaborate with the health and productivity functions within their organization. Partnering with their company's EAP program was of great interest. The next section provides an excellent example of the heroic role corporate security can play in protecting employee health and resiliency in the face of terrorism.

The third organizational barrier to workplace preparedness is employer and employee attitudes about such activities that range from complacency to fear to lack of fitness An interesting, newly reported phenomenon among employers who have tried to institute evacuation drills since 9/11 is employee resistance due to lack of fitness (Ursano and Vineburgh 2003). A woman who experienced the burning of the Twin Towers and works in New York City remarked that her workplace subsequently engaged employees to practise evacuation from the 42nd floor. She commented that 'employees are not conditioned for terrorism, and most colleagues reported feeling the effects of this drill for an entire weekend' (Hall, personal communication, December 2003).

Fear is another barrier to preparedness. A number of employee assistance and occupational health professionals of Fortune 500, multi-national corporations interested in workplace preparedness expressed their primary concern as a question: how to raise awareness of this topic without raising undue anxiety in the workplace (Bender 2003). This is the subject of the next section.

Integrated workplace resiliency model: addressing and overcoming barriers to workplace preparedness for disaster and terrorism

In this section we introduce a practical approach for equipping organizations and workers to deal with the impact of terrorism. This approach, an Integrated Workplace Resiliency Model (see Table 11.1), draws upon many concepts outlined in this chapter. The model also describes the role that workplace health and productivity professionals can play in each phase: pre-event, event and post-event.

The cornerstone of this integrated model is its focus on resiliency as an *outcome* of preparedness planning. Resiliency has a positive connotation and can provide a positive framework for engaging reluctant corporations and employees to participate in terrorism preparedness. Resiliency is a meaningful disaster metaphor for workplace preparedness and response to disaster (Ursano and Vineburgh 2004a; Vineburgh 2004). Resiliency involves two perspectives that have workplace-specific implications. From a clinical perspective, resiliency is the expected outcome of disaster and terrorism (North 2003; Ursano and Norwood 2003), and aligns with workplace health and productivity. From an organizational perspective, resiliency is integral to corporate continuity and refers to the human capital of the organization and its continuity (see '3Rs').

Pre-event phase: educate

In the pre-event phase, workplace health professionals must *educate* the workplace – senior management, management and employees – about the importance of preparedness, including practical interventions. It is important to educate senior management in order to achieve executive level buy-in and participation. A large financial corporation undergoing a restructuring of its disaster preparedness planning in a major city of terrorist threat commented that the role of their medical and mental health functions is miniscule in contrast to the organization's emphasis on operational functions. Given the expanded threat of terrorism, it would seem that the human capital of the organization – employee health, especially its mental health – would be paramount in such crisis planning. Educating senior management to integrate human continuity functions (employee assistance, medical, occupational health) within their business continuity planning is an essential first step to organizational preparedness for terrorism.

Workplace health providers must also *educate* employees about preparedness, both its psychological and behavioural implications. Working in collaboration with other functions like human resources or corporate security, EAPs can provide information on important disaster

217

behaviours such as evacuation, shelter-in-place and family communication plans. Disaster behaviours can be taught in conjunction with corporate security who can facilitate the actual practising of the drills. Existing health awareness events or a dedicated day on workplace preparedness can provide the vehicle for this activity (Vineburgh 2004). Such a campaign on workplace resiliency incorporating terrorism preparedness could even be conducted as a global workplace initiative.

Morgan Stanley case study: pre-event preparedness and resiliency
The 9/11 response of Morgan Stanley, a global financial services corporation, illustrates how a collaborative approach involving operational and human continuity planning greatly enhanced the resiliency of the business and its people. Soon after the 1993 World Trade Center bombings, Morgan Stanley launched a preparedness programme involving serious evacuation drills directed by its corporate security department. On the morning of 9/11, one minute after the North Tower was struck, Rick Rescorla, security Vice President, instructed Morgan Stanley's employees to evacuate the South Tower immediately, to stay calm and follow their well-practised drills. This resulted in a loss of only seven of its 2,700 employees.

This example represents the successful integration of security, facilities, human health and behaviour and employee preparedness. Moreover, Morgan Stanley exhibited a trait attributable to corporations that are resilient: an ability to stare down reality and plan for the worst (Coutu 2002). This kind of attitude coupled with pre-event preparedness planning among senior leadership, management and employees creates social cohesion and shared values, which are two important ingredients of organizational and individual resiliency (see Table 11.1).

Event phase: communicate

In the event phase, the immediate, actual response to the terrorist event, workplace health professionals must *communicate* on behalf of corporate leadership. It is essential to stay on the corporate message to reinforce information on employee safety, workplace resumption and schedules, and employee resources for information and help-seeking. Employee assistance programmes and human resources departments can integrate the corporate communication message into existing EAP employee helplines and benefits websites. An important role in this phase is provision of psychological first aid: promoting personal care, sleep, exercise and return to normal routine (National Institute of Mental Health 2002).

Event communication and resiliency
Two case studies on corporate responses to 9/11 in the *Harvard Business*

Review (Argenti 2002; Greenberg 2002) underscore the importance of communications and communication strategies in the immediate aftermath of workplace disasters, and how such communication fosters organizational recovery and resilience. The CEO of Marsh & McLennan Companies, a corporation that suffered severe losses (295 employees), emphasizes the importance of CEO visibility in communicating during the immediate aftermath of a disaster (Greenberg 2002; Argenti 2002). Improvization and creativity were touted as essential among CEOs of affected corporations with downed power and telephone lines. Public address systems became important, and the media became partners with corporations to communicate information about employee whereabouts and safety issues (Argenti 2002). Communication through leadership visibility that is clear, honest and compassionate reassures employees. Reassuring employees helps re-establish operational continuity, enhancing the resiliency of people and business.

Post-event phase: evaluate

In the post-event phase, workplace health and productivity professionals must evaluate the impact of the event and provide necessary resources to aid in the recovery. EAPs can provide health promotion materials on normal distress reactions of trauma and how to distinguish between normal distress and more serious psychiatric problems requiring evaluation and treatment. They can provide information on escalation of health risks such as increased smoking, alcohol intake and even family violence. EAPs can promote the use of existing anonymous and interactive screening resources for case finding and referral and treatment resources.

Human resource professionals must stay alert to the opening of fault lines from terrorist events. Terrorism opens the fault lines of a society, revealing its vulnerabilities and divisive tendencies along racial, ethnic and religious lines (Ursano 2002). This can result in scapegoating, discrimination against ethnicities perceived akin to the terrorist agent, as well as fallout around perceived inequities in disaster treatment responses.

In the aftermath of the anthrax attacks of 2001, US postal workers became disgruntled, perceiving their medical treatment inferior to that given to employees on Capitol Hill despite the fact that theirs may have been a technically more effective protocol. This perception has historical roots around the fault lines of race and ethnicity in the United States. It resulted in serious and persistent mistrust that undermined the cohesion of the postal service workplace, including legal ramifications (Holloway and Waldrep 2004; Steury *et al.* 2004). These behavioural consequences of terrorism have important implications for the human capital and continuity of organizations about which human resource personnel must be knowledgeable.

Employee assistance programmes and human resources departments must reach out to vulnerable populations. Gender and pre-disaster psychiatric history are strong predictors of post-trauma psychiatric difficulties (North 2003; North *et al.* 1999). After disasters, women are more likely to experience PTSD and major depression, and men are at greater risk for substance abuse. Individuals with pre-existing mental disorders are more likely to experience renewed difficulties. Because some workplaces are predominantly male or female, such findings can inform pre- and post -disaster interventions.

Specific groups may require special interventions. These include identified cultural groups whose perception of the disaster may be markedly different as a result of past experiences with disasters (i.e. refugees, individuals recently exposed to traumas, ethnic groups). The number of refugees worldwide is growing, and many are relocated in the United States, as well as in workplaces throughout the world. The unique characteristics of refugees groups, including cultural, ethnic and language considerations, torture or trauma experiences, multiple losses, minimal resources and an uncertain future, need to be considered in developing mental health services (Gerrity and Steinglass 2003).

Post-event interventions and resiliency

While resiliency is the expected outcome of disaster, attention to the psychological and behavioural implications of trauma are important. Employee assistance, occupational health and wellness programmes can provide information on stress management, depression, anxiety, post-traumatic stress and alcohol misuse or abuse, as well as publicize resources for self-identification to promote help-seeking. Human resource professionals must plan for and anticipate the opening of fault lines and the potential vulnerabilities represented by their workplace populations. Attention to these issues fosters employee and organizational resiliency (Coutu and Hyman 2002; Ursano 2002; Vineburgh 2004).

Workplace preparedness for terrorism in the 21st century: population health partnership and global implications

The workplace is an important disaster preparedness setting for managing the organizational and human consequences of terrorism. Workplace health and productivity providers can play an important role in equipping organizations and employees to deal with the impact of such trauma. Because terrorism continues to be a global threat and one that frequently targets, disrupts and in some instances destroys the workplace, this role will be increasingly important worldwide.

At a 2003 global symposium on workplace mental health held at the International Labour Organization in Geneva, Switzerland, attendees, including medical directors from multi-national corporations, EAP providers and ministers of health, expressed concern about terrorism as an extreme form of workplace violence with global consequences. Recommendations included preparing employees through workplace drills in evacuation, shelter-in-place, as well as training for employee health and productivity professionals in disaster mental health (Vineburgh 2003).

Workplace preparedness for terrorism is an important dimension of and vehicle for population health in the 21st century. Employed individuals spend more than a third of their day at work (IOM 2003b), and work is most often the source of one's health benefits. In addition, employees are avid health consumers for themselves and their families (Vineburgh 2002). Interestingly, more than twice as many individuals experiencing persistent distress after 9/11 accessed information at work rather than from a medical practitioner, and over three times as many sought information and counselling at work rather than from a mental health provider assumably in a community setting (Stein *et al.* 2003). There is increasing evidence that workplace health promotion activities and programmes can change behaviour and psycho-social risk factors for individual employees and the collective risk profile of the employee population (IOM 2003b).

This is very encouraging for workplace health professionals seeking a pro-active role in equipping organizations and workers to deal with the impact of terrorism. Workplace health and productivity professionals can provide the health promotion context and health promotion content to educate management, employees and even families on preparedness for terrorism. Organizational planning for terrorism must address and incorporate the human element of disasters in order to manage the human consequences. Because many corporations are multinational and/ or engage in global trade, employee preparedness for terrorism must extend across organizations and geographical boundaries and encompass culturally sensitive and culturally relevant preparedness information and response interventions to terrorist events.

Language is an important element, if not the precursor in communicating new ideas aimed at motivating systems and attitudinal change. Language is a necessary precondition to the establishment of socio-cultural organization, and critical to preparing for, responding to and recovering from the effects of disastrous events (Holloway and Waldrep 2004). The language of terrorism is frightening, conjuring up images and events that provoke anxiety among large populations, which can be a barrier to preparedness. Therefore the language used by health promotion professionals and public education campaigns aimed at preparedness for terrorism must strike a chord that engages organizations and individuals to take action in a way that does not provoke unnecessary anxiety.

This chapter introduces new language (see Table 11.2) to communicate the significance of workplace preparedness. In using language that engages the attention of our intended audience, in this case employers, management and employees, we join with them to respect and integrate their concerns, needs and objectives into a greater vision for the common good.

Employers and workplace health and productivity professionals can play a vital role in protecting their workplace and fostering organizational and employee resiliency in the face of terrorism and its threat in the 21st century. These efforts will also strengthen relationships between global

Table 11.2 New language to promote workplace preparedness for terrorism and population health partnerships for the 21st century

• **Disaster Behaviours**: Behaviours manifest at the time of disasters. Disaster behaviours may increase or decrease risk to life and are the result of psychological and social processes, including training and past experience.

• **Human Continuity**: Sustaining the health, safety and ability to perform of individuals in a group or community after a critical incident, disaster or terrorist attack

• **Population Health**: A term that refers to 'the health of the population' or 'the population's health' for which public health and public health interventions are developed. Employers and employee health and productivity providers are important partners in population health who can provide disaster education to enhance the health of their workplace, their community and their nation.

• **Organizational Continuity**: Sustaining the function and performance of an organization after a critical incident, disaster or terrorist attack.

• **Preparedness**: Education about disasters, including terrorism and bioterrorism, as well as actions taken to prevent, mitigate and foster recovery from disaster. This includes knowledge of proper evacuation techniques; understanding and voluntary compliance with life-saving disaster behaviours, including shelter-in-place, quarantine; the creation of family communication plans and disaster kits.

• **Resiliency**: In its most general sense, bouncing back from adversity. In the context of disaster mental health, resiliency is the expected, clinical outcome of disaster. In an organizational context, resiliency applies to the human element of the organization, in addition to its operational components (redundancy and reliability). The human element is the most resilient component of an organization.

workplace colleagues who can positively impact the health of their respective communities and nations. Workplace preparedness for terrorism is an important population health intervention of the 21st century that can make a significant contribution to homeland and global security.

References

Aguirre, B.E., Wenger, D. and Vigo, G. (1998) 'A Test of the Emergent Norm Theory of Collective Behaviour', *Sociological Forum*, 13, pp. 301–20.

American Psychological Association Help Center (2004) *The Road to Resilience*. http://www.apahelpcenter.org (accessed 10 October 2004).

Argenti, P. (2002) 'Crisis Communication: lessons from 9/11', *Harvard Business Review*, Harvard Business School of Publishing Corporation.

Bender, E. (2003) 'Employers See Value in Raising Workers' Awareness of Mental Health Issues', *Psychiatric News*, 38(7), pp. 8–9.

Brenda Blair Consulting Group (2003) *Stress and Resilience Benchmarking Project for Chevron Texaco*.

Cavanagh, T.E. (2003) 'Corporate Security Management: organization and spending since 9/11', *The Conference Board Executive Summary*.

Cohen, D. (2002) 'HR Implications of the Attack on America: one year later', *Society for Human Resource Management*, Alexandria, VA.

Council for Excellence in Government (2004) *From the Home Front to the Front Lines: America speaks out about homeland security*. Hart-Teeter Research.

ComPsych Survey (2004) *Employees Feel Sense of Inertia Around Terror Warnings*.

Coutu, D.L. (2002) 'How Resilience Works', *Harvard Business Review On Point*, Harvard Business School Publishing Corporation.

Coutu, D.L. and Hyman, S.E. (2002). 'Managing Emotional Fallout: parting remarks from America's top psychiatrist', *Harvard Business Review*, Harvard Business School Publishing Corporation.

Fullerton, C.S., Ursano, R.J. and Norwood, A.E. (2003) 'Workplace Interventions Following Trauma: A Review of Interventions to Prevent or Treat Psychological and Behavioural Consequences of Occupational or Workplace Exposure to Mass Traumatic Events', *Final Report to NIOSH* (Uniformed Services University of the Health Sciences), Bethesda, MD.

Galea, S., Ahern, J., Resnick, H., Kilpatrick, D., Bucuvalas, M., Gold, J. and Vlahov, D. (2002) 'Psychological Sequelae of the September 11 terrorist Attacks in New York City', *New England Journal of Medicine*, 346, pp. 982–7.

Gerrity, E.T. and Steinglass, P. (2003) 'Relocation Stress Following Catastrophic Events', in R.J. Ursano, C.S. Fullerton and A.E. Norwood (eds), *Terrorism and Disaster: Individual and Community Mental Health Interventions*, Cambridge: Cambridge University Press.

Greenberg, J.W. (2002) 'September 11 2001: a ceo's story', *Harvard Business Review*, Harvard Business School of Publishing.

Hall, M.J., Norwood, A.E., Ursano, R.J. and Fullerton, C.S. (2003) 'The Psychological Impacts of Bioterrorism'. *Biosecurity and Bioterrorism: Biodefense Strategy, Practice, & Science*, 1(2), pp. 139–44.

Holloway, H.C. and Waldrep, D.A. (2004) 'Biopsychosocial Factors in Bioterrorism: Consequences for Psychiatric Care, Society and Public Health', in R.J. Ursano, A.E. Norwood and C.S. Fullerton (eds) *Bioterrorism: Psychological and Public Health Interventions*, Cambridge: Cambridge University Press.

Holloway, H.C., Norwood, A.E., Fullerton, C.S., Engel, C.C. and Ursano, R.J. (1997) 'The Threat of Biological Weapons: prophylaxis and mitigation of psychological and social consequences', *Journal of the American Medical Association*, 278, pp. 425–7.

Institute of Medicine of the National Academies (IOM) (2003a). *Preparing for the Psychological Consequences of Terrorism: A Public Health Strategy*, Washington, DC: National Academies Press.

Institute of Medicine of the National Academies (IOM) (2003b) *The Future of the Public's Health in the 21st Century*, Washington, DC: The National Academies Press.

Masi, D.A. (ed) (2000) *International Employee Assistance Anthology*, 2nd edition, Washington, DC: Dallen Inc.

Mankin, L.D. and Perry, R.W. (2004) 'Terrorism Challenges for Human Resource Management', *Review of Public Personnel Administration*, 24(1), pp. 3–17.

Monaghan, S. (2003) 'Developing an EAP Strategy', *Journal of Employee Assistance*, 2nd Quarter, pp. 14–15.

National Center for Disaster Preparedness (NCDP) (2003) *How Americans Feel About Terrorism and Security: two years after 9/11*, Mailman School of Public Health in collaboration with The Children's Health Fund, New York City: Columbia University.

National Institute of Mental Health (2002) *Mental Health and Mass Violence: evidence-based early psychological interventions for victims/survivors of mass violence*. Washington, DC: NIH Publications.

North, C.S., Nixon, S.J., Shariat, S., Mallonee, S., McMillen, J.C., Spitznagel, E.L. and Smith, E.M. (1999) 'Psychiatric Disorders among Survivors of the Oklahoma City Bombing', *Journal of the American Medical Association* 282, pp. 755–62.

North, C.S., Tivis, L., McMillen, J.C., Pfefferbaum, B., Spitznagel, E.L., Cox, J., Nixon S., Bunch, K.P. and Smith, E.M. (2002) 'Psychiatric Disorders in Rescue Workers after the Oklahoma City Bombing', *American Journal of Psychiatry*, 159, pp. 857–9.

North, C.S. (2003) 'Psychiatric Epidemiology of Disaster Responses', in R.J. Ursano and A.E. Norwood (eds) *Trauma & Disaster: Responses & Management*, Arlington, VA: American Psychiatric Publishing, Inc.

Pfefferbaum, B. and Doughty, D.E. (2001) 'Increased Alcohol Use in a Treatment Sample of Oklahoma City Bombing Victims', *Psychiatry*, 64, pp. 296–303.

Raskin, E., and Williams, L. (2003) *Ensuring Solutions to Alcohol Problems: Issue Brief 3*, George Washington University Medical Center.

Reddy, M. (2003) 'A Business Strategy for Workplace Efficiency: innovative global EAP application by increasing mental wellbeing at work', *The Third Annual Gobal Symposium on Business and Mental Energy at Work*, ILO: Geneva, Switzerland.

Roman, P.M. and Blum, T.C. (2002) 'The Workplace and Alcohol Problem Prevention', *Alcohol Research and Health* 26(1), pp. 49–57.

Silver, R.C., Holman, E.A., McIntosh, D.N., Poulin, M. and Gil-Rivas, V. (2002) 'Nationwide Longitudinal Study of Psychological Responses to September 11', *Journal of American Medical Association*, 288(10), pp. 1235–44.

Stein, B.D., Elliott, M.N., Jaycox, L.H., Collins, R., Berry, S., Klein, D.J. and Schuster, M.A. (2003) 'A National Longitudinal Study of the Psychological Consequences of the September 11 2001 Terrorist Attacks: reactions, impairment, and help-seeking', RAND Corporation.

Steury, S., Spencer, S. and Parkinson, G.W. (2004) 'The Social Context of Recovery', *Psychiatry*, 67(2), pp. 158–63.

The Conference Board (2003) *Corporate Security and Crisis Management Conference: Emerging Issues and Strategic Imperatives*, New York City, NY.

Ursano, R.J. (2002) 'Terrorism and Mental Health: public health and primary care', *Status Report: Meeting the Mental Health Needs of the Country in the Wake of September 11 2001*, The Eighteenth Annual Rosalynn Carter Symposium on Mental Health Policy, Atlanta: The Carter Center.

Ursano, R.J., Fullerton, C.S. and Norwood, A.E. (eds) (2003) *Terrorism and Disaster: Individual and Community Mental Health interventions*, (Cambridge: Cambridge University Press.

Ursano, R.J. and Norwood, A.E. (eds) (2003) *Disaster: Responses and Management*, Washington, DC: American Psychiatric Publishing, Inc.

Ursano, R.J. and Vineburgh, N.T. (2003) 'Corporate Preparedness for Terrorism', *Workplace Response Teleconference Series*, Wellesley, MA: Screening for Mental Health.

Ursano, R.J., Vineburgh, N.T., Fullerton, C.S. (2004a) 'Corporate Health and Preparedness: bioterrorism preparedness', The Imperative for a Public Private partnership: Sam Nunn Bank of America Policy Forum. Atlanta, GA.

Ursano, R.J., Fullerton, C.S., Vineburgh, N.T. and Flynn, B. (2004) 'Preparing for the Psychological Consequences of Terrorism: preparedness for mental health, behavioural change and distress related responses – neurobiology and public health', *Congressional Briefing*, Washington, DC.

Ursano, R.J. and Vineburgh, N.T. (2004a) 'Fostering Resiliency: new concepts in disaster preparedness and response', *Resiliency in the World of Work: EASNA 16th Annual Institute*, Ottawa, Canada.

Ursano, R.J. and Vineburgh, N.T. (2004b) 'Workplace Resiliency in the Face of Terrorism: the role and integration of health promotion and natural debriefing', In-service EAP Presentation: *US House of Representatives, US Senate, Library of Congress*, Washington, DC

Vineburgh, N.T. (2002) 'Fall Teleconference Series Examines Workplace Impact of Sept. 11', *Mental Health Weekly*, 12(35), pp. 5–6.

Vineburgh, N.T. (2003) 'Threat of Mental Illness, Stress, Violence and Terrorism', *The Third Annual Global Symposium on Business and Mental Energy at Work*, ILO: Geneva, Switzerland.

Vineburgh, N.T. (2004) 'The Power of the Pink Ribbon: raising awareness of the mental health implications of terrorism', *Psychiatry*, 67(2), pp. 137–46.

Vlahov, D., Galea, S., Resnick, H., Boscarino, J.A., Bucuvalas, M., Gold, J. and Kilpatrick, D. (2002) 'Increased Use of Cigarettes, Alcohol, and Marijuana among Manhattan, New York Residents after the September 11th Terrorist Attacks', *American Journal of Epidemiology*, 155, pp. 988–96.

Weisaeth, L. (1989) 'The Stressors and the Post-Traumatic Stress Syndrome After an Industrial Disaster', *Acta Psychiatrica Scandinavica*, 80 (Suppl. 355), pp. 25–37.

Section 4

Bullies at work

Chapter 12

Workplace bullying: individual pathology or organizational culture?

Ståle Einarsen, Helge Hoel, Dieter Zapf and Cary L. Cooper

Introduction

During the last 10 years, a wide range of studies have documented the existence of bullying as a salient problem in contemporary working life (Einarsen, Hoel, Zapf and Cooper, 2003). This problem, which has also been labelled 'emotional abuse', 'harassment at work' or 'victimization at work', seems to affect as many as 5–10 per cent of the workforce at any point in time (Zapf, Einarsen, Hoel and Vartia 2003). Studies have also shown that exposure to bullying leads to a host of negative effects in targets (Einarsen and Mikkelsen 2003) as well as having detrimental effects on the organization and its working environment (Hoel, Einarsen and Cooper 2003). Exposure to such treatment has been claimed to be a more crippling and devastating problem for employees than all other kinds of work-related stress put together, and is seen by many researchers and targets alike as an extreme type of social stress at work (Zapf, Knorz and Kulla 1996). Although the phenomenon is likely to be as old as mankind, public awareness on the issue of bullying at work among adults was first raised in the Nordic countries in the late 1980s (Leymann 1990; Matthiesen, Raknes and Røkkum 1989). During the 1990s interest also spread to countries such as the UK (Adams 1992; Rayner 1997), Australia (McCarthy, Sheehan and Wilkie, 1996), Germany and Austria (Neidl 1995; Zapf, Knorz and Kulla 1996). The systematic mistreatment of employees by colleagues and superiors has however only recently been in focus in the US (Rayner and Keashly 2004), although the issue was raised as early as 1976 in the book *The harassed worker* by Carroll Brodsky. The aim of the present chapter is to provide an overview of research results relating to the very nature and causes of bullying at work. After focusing on the key characteristics of the phenomenon, we discuss two different but not necessarily mutually exclusive rationales as to why bullying occurs within the work environment; the role of individuals and the role of the organization.

A typical feature of many newly discovered social problems is the creation of a public demonizing process where 'folk devils' and 'disaster mentality' prevails (Lewis 2000). In the case of bullying at work, such folk devils have been evident in the focus on the 'psychopaths at work' (e.g. Field 1996) and 'neurotic victims' as explanations of why bullying occurs in an organization (see also Einarsen 2000). The late Heinz Leymann (1990), one of the pioneers in this field, strongly believed otherwise as he argued vigorously against individual factors as antecedents of bullying, especially when they are linked to issues of victim personality. Instead he advocated a situational outlook, where organizational factors relating to leadership, work-design and organizational culture were seen as the main causes.

The nature of the beast

Bullying at work may be defined as repeated actions and practices that are directed at one or more workers, which may be done deliberately or unconsciously, but are unwanted by the victim, and manifestly cause humiliation, offence and distress, and that may interfere with job performance and/or cause an unpleasant working environment (Einarsen and Raknes 1997). Hence, the concept refers to situations where an employee is subjected to repeated and unwanted actions and practices solely directed against them or towards a group of employees. These acts may be deliberate or unconscious. However, they result in creating an unpleasant psycho-social working environment, as well as humiliation, resentment and distress in the targets. The key element of the bullying concept is therefore about persistent exposure to negative and aggressive behaviours of a primarily psychological nature leading to stigmatization and victimization of the focal person(s) (Björkqvist, Österman and Hjelt-Bäck 1994).

The frequency and the duration of the experience are key dimensions of bullying. Bullying is not about single acts of aggression. It is about behaviour directed against a target repeatedly and over a long period of time (Björkqvist *et al.* 1994; Niedl 1995). Although single acts of aggression and harassment occur fairly often in everyday interaction at work, they seem to be associated with severe health problems in the target when they are experienced on a regular basis. Yet, the very nature of the behaviours may be quite diverse as they seem to involve both work-related and person-related behaviours (Einarsen *et al.* 2003). Work-related behaviours include such things as being subjected to unreasonable deadlines, unmanageable workloads, excessive monitoring of work, meaningless tasks or even a void of tasks altogether. Personal bullying consists of behaviours such as insulting remarks, excessive teasing, gossip or rumours, persistent criticism, practical jokes and intimidating behaviours (Einarsen *et al.* 2003). These behaviours are then 'used with the aim or at least the effect of persistently humiliating, intimidating, frightening or punishing the victim' (Einarsen 2000b: 8). To single someone out as a 'deserving' target is seen as another key characteristic of bullying (Leymann 1996; Zapf 1999a).

Bullying is also not an 'either or' phenomenon, but rather a gradually evolving process (Leymann 1990; Zapf and Gross 2001). During the early phases of the process, targets are typically subjected to aggressive behaviour that is difficult to pin down because of its indirect and discrete nature (Einarsen 2000). Progressively more direct aggressive acts appear. The victims are clearly isolated and avoided, humiliated in public by excessive criticism or by being made a laughing stock. In the end both physical and psychological means of violence may be used.

> The stigmatising effects of these activities, and their escalating frequency and intensity, make the victims constantly less able to cope with his or her daily tasks and co-operation requirements of the job, thus becoming continually more vulnerable and 'a deserving target' (Einarsen 2000b: 8).

Another defining feature is an imbalance of power between the parties (Leymann 1996; Niedl 1995), where the target finds it difficult to defend him or herself against the behaviour, probably as the opportunity for retaliation may be ruled out. Typically, a victim is constantly teased, tormented and insulted and perceives that he or she has little recourse to retaliate in kind (Einarsen 1999). The imbalance of power may of course mirror the formal power-structure within the organizational context in which the bullying scenario unfolds, for example when someone is on the receiving end of illegitimate negative acts from a person in a superior organizational position. Alternatively, the source of power may be informal as in situations where a group of colleagues bully a single individual and the target finds it difficult to defend against an 'overwhelming' group of antagonists. Einarsen (1999) also argues that knowledge of someone's 'weak point' may become a strong source of power in a bullying situation as it may help the perpetrator to exploit the perceived inadequacies of the target's personality or work performance, which in itself indicates powerlessness on the part of the target. In such cases, the behaviours may be both 'subtle, devious and immensely difficult to confront' (Adams 1992: 17) and they may even be difficult to recognize at least by non-affected colleagues or supervisors. Hence, bullying may result from the exploitation of power by an individual or by a group, or it may be a result of someone taking advantage of a power deficit on the part of the target (Einarsen *et al.* 2003). In line with this we have defined bullying as follows:

> Bullying at work means harassing, offending, socially excluding someone or negatively affecting someone's work tasks. In order for the label bullying (or mobbing) to be applied to a particular activity, interaction or process, it has to occur repeatedly and regularly (e.g. weekly) and over a period of time (e.g. about six months). Bullying is an escalating process in the course of which the person confronted ends up in an inferior position and becomes the target of systematic negative social acts. A conflict cannot be called bullying if the incident is an isolated event or if two parties of approximately equal 'strength' are in conflict (Einarsen, Hoel, Zapf and Cooper, 2003: p. 15).

Individual antecedents of bullying: the bully

Psychological literature presents a wide range of concepts relating to the personality of bullies, such as 'the abrasive personality', 'the authoritarian personality' and 'the petty tyrant' (see also Ashforth 1994). The concept of petty tyranny refers to leaders who lord their power over others through arbitrariness and self-aggrandizement, the belittling of subordinates, lack of consideration and the use of an authoritarian style of conflict-management. In behavioural terms these leaders shout and scream at subordinates, they criticize, complain and demean them, and they lie and manipulate others in order to have their way. In a book called *Corporate hyenas at work*, which uses a South African metaphor for bullies at work, Marais and Herman (1997) ask whether such behaviours are caused by a dysfunctional personality and whether it is the actions of a psychopath at work. They conclude by stating:

Corporate hyenas use all of the narcissistic, immature and neurotic defences to survive. They are a danger to themselves and to others. They most probably carry scars of a dysfunctional childhood and societal maladjustment embedded in their behaviour and they survive workplace politics with anti-social strategies (p. 13).

Also, Tim Field, a former UK victim of bullying, strongly advocates such a view when claiming that most bullying is caused by the psychopathic personality of the bully (Field 1996).

In an interview study among 30 Irish victims of bullying, all interviewed targets blamed the difficult personality of the bully (O'Moore, Seigne, Mcguire and Smith 1998). Many targets also refer to envy on behalf of the bullies as the main reason behind bullying (Björkqvist *et al.* 1994). In a study by Vartia (1996), this was the case in 68 per cent of the reported cases. 'They wanted to push me out of the company' was the most frequent reason for being bullied in a study by Zapf (1999b). A weak superior, competition for tasks, status or advancement, or competition for the supervisor's favour are other perceived reasons for bullying given by targets (Einarsen 2000). However, not much is actually known about the characteristics of bullies. Most available information has so far been provided by targets or by stories told in popular self-help books. Obviously, we can only rely to some extent on such descriptions when we try to understand the psychology of a perpetrator.

What we do know is that bullies seem to be men more often than women, and supervisors and managers more often than colleagues (Zapf *et al.* 2003). In a study among 2,200 Norwegian employees, some 5 per cent of the respondents admitted that they had bullied others at work (Einarsen, Raknes, Matthiesen and Hellesøy 1994). These self-reported bullies differed from other employees in many respects, describing themselves as anxious in social situations, with low social competence and a low self-esteem. However, they also described themselves as highly aggressive compared to others, reacting with aggressiveness in a wide range of situations and towards a wide range of perceived provocations. Similar results were found by Stucke (2002) in a study where employees first indicated whether or not they actively used different kinds of bullying behaviours and whether or not they were the receivers of such behaviour. In addition, measures of narcissism and stability of self-esteem were measured. Narcissism implies high self-esteem going along with the disregard of others. Active bullying behaviour was highest for those high in narcissism but low in self-esteem stability. Perhaps these individuals had to balance their high but unstable self-esteem by mistreating others. Such an interpretation builds on an assumption that aggressive behaviour often results from threatened self-esteem:

In all spheres we examined, we found that violence emerged from threatened egotism, whether this was labelled as wounded pride, disrespect, verbal abuse, insults, anger manipulations, status inconsistency, or something else. Violence resulted most commonly from feeling that one's superiority was somehow being undermined, jeopardized, or contradicted by current circumstances. (Baumeister, Smart and Boden 1996: p. 26).

Bullying due to such aspects of self-esteem protection may occur especially frequently if the bullies are at management level, because being dominant, self-assertive, having high self-esteem and protecting this self-esteem is normally expected from this group (Zapf and Einarsen 2004). Yet, in a British questionnaire study where subordinates evaluated and nominated 37 managers anonymously, no differences were found between bullies and non-bullies regarding the managers' self-reported mental health, stress levels or personality (Rayner 1999). Hence, we must conclude that although targets often perceive the causes of bullying as related to the individual perpetrator and although we have a few studies that may support such a view, we still do not have enough evidence to substantiate such a view. Even if there may exist a propensity to bully in most perpetrators, they will probably only exhibit such behaviours at work if the organization allows or even rewards such behaviour (Brodsky 1976).

Individual antecedents of bullying: the targets

Several studies have pointed to potential causes of bullying within the target (Coyne, Seigne and Randall 2000; Vartia 1996; Matthiesen and Einarsen 2001; Zapf 1999b). Although these studies do not have a longitudinal design and therefore cannot conclude on cause and effect, the observed differences between targets and non-targets seem to be more likely a cause than a consequence of bullying (Zapf and Einarsen 2004). For instance, a German study revealed that many targets perceived themselves as being different from their colleagues in many respects, even more so than a control group (Zapf and Bühler, in Zapf 1999). One subgroup of targets claimed to be low in social competencies and conflict-management skills, as well as being unassertive, weak and neurotic. A total of 33 per cent of the 45 participants in the study saw themselves as less assertive and worse conflicts managers than their colleagues, compared to only 16 per cent of the control group. Another group of targets described themselves as more achievement oriented and more conscientious than their colleagues, probably leading them to clash with the norms in their work group. Notably, only 2 per cent of the 45 targets 'admitted' that their performance was below average. If this conscientiousness goes along with rigidity, these targets may be a constant hassle to their colleagues. Consequently, the group may start to harass these persons, either to enforce conformity or to get rid of them (Zapf and Einarsen 2004). Such a conclusion also fits well with Brodsky's (1976: 89) qualitative observations:

> The harassed victim generally tends to be conscientious, literal-minded, and somewhat unsophisticated. Often, he is an overachiever who tends to have an unrealistic view of himself and of the situation in which he finds himself. He may believe he is an ideal worker and that the job he is going to get will be the ideal job. As a result, he has great difficulty in adjusting not only to the imperfections of the situation but to the imperfections of his own functioning as well.

In a study of the personality of 60 Irish targets of bullying using the five-factor framework of personality, Coyne *et al.* (2000) found targets to be more rule-bound, honest, punctual and accurate in comparison with a control group.

In a Norwegian survey among 2,200 participants, targets of bullying described themselves as being low on self-esteem, high on social anxiety and low on social competence (Einarsen *et al.* 1994). In the study by Coyne *et al.* (2000), targets were described as more anxious, suspicious, and reported having more problems coping with difficult situations. Moreover, targets were less assertive, competitive and outspoken than non-targets. Based on medical records of 87 targets of bullying, Lindemeier (1996) found that 31 per cent of the patients reported a general tendency to avoid conflicts, while 27 per cent reported problems with a low self-esteem even before the bullying began. Another 23 per cent had always been emotionally labile and somewhat serious-minded. Based on interviews with American targets of bullying, Brodsky (1976) claimed that many targets are of a humourless nature, which may render them susceptible to bullying, especially when meeting an artless teaser or when working in a team characterized by 'humour gone sour'.

A study of personality and personality disorders among 85 Norwegian targets of bullying at work using a comprehensive measure of personality called the MMPI-2 revealed that there is probably more than one target-profile (Matthiesen and Einarsen 2001). As a group they were described as psychologically naive with a tendency to blame others for their misfortune as well as reacting with psychosomatic complaints when facing psychological problems. However, the targets were not a homogeneous group. One group, labelled the 'seriously affected', reported a range of emotional and psychological problems although they reported a relatively low exposure to specific bullying behaviours, a result indicating that personality is of importance in determining how bullying is experienced and how it is dealt with. These targets were depressive, anxious, suspicious, uncertain of themselves, and troubled by confused thoughts. A second group, referred to as the 'disappointed and depressed', were depressed and somewhat suspicious of the outside world. The third group, called the 'common group', portrayed a quite normal personality, in spite of having experienced the largest number of specific bullying behaviours. Such results may indicate that a specific vulnerability/hardiness factor may exist among some but not all targets of bullying at work. Persons who are already suffering from psychological problems are probably more likely to suffer long-term psychological and physical problems in the wake of bullying and serious personal conflicts. Persons with psychological problems, low self-confidence and a high degree of anxiety in social situations may also be more likely than others to feel bullied and harassed, and they may find it more difficult to defend themselves when exposed to the aggression of other people.

Hence, it may be concluded that individuals low in self-esteem, self-assertion and social competencies, and high in anxiety and depression may be defenceless and 'easy targets' of bullying. A power deficit seems to be intrinsic to the very nature of their personality. The behaviour of a target may of course also cause frustration and irritation in others, who may then respond to them by means of aggression and bullying. However, a personality deficit in a target does not in itself allow others to misbehave against them. Bullying should be considered 'out of line' even if the target is vulnerable or someone who easily causes frustration in others. Furthermore, Leymann and Gustafsson (1996) argue that what we are observing in the studies reported above is not the pre-morbid personality of the target, but rather signs of the destruction of the target's personality as a result of a highly traumatic experience. Since longitudinal studies are limited, this may very well be a relevant explanation, at least in some cases. The data so far does only implicate that personality may be involved in some cases. The observed personal characteristics of the targets cannot be viewed as a general explanation of bullying (Zapf and Einarsen 2003), and they count for even less when used as an excuse for bullying.

Organizational antecedents of bullying

Leadership and employer responsibilities

Although individual factors may indeed play a part in some bullying scenarios, bullying is a complex social process which must be understood within the social and situational context where it arises (Einarsen *et al.* 2003). Although bullying is exhibited and perceived by specific individuals and is something that occurs within an inter-personal relationship, it is connected to work and it does happen in an organizational context with formal power relationships and with formal responsibilities. The latter fact also implies that whatever the antecedents of bullying may be, employers and managers do have a formal role to play in all such cases. It was such a line of argument that led Leymann (1990) to conclude that since bullying takes place within a situation regulated by formal behavioural rules and responsibilities, it is always and by definition the responsibility of the organization and its management.

Such a relationship between the existence of bullying and the role of the organization has seldom been more clearly expressed than by Brodsky (1976), who argued that bullying or harassment could only take place in organizations which allowed such behaviour and processes to be carried out in their midst. The power of this argument was brought to the fore when in their assessment of potential causes of bullying, nine out of ten respondents in a large-scale trade union survey in the UK agreed to the statement that bullying exists because 'the bully can get away with it' and because targets are 'too afraid to report it' (Unison 1997). Furthermore, when as many as 50–80 per cent of all targets of bullying claim to be bullied by a superior, bullying is evidently an organizational issue.

Whether conscious of their own role or not, leaders do play an essential role in the creation and manifestation of any organizational culture (Schein 1985). However, as opposed to the evidence on the role of leadership in bullying, traditional leadership research has paid little attention to potentially abusive or negative leadership styles, as most leadership research has been focused on the effectiveness of leaders (Ashforth 1994). However, as shown in a study by Einarsen *et al.* (1994), dissatisfaction with leaders was found to be one of the strongest predictors of bullying. Based on survey data, bullying has also been associated with lack of involvement in decision-making processes, with work-environments where employees are afraid of expressing their opinions and where an authoritarian way of settling conflicts prevails (Vartia 1996). Satisfaction with supervisors' ability to resolve work-related conflict has been found to account for the largest difference between bullied and non-bullied respondents (O'Moore *et al.* 1998). An authoritarian leadership or style

237

of management may also create a climate of fear, where there is no room for criticism and where complaining may be considered futile. Of course, there will always be disagreement with regard to where to draw the line between bullying and firm management as 'people with different social interests are likely to draw the boundaries between types of behaviour differently' (Lee 2000: 597). Nevertheless, Hoel and Cooper (2000) reported that senior managers were the group who reported the highest levels of witnessing bullying, suggesting that managers themselves in many cases have less of a problem in distinguishing bullying from so-called 'firm' management than may at first be anticipated. By contrast, in some cases bullying may not reflect an abuse of power but be the result of leaders' weakness or perceived lack of powers. It is unsurprising that in such situations they may sometimes resort to unacceptable treatment of their staff in order to stay in control (Ashforth 1994). Hence bullying may be a result of a highly aggressive leadership style with an abuse of power, as well as the acts of a manager desperate to regain his or her power.

The work environment perspective

A dominating explanatory framework of bullying in the early Nordic research on bullying was related to the psycho-social work environment (Einarsen 2000). The basis of the work environment hypothesis first put forward by Leymann (1990, 1993) is that the stress and frustration caused by a negative psycho-social environment may lead to bullying of an exposed target, especially if management do not handle the situation in a firm and just way. Work-related stress makes workers become tense, thus increasing the likelihood of confrontations with superiors and peers which again may offset or feed bullying processes (Hoel, Zapf and Cooper 2002). According to the frustration-aggression hypothesis, bullying may then flourish due to the effect of this environment on the aggressive behaviour of the perpetrators (Einarsen 2000). Alternatively, a social-interaction approach to aggression would argue that a stressful environment will indirectly affect aggression through its effect on the victim's behaviour. Distressed persons may violate expectations, annoy others, perform less competently and even violate social norms describing polite and friendly interactions and hence elicit aggressive behaviour in others (Einarsen 2000).

Within this framework, four factors are commonly claimed to be predictors of bullying at work: (1) deficiencies in work design, (2) deficiencies in leadership behaviour, (3) a socially exposed position of the victim, and (4) a negative social climate in the department (Einarsen 1999; Leymann 1993). Support for this view has been generated from a couple of studies. For instance, Zapf, Knorz and Kulla (1996) found that

German targets of bullying reported to have little control over their own time combined with high cooperation requirements. A situation where people are forced to work closely together offers more possibilities for unresolved conflicts. As a consequence of people's restricted control over their own time, unresolved conflicts may escalate into harassment, particularly if the workgroup climate is characterized by 'humour going sour' (Brodsky 1976). In a study among Irish targets of bullying, the targets described their workplace as a highly stressful and competitive environment, plagued with inter-personal conflicts and a lack of a friendly and supportive atmosphere, undergoing organizational changes and managed by means of an authoritarian leadership style (O'Moore *et al.* 1998). In a survey among 2,215 randomly chosen Norwegian members of six different labour unions, Einarsen, Raknes and Matthiesen (1994) found that work environments where bullying existed had employees who reported an elevated level of role conflict and who were dissatisfied with their social climate, their superior's leadership behaviour, and the possibility of self-monitoring one's work. A high degree of ambiguity or incompatible demands and expectations around roles, tasks and responsibilities may create a high degree of frustration within the workgroup, especially in connection to rights, obligations, privileges and positions. A high level of role conflict, lack of self-monitoring possibilities and poorly performing supervisors may also lead to high levels of inter-personal conflict which combined with a negative social climate may easily turn into a bullying situation. Frustration may also give rise to scapegoating processes, where frustrations are displaced and projected against a fellow worker, especially if this person is in a socially exposed position.

Salin (2003a) divides possible work-related antecedents of bullying into three groups: enabling, motivating and triggering factors (see also Hoel and Salin 2003). Enabling factors describe factors which may increase the likelihood of bullying without being able to cause bullying on their own. A perceived power imbalance between perpetrator and victim, a low perceived risk when behaving aggressively, and frustration with, for example, work control and the social climate may be examples of such factors. Motivating factors are factors that may make it worthwhile for a perpetrator to engage in bullying, for instance in order to eliminate subordinates or colleagues perceived as 'burdens', 'threats' or plain annoyance. A high level of internal competition and rivalry may for instance constitute such a factor. From a social interactionist perspective, bullying behaviours may actually be seen as instrumental behaviour used in order to achieve certain goals or values. Hence bullying, or systematic aggressive behaviour, may then be used to influence others, to achieve justice or to protect one's own self-esteem or identity (Felson and Tedeschi 1993). Salin (2003b) also argues that bullying may actually evolve out of organizational politics, that is, the deliberate use of aggression in order to improve and promote one's own interest. Finally, triggering factors increase insecurity, thereby making it more likely for bullying processes actually to evolve. Organizational changes such as a change in manager, restructuring and downsizing are examples of such factors (Hoel and Salin 2003).

Unresolved conflicts

Inter-personal conflicts are part of everyday life in all organizations and workgroups. In some instances, these conflicts escalate into harsh personified bullying struggles (Einarsen 2000). Although inter-personal conflicts must not be considered bullying, there may be a thin line between the battles between two parties in an inter-personal conflict, and the aggressive behaviour used in bullying (see also Zapf and Gross 2001). Both Leymann (1990) and Einarsen *et al.* (1994) have argued that long-term unresolved inter-personal conflicts may escalate into bullying if proper interventions and conflict-management strategies are not implemented. Moreover, if the probability of conflicts is high in an organization then the probability that a conflict might not be solved but will escalate is also high (Zapf and Einarsen 2004). Hassles in the work organization might make cooperation more difficult, unclear or contradictory goals might induce rivalry, and high time pressure might imply that there is little time for conflict management. An organization with such characteristics should in theory therefore have a higher risk for bullying compared to an organization with no such characteristics (Hoel *et al.* 2002; Zapf and Einarsen 2004). As shown above, many studies show that targets work under conditions conducive to conflicts at work (high job stressors such as time pressure, high cooperational dependencies, high levels of role conflict and role ambiguity and low control at work).

A change in the nature of work organizations

While the early Scandinavian work on bullying focused on causes of bullying in the proximal workgroup or department, Anglo-Saxon researchers have lately taken on a broader perspective, arguing that any investigation of bullying needs to acknowledge the rapidly changing nature of work and its impact on organizational structures and work processes (Lewis and Rayner, 2003; Hoel and Salin, 2003). Pressures arising from intensified global competition have contributed to wide-reaching restructuring processes, with downsized and leaner organizations emerging in the private as well as the public sector, with greater pressures on managers and workers alike. As a parallel move, the demands for managerial accountability have increased as a wider range of responsibilities are devolved down the line with tasks which were previously taken care of by the personnel function. Consequently the nature of the relationship between first-line managers and workers has changed, often in the direction of more autocratic practices among managers. Lewis and Sheehan (2003) argue that a culture where 'achievement of organizational goals justifies its means' (p. 3) may very well foster bullying behaviours. In such a climate, managers may be more likely to wield their power and control to excess. In addition, workers' opportunity to resist and challenge what they may consider unacceptable or even bullying behaviours from their superiors may also have become more limited (Hoel and Salin 2003), increasing the power deficit of employees.

In a study on the nature and causes of aggression at work, Baron and Neuman (1976) discovered that the greater extent to which several changes had recently occurred in the participants' organization, the greater the incidence of workplace bullying they reported. Also, Brodsky (1976) saw work pressure as a type of work harassment in its own respect, as work pressure may be used as a 'legitimate' means to punish subordinates. However, when attributed to negative intentions, work stress may also easily be perceived as bullying by employees.

Organizational implications

The argument and evidence provided in this chapter give a clear indication that bullying may emerge from or be the product of a number of factors which on their own or in combination may contribute to its presence. However, from an organizational perspective, the most important issues are those that are influenced or controlled by the organization. In this respect many of the factors associated with individual predisposition and personality, albeit sometimes central to the development of bullying, are normally beyond the control and influence of the organization. To some extent it may of course be possible to influence the range of personalities and personal characteristics within an organization by means of selection and promotion processes. Nevertheless, with respect to the prevention of bullying we consider such approaches at best insufficient and at worst a self-illusion.

In our view, a far more productive approach would be to consider bullying as an inherent organizational problem which should be met by organizational measures. In this respect, approaches which aim to identify, prevent, minimize and control organizational risk factors and behaviours associated with bullying would be more productive (see also Hubert 2003). First of all, we need to identify and analyse risk factors for bullying in the working environment, for instance by the use of risk assessments (see also Spurgeon 2003). Where a risk-assessment approach is applied, the focus is primarily on minimizing the presence of the problem more than actually eliminating it altogether. A first step in a risk assessment is to define the problem. Having an organization discussing and defining the nature of bullying at work may in itself be an important intervention. Then the organization needs to assess the prevalence of aggressive behaviour and bullying, for example by means of a questionnaire survey and to identify factors which may increase its occurrence (Spurgeon 2003). Proper preventions or remedial actions must then follow from this assessment. Based on the research conducted so far, preventive interventions would most likely include general efforts to improve leadership quality and organizational climate, as well as psycho-social working conditions associated with stress and inter-personal conflicts in workgroups (Hoel and Salin 2003). A focus on leadership quality must combine a focus on conflict-management skills with a focus on identifying and controlling aggressive and undesired behaviours among both superiors and subordinates.

Although preventive actions in the form of reducing risk factors for aggressive behaviour and inter-personal conflicts may be helpful, there will always be a need to stop and control aggressive and violent behaviour in organizations. One mechanism that regulates behaviour in organizations is the organizational culture, which through its prevailing norms and values may both permit and even reward bullying behaviours. In a study of fire brigades, Archer (1999) found that bullying of females and non-white males was deeply embedded in the very nature of the organizational culture in the fire service, caused especially by a desire to perpetuate the white male culture. The impact of socialization processes, whereby newcomers take on established norms and values, suggests that organizations need to pay more attention to how they may prevent negative norms taking a hold (Hoel and Salin 2003). Organizations must also pay attention to how they may promote a positive culture which may help prevent bullying while embracing diversity and the dignity of all organization members. Yet, organizations must also be prepared to intervene directly in situations where bullying occurs by supporting targets, by conducting informal mediation, by managing formal complaints and by issuing sanctions to perpetrators if necessary (see also Hubert 2003).

Hence, if we are to manage the problem of bullying at work effectively, a systematic and comprehensive approach is needed. In this respect, policies have often been considered a way forward (Richards and Daley 2003). Included in such policies must be a description of an expected organizational culture and its most important values combined with a code of conduct identifying what is to be considered as undesirable behaviour among superiors and subordinates (Hubert 2003). Furthermore, an effective policy needs to deal with the safe reporting of bullying, as well as the possibility for targets to receive counselling and social support. A policy must contain directions for more informal solutions of the problem, as well as an independent system for the management of formal complaints (see also Merchant and Hoel 2003).

However, the presence of policies and procedures is no guarantee against bullying and abusive behaviours per se (Lewis and Rayner 2003). For such policies to become an effective instrument against bullying, they need to reflect a shared organizational understanding of the problem. Furthermore, they must be enforced in a fair and consistent manner and adjusted according to feedback received as part of regular monitoring practices. To the extent that organizational policies on bullying are developed though involvement and in collaboration with all groups of employees, and thus represent some degree of shared values in the organization, such policies may contribute to a culture shift in this area. Where properly communicated and enforced they may, therefore, in their own right contribute to a reduction in negative behaviour and bullying.

However, at the end of the day the existence, prevention and constructive management of bullying at work resides with the managers and supervisors of the organization and the organizational culture they create or permit. Instead of relying on a strategy for restricting the employment of potential bullies and targets, the focus must be on the acceptance and management of diversity in the workforce, combined with clear norms for acceptable behaviours, as well sanctions against behaviours deemed unacceptable by the organization.

References

Adams, A. (1992) *Bullying at work: how to confront and overcome it*, London: Virago Press.

Archer, D. (1999) 'Exploring "bullying" culture in the para-military organization', *International Journal of Manpower*, 20(1/2), pp. 94–105.

Ashforth, B. (1984) 'Petty tyranny in organizations', *Human Relations*, 47(7), pp. 755–78.

Baron, R.A. and Neuman, J.H. (1996). 'Workplace violence and workplace aggression: Evidence on their relative frequency and potential causes', *Aggressive Behavior*, (2), pp. 161–73.

Björkqvist, K., Österman, K. and Hjelt-bäck, M. (1994). 'Aggression among university employees', *Aggressive Behavior* (20), pp. 173–84.

Brodsky, C.M. (1976) *The Harassed Worker*, Toronto: Lexington Books, D.C. Heath and Company.

Baumeister, R.F., Smart, L. and Boden, J.M. (1996) 'Relation of threatened egotism to violence and aggression: The dark side of high self-esteem', *Psychological Review*, (103), pp. 5–33

Coyne, I., Seigne, E. and Randall, P. (2000) 'Predicting workplace victim status from personality', *European Journal of Work and Organizational Psychology*, 9, 335–49.

Einarsen, S. (1999) 'The nature and causes of bullying at work', *International Journal of Manpower*, 20(1/2), pp. 16–27.

Einarsen, S. (2000) 'Harassment and bullying at work: a review of the Scandinavian approach', *Aggression and Violent Behavior*, 5(4), pp. 371–401.

Einarsen, S. (2000b) 'Bullying and harassment at work: unveiling an organizational taboo', in M. Sheehan, S. Ramsey and J. Partick (eds), *Transcending boundaries. Integrating people, processes and systems*, Brisbane: The School of Management, Griffith University.

Einarsen, S., Hoel, H., Zapf, D. and Cooper, C.L. (2003) *Bullying and emotional abuse in the workplace. International perspectives in research and practice*, London: Taylor and Francis.

Einarsen, S. and Mikkelsen, E.G. (2003) 'Individual effects of exposure to bullying at work', in S. Einarsen, H. Hoel, D. Zapf and C.L. Cooper (eds) *Bullying and emotional abuse in the workplace. International perspectives in research and practice*, London: Taylor and Francis.

Einarsen, S. and Raknes, B.I. (1997) 'Harassment in the workplace and the victimization of men', *Violence and Victims*, (12), pp. 247–263.

Einarsen, S., Raknes, B.I. and Matthiesen, S.B., (1994) 'Bullying and harassment at work and their relationships to work environment quality: an exploratory study', *European Work and Organizational Psychologist*, 4(4), pp. 381–401.

Einarsen, S., Raknes, B.I., Matthiesen, S.B. and Hellesøy, O.H. (1994) *Mobbing og harde personkonflikter. Helsefarlig samspill pa arbeidsplassen*, Soreidgrend: Sigma Forlag.

Felson, R.B. and Tedeschi, J.T. (1993). *Aggression and violence. Social interactionst perspectives*, Washington DC: American Psychological Association.

Field, T. (1996) *Bullying in sight*, Wantage, Oxon: Success Unlimited.

Hoel, H. and Cooper, C.L. (2000) *Destructive Conflict and Bullying at Work*, Manchester School of Management, University of Manchester Institute of Science and Technology.

Hoel, H. and Salin, D. (2003) 'Organizational antecedents of workplace bullying', in S. Einarsen, H. Hoel, D. Zapf and C.L. Cooper (eds) *Bullying and emotional abuse in the workplace. International perspectives in research and practice*, London: Taylor and Francis.

Hoel, H., Einarsen, S. and Cooper, C.L. (2003) 'Organizational effects of bullying', in S. Einarsen, H. Hoel, D. Zapf and C.L. Cooper (eds), *Bullying and emotional abuse in the workplace. International perspectives in research and practice'*, London: Taylor and Francis.

Hoel, H., Zapf, D. and Cooper, C.L. (2002) 'Workplace bullying and stress', in P.L. Perrewe and D.C. Ganster (eds) *Historical and Current Perspectives on Stress and Health. Research in Occupational Stress and Well-being Volume 2* (293–233), New York: Jai, Elsevier Science Ltd.

Hubert, A. (2003) 'To prevent and overcome undesirable interaction: a systematic approach model', in S. Einarsen, H. Hoel, D. Zapf and C.L. Cooper (eds) *Bullying and emotional abuse in the workplace. International perspectives in research and practice*, London: Taylor and Francis.

Lee, D. (2000) 'An analysis of workplace bullying in the UK', *Personnel Review*, 29(5), pp. 593–612.

Lewis, D. (2000) 'Bullying at work: A case of moral panic?', in M. Sheehan, S. Ramsey and J. Partick (eds) *Transcending boundaries. Integrating people, processes and systems*, Brisbane: The School of Management, Griffith University.

Lewis, D. and Rayner, C. (2003) 'Bullying and human resoure management: a wolf in sheep's clothing', in S. Einarsen, H. Hoel, D. Zapf and C.L. Cooper (eds), *Bullying and emotional abuse in the workplace. International perspectives in research and practice*, London: Taylor and Francis.

Lewis, D. and Sheehan, M. (2003) 'Workplace bullying: theoretical and practical approaches to a management challenge', *International Journal of Management and Decision Making*, (4), pp. 1–10.

Leymann, H. (1990) 'Mobbing and psychological terror at workplaces', *Violence and Victims*, (5), pp. 119–26.

Leymann, H. (1993) *Mobbing – Psychoterror am Arbeitsplatz und wie man sich dagegen wehren kann*, Reinbeck: Rowohlt.

Leymann, H. (1996) 'The content and development of mobbing at work', *European Journal of Work and Organizational Psychology*, 5(2), pp. 165–84.

Leymann, H. and Gustafsson, A. (1996) 'Mobbing and the development of post-traumatic stress disorders', *The European Journal of Work and Organizational Psychology*, (5), pp. 251–76.

Lindemeier, B. (1996) 'Mobbing, Krankheitsbild und intervention des betriebsarztes', *Die Berufsgenossenschaft*, June, pp. 428–31.

Marais, S. and Herman, M. (1997) '*Corporate hyneas at work*, Pretoria: Kagiso Publishers.

Matthiesen, S.B. and Einarsen, S. (2001) 'MMPI-2-configurations among victims of bullying at work', *European Journal of Work and Organizational Psychology*, (10), 467–84.

Matthiesen, S.B., Raknes, B.I. and Røkkum, O. (1989). 'Mobbing på arbeidsplassen', *Tidskrift for Norsk Psykologforening*, (26), pp. 761–74.

McCarthy, P., Sheehan, M.J. and Wilkie, W. (1996) *Bullying: from backyard to boardroom*, Alexandria, Australia: Millennium Books.

Merchant, V. and Hoel, H. (2003) 'Investigating complaints of bullying', in S. Einarsen, H. Hoel, D. Zapf and C.L. Cooper (eds) *Bullying and emotional abuse in the workplace. International perspectives in research and practice'*, London: Taylor and Francis.

Niedl, K. (1995) *Mobbing/Bullying am Arbeitsplatz. Eine empirische Analyse zum Phänomen sowie zu personalwirtschaftlich relevanten Effekten von systematischen Feindseligkeiten.* Munich: Hampp.

O'Moore, M., Seigne, E., Mcguire, I. and Smith, M. (1998) 'Victims of bullying at work in Ireland', *Journal of Occupational Health and Safety – Australia and New Zealand*, 14(6), pp. 569–74.

Rayner, C. (1997) 'The incidence of workplace bullying', *Journal of Community and Applied Social Psychology*, (7), 199–208.

Rayner, C. (1999) *Bullying in the workplace*. Unpublished doctoral thesis. University of Manchester Institute of Science and Technology, Manchester, England.

Rayner, C. and Keashly, L. (2004) 'Bullying at work: A perspective from Britain and North America', in S. Fox and P.E. Spector (eds) *Counterproductive work behaviour. Investigations of actors and targets*, Washington, DC: American Psychological Association.

Richards, J. and Daley, H. (2003) 'Bullying policy: development, implementation and monitoring', in S. Einarsen, H. Hoel, D. Zapf and C.L. Cooper (eds) *Bullying and emotional abuse in the workplace. International perspectives in research and practice*, London: Taylor and Francis.

Salin, D. (2003a) 'Ways of explaining workplace bullying: a review of enabling, motivating and precipitating structures and processes in the work environment', *Human Relations*, 56(10) pp. 1213–32.

Salin, D. (2003b) 'Bullying and organizational politics in competitive and rapidly changing work environments', *International Journal of Management and Decision Making*, (4), pp. 35–45.

Schein, E. (1985) *Organizational Culture and Leadership*, San Francisco: Jossey-Bass Inc. Publishers.

Spurgeon, A. (2003) 'Bullying and risk management', in S. Einarsen, H. Hoel, D. Zapf and C.L. Cooper (eds) *Bullying and emotional abuse in the workplace. International perspectives in research and practice*, London: Taylor and Francis.

Stucke, T. (2002) 'Persönlichkeitskorrelate von Mobbing. Narzissmus und Selbstkonzeptklarheit als Persönlichkeitsmerkmale bei Mobbingtätern', *Zeitschrift für Arbeits- und Organizationspsychologie*, (46), pp. 216–221.

Unison (1997) *Unison Members' Experience of Bullying at Work*, London: UNISON.

Vartia, M. (1996) 'The sources of bullying: psychological work environment and organizational climate', *European Journal of Work and Organizational Psychology*, 5(2), pp. 203–14.

Zapf, D. (1999a) Mobbing in Organizationen. Ein Überblick zum Stand der Forschung', *Zeitschrift für Arbeits- und Organizationspsychologie*, (43), 1–25.

Zapf, D. (1999b) 'Organizational, work group related and personal causes of mobbing/bullying at work', *International Journal of Manpower*, 20(1/2), pp. 70–85.

Zapf, D. and Einarsen, S. (2003) 'Individual antecedents of bullying: targets and perpetrators', in S. Einarsen, H. Hoel, D. Zapf and C.L. Cooper (eds) *Bullying and emotional abuse in the workplace. International perspectives in research and practice*, London: Taylor and Francis.

Zapf, D. and Einarsen, S. (2004) Mobbing at work: escalated conflicts at work', in S. Fox and P.E. Spector (eds) *Counterproductive work behaviour. Investigations of actors and targets*, Washington, DC: American Psychological Association.

Zapf, D., Einarsen, S., Hoel, H. and Vartia, M. (2003) 'Empirical findings on bullying in the workplace', in S. Einarsen, H. Hoel, D. Zapf and C.L. Cooper (eds) *Bullying and emotional abuse in the workplace. International perspectives in research and practice*, London: Taylor and Francis.

Zapf, D. and Gross, C. (2001) 'Conflict escalation and coping with workplace bullying: A replication and extension', *European Journal of Work and Organizational Psychology*, (10), pp. 497–522.

Zapf, D., Knorz, C. and Kulla, M. (1996) 'On the relationship between mobbing factors, and job content, social work environment, and health outcomes', *European Journal of Work and Organizational Psychology*, 5(2), pp. 215–37.

Chapter 13

Cyber-harassment in the workplace

Monica T. Whitty and Adrian N. Carr

Introduction

Cyberspace can be a great tool for an organization; however, workplaces have not yet come to grips with how to use electronic communication in the most productive manner. On the one hand, the introduction of electronic communication within our places of work has improved communication, the pace at which we conduct our work, and provided greater access to important information. However, on the other hand, workplaces have experienced problems with how individuals from both within and external to the organization have utilized these new types of communication.

In this chapter, we consider electronic bullying in the workplace. More specifically, we focus on two extreme forms of bullying: cyberstalking and cyber-terrorism. Unfortunately, dealing with the full range of electronic bullying behaviours is beyond the scope of this chapter. Although we do acknowledge that other forms of electronic bullying, such as, flaming (which is essentially when an individual online writes with hostility towards a particular person or a group of people) do exist. We begin this chapter by highlighting that academics, legislators, policy makers and the like are still developing definitions for cyber-harassment. The more severe forms of harassment, cyberstalking and cyber-terrorism are outlined and examples of how these have affected workplaces are provided.

We then move towards developing a theory on how better to manage cyberspace within our places of work. While we would not dismiss the usefulness of policies, filtering software and the monitoring of workers to help prevent cyber-harassment and bullying in the workplace, we believe that this is not the final solution. Instead, we argue that if we are better able to conceptualize cyberspace and the relationships workers have with this space, then we may be able to develop more effective solutions in dealing with these new workplace violence issues. We make an attempt here to do just that by drawing on object relations theories developed by Winnicott, Bollas and Klein. We make the case here that while cyberspace is a unique and important tool for organizations to utilize, if not understood well the problems that have already emerged will remain and potentially increase.

What is cyber-harassment?

Electronic communication can be used to harass in both similar and new ways to offline traditional harassment. Before exploring how cyber-harassment might take place in our places of work, this paper outlines two severe forms of cyber-harassment: cyberstalking and cyber-terrorism.

Defining cyberstalking

Currently there is no universal definition of cyberstalking. McGrath and Casey (2002) have argued that:

> Stalking is the repeated uninvited monitoring and/or intrusion into the life and activities of a victim that is usually, but not always, undertaken for the purpose of frightening or intimidating the victim or those around the victim … Cyberstalking is merely stalking that uses the Internet for information gathering, monitoring, and/or victim contact (pp. 88–89).

Deirmenjian (1999) defined cyberstalking as 'harassment on the Internet using various modes of transmission such as electronic mail [e-mail], chat rooms, newsgroups, mail exploders, and the World Wide Web' (p. 407).

We agree with McGrath and Casey's (2002) notion that cyberstalking uses the Internet for information gathering, monitoring and/or victim contact. We also believe, akin to Deirmenjian's view, that cyberstalking, like stalking, is a form of harassment. However, we contend here that these definitions are too narrow, and instead a definition of cyberstalking should not be restricted to the Internet but should include any electronic communication device (which would also include, for instance, the text-messaging feature of mobile phones). We also recognise here that cyberstalking can be accompanied by traditional forms of stalking and harassment.

A more comprehensive view of cyberstalking has been offered by Bocij (2004: 14):

> A group of behaviors in which an individual, group of individuals, or organization uses information and communications technology to harass another individual, group of individuals, or organization. Such behaviors may include, but are not limited to, the transmission of threats and false accusations, identity theft, damage to data or equipment, computer monitoring, solicitation of minors for sexual purposes, and any form of aggression. Harassment is defined as a course of actions that a reasonable person, in possession of the same information, would think causes another reasonable person to suffer emotional distress.

Bocij's definition is not restricted to the Internet. Moreover, he quite rightly points out that cyberstalking can also be directed at groups or organizations as well as committed by groups or organizations.

Some of the current available legislation, which has been rewritten to include cyberstalking, is not restricted to just the Internet. For example, in South Australia the legislation defines cyberstalking as:

> … where stalkers take advantage of information technology either to cause physical or mental harm to the victim, or to cause the victim to feel serious apprehension or fear. Cyberstalking occurs when a person on at least two separate occasions with an intent to cause serious harm, uses the internet or some other form of electronic communication to publish or transmit offensive material, or communicates with the person, or to others about that person in a manner that could reasonably be expected to arouse apprehension or fear (SA Crimes Act 1990).

In a US Attorney General Report (1999), cyberstalking was defined as 'the use of the Internet, e-mail, or other electronic communications devices to stalk another person'.

It is also important to note that cyberstalking does not necessarily remain online. Stalking behaviour can potentially initiate online and progress to offline methods of stalking, including all traditional offline stalking behaviours, such as the phone, being followed, sending letters and so forth. In addition, the potential victim might simply be identified online and then stalked offline (Griffiths 2000).

To give an example of cyberstalking we outline here a classic case which occurred between Woodside Literacy Agency's dealings with Jayne Hitchcock (Bocij 2004; Deirmenjian 1999). When Jayne Hitchcock sent her book proposal to the Woodside Literacy Agency, she received a reply complimenting her on her proposal and a request for a reading fee. A few months later, post emerged on Usenet groups warning writers of this company, which prompted writers to test the company's credibility by sending their worst manuscripts. They too were complimented on their work and were requested to pay a reading fee. When Woodside discovered what was happening, the owner Leonard retaliated by spamming individuals. He then impersonated Hitchcock in various newsgroups and sent messages containing inflammatory comments. In one such message, it claimed that Hitchcock was into sadomasochistic practices and provided her phone number. This led to a barrage of phone calls to Hitchcock, which she obviously found harassing. Leonard was arrested in 2000 on charges of conspiracy to commit mail fraud.

While we still know little about the crime of cyberstalking, authors warn us that we should not trivialise this crime (Bocij 2004). For example, Bocij (2004) has argued that the harm caused to cyberstalked victims is often equal to or sometimes more harmful than traditional stalking. He also makes the point that even if the cyberstalker lives in another country this does not make his/her threats less credible.

Defining cyber-terrorism

Cyber-terrorism is perhaps even more difficult to define than cyberstalking. As Knight (2001) reports, the UK Terrorism Act 2000 is 'designed to prevent dissident political groups from using the UK as a base for terrorism and recognizes a new threat from cyber-terrorists for the first time. But the Act also significantly widens the definition of terrorism to include those actions that "seriously interfere with or seriously disrupt an electronic system".' The problem is that there is still little agreement on what is considered as cyber-terrorism. For instance, Bocij (2004) raises the question of whether electrohippies or hacktivists should be considered as cyber-terrorists. Bocij (2004) also makes the important point that if convicted for cyber-terrorism, individuals would face more severe punishments than they would for hacking activities.

Despite this fine line between who ought to be called a hacktivist, electrohippy or cyber-terrorist, the media have not held back on raising concerns about the potential harm cyber-terrorists might cause. For example, it was recently reported in Australian papers that during 2000 an Australian man, Vitek Boden, pumped for two months hundreds of thousands of litres of raw sewage into public waterways (Wyld 2004). In the meantime, the shire he was causing the problem in was employing him in a consultancy job to clean up the pollution that, little known to them, he was causing. Wyld reports that 'using a stolen computer and radio transmitter, Boden had set his car up as a remote command centre for sewage treatment along the Sunshine Coast.' Boden was arrested and found to be guilty of 30 charges of computer hacking and causing serious environmental harm. Wyld argues that although 'Boden may have had an individual agenda, his activities – theoretically – could just as easily have been carried out by operatives backed by a terrorist organization.'

Cyber-harassment in the workplace

Cyber-harassment is not just a concern for legislators, but also a problem that employers need to acknowledge more. As examples already presented in this paper illustrate, harassment in the workplace can occur on a number of levels. It can be on an inter-personal level and can even lead to more severe harassment, such as cyberstalking. It can also occur by having a group attacking an individual within an organization, or an individual, for example, Vitek Boden, attacking the shire. This chapter now turns to consider how we might more specifically consider cyber-harassment in the workplace.

Bocij (2004) warns us that the harm caused by cyberstalking must not be underestimated. An organization's reputation can be completely destroyed. Bocij gives an interesting example of an organization stalked by proxy, as he describes:

> ... it was alleged that Procter & Gamble had sponsored a web site that encouraged complaints against Amyway. It is alleged that the site featured negative news stories, personal testimonials, and even confidential documents belonging to Amyway. This kind of behaviour can be considered corporate stalking-by-proxy since it involved a company using a third party to harass a competitor (p. 143).

To add to the examples given earlier in this chapter, in the workplace cyber-harassment can take the form of obscene or hate e-mail/text messages that threaten or frighten, or e-mails/text messages that contain offensive content, such as sexist or racist material. What is unique about this type of workplace harassment, compared to more traditional forms of harassment, is that this material can be sent by people in addition to work colleagues, by other individuals outside the workplace (either known or not known to the person) or even in the form of spam. In 1998, Novell carried out a study in the UK on spamming. A serendipitous finding was that 41 per cent of the women in their sample had been sent pornographic material or had been harassed or stalked on the Internet (cited in Driscoll 1999). The problem with spam is that it can (and often does) contain sexual and/or illegal material. However, it is an extremely difficult problem to obviate and it is difficult to locate the source of the e-mail.

Other studies have more recently identified similar problems with the Internet and e-mail in the workplace. In 2001, Elron reported that about one in ten participants stated they had seen fellow workers accessing adult websites (Elron Software 2001). Moreover, one out of three participants stated that they received sexist material via e-mail and one out of eight participants stated that they received racist material via e-mail. In Whitty's (2004) recent research, similar concerns arose. In this Australia-wide study, 17 per cent of participants stated that they had been harassed in emails in their workplace, while 49 per cent said they had received offensive e-mails. In response to what type of material should be banned in the workplace, a significant proportion of women (67 per cent) compared to men (55 per cent) stated that offensive material, such as porn, should be banned. Furthermore, women disagreed more strongly than men did in their responses to whether workers should be permitted to access sexual material from the web at work.

While individuals are overall concerned about the material available at work on the Internet and the types of annoying e-mails they receive, they nevertheless approve of using the Internet and e-mail for personal usage. What appears to be a stark contradiction is that some of this personal usage could, in turn, annoy, offend or potentially harass others. For example, in the aforementioned Elron study, 70 per cent of participants stated that they commonly send jokes and chain mail via e-mail (Elron Software 2001). In Whitty's (2004) study it was found that one-third of her participants believed it was acceptable for workers to discuss sexual matters at work. What is particularly concerning about this result includes: (1) What kind of sexual details are being discussed?; (2) Are these e-mails ever seen by other employees and if so, is this construed as harassment?; and (3) Have there been instances when employees have accidentally sent these e-mails to someone for whom they were not intended?

In considering the above empirical research, there is a noteworthy corollary of ignoring this form of harassment. If effective strategies are not implemented to prevent cyber-harassment, individuals could begin to fear using the Internet (even if this type of harassment has not directly affected them). There are a number of disadvantages that accompany fear of using the Internet. For example, individuals are disadvantaged in the workplace, where the Internet is a resource that is increasingly being utilized. Furthermore, people are disadvantaged in educational settings where educators are required to use the Internet as an educational tool.

Drawing from object-relations theory to conceptualize cyberspace

So far, this chapter has highlighted the types of harassment that can take place in cyberspace and has considered, in particular, how this might cause problems in the workplace. We would not want to, however, dismiss the importance of cyberspace or under-emphasize the utility of the Internet and e-mail and other electronic communication in the workplace. Both the Internet and e-mail are great assets to an organization, especially when it comes to creating new knowledge (Whitty and Carr, forthcoming). Employers have attempted to obviate these problems by developing Internet usage policies, implementing filtering software and monitoring their workers. Some researchers have even suggested that psychological tests could assist employers in identifying potentially 'problem' employees. Each of these methods has its uses. However, none of them has been very successful in adequately dealing with Internet and e-mail usage problems (see Whitty 2004; Whitty and Carr, forthcoming). We propose in this chapter that if we are better able to conceptualize cyberspace and the relationship workers have with this space, then we may be able to develop solutions that are more effective in dealing with these new workplace harassment concerns. In grappling with how people understand and work within cyberspace, we think it is instructive to draw from object-relations theory, in particular to use a conceptual lens that comes from the work of Donald Winnicott, Christopher Bollas and Melanie Klein.

Donald Woods Winnicott used the term 'potential space' to mean the space between the mother and the infant. He contrasted this 'potential space (a) with the inner world (which is related to the psychosomatic partnership) and (b) with actual, or external reality' (1971/1997: 41). Winnicott understood potential spaces to be an area of intermediate experiencing that is between inner and outer worlds, 'between the subjective object and the object objectively perceived' (Winnicott 1971/1997: 100). Winnicott (1971/1997) argued that the potential space is:

the hypothetical area that exists (but cannot exist) between the baby and the object (mother or part of mother) during the phase of the repudiation of the object as not-me, that is, at the end of being merged in with the object (p. 107).

Although Winnicott believed that potential space originates between the mother and the infant, he also argued that later on it becomes possible for the individual child or adult to develop his/her own capacity to generate potential space. For example, he proposed that such spaces could exist between the patient and analyst.

According to Winnicott, potential space is the place where play takes place. He also stated that potential space is not inner psychic reality, rather, it 'is outside the individual, but it is not the external world' (1971/1997: 51). Potential space is not pure fantasy, but nor is it pure reality.

Winnicott (1971/1997) also believed that play is as important an activity during adulthood as it is in childhood. He went as far as to argue that play is central to individual growth. It is in Winnicott's potential space that meanings and self are continually being created and re-created. Winnicott (1971/1997) strongly contended that 'it is only in being creative that the individual discovers the self' (p. 54). Hence, he argued that given a 'good enough' environment the interplay of the inner world and external reality promotes the development of self and facilitates growth. In other words, *it is play that is the universal*, and that belongs to health.

The rules that are formed during play are also a notable aspect of Winnicott's theory. How we play the game and what rules we develop in order for play to take place, are questions we need to consider when we explore Winnicott's potential space. However, while play does have a sense of freedom, it is nonetheless constrained by rules. As Carr and Downs (forthcoming) argue, 'On the one hand the fundamental essence of play is the freedom and the license to create. Yet, on the other hand, constraint in the form of rules is required.' Given this juxtaposition between play and constraint, Carr (2001) contends that play transcends the serious and non-serious oppositional binary as it is a differentiated level of reality. As Freud (1908/1985) remarks:

Every child at play … creates a world of his own … It would be wrong to think he does not take that world seriously; on the contrary, he takes his play very seriously and he expends large amounts of emotion on it. The opposite of play is not what is serious but what is real (p. 132).

Winnicott used the term 'transitional object' to refer to the object that connects self and other. Winnicott noticed, for example, how an infant would suck and hug a doll or blanket. He suggested that the doll or blanket did not represent a doll or blanket as such, but is rather an *as-if object*. The infant makes use of the illusion that although this is not the breast, treating it as such will allow an appreciation of what is 'me' and what is 'not-me' (Winnicott 1971/1997: 41). Although referred to as a transitional object, 'it is not the object, of course that is transitional' (Winnicott 1971/1997: 14). The object is the initial manifestation of a different positioning of the infant in the world. The doll or blanket thus connects to subjective experience, but is in the objective world.

Christopher Bollas has elaborated further on Winnicott's work, with a particular focus on the nature of transitional objects. According to Bollas (1987, 1992), transitional objects, like all objects, themselves leave a trace within us. Bollas (1992: 59) argues that 'as we encounter the object world ... we are substantially metamorphosed by the structure of objects; internally transformed by objects that leave their trace within us'. Some objects seem to have much more inner meaning for us and unlock unconscious thought processes and affective states. In a sense, Bollas argues, these objects are 'transformational' and may act like 'psychic keys' (see also Carr 2003). The objects themselves, in acting as psychic keys, appear to enable past unconscious experiences to be released to inform present behaviour. In respect to online interactions, we would suggest that the transitional objects such as computers, monitors, keyboards, mice, modems and so forth 'leave a trace' within us such that they trigger emotional responses such as expectations, passion and curiosity which are reminders of previous Internet 'encounters'.

Another theory we would like to draw up in this paper is Melanie Klein's (1975) well-known object-relations theory. One of the aspects of her theory that we are utilizing in this paper is her notion of splitting. According to Klein, splitting behaviour involves dichotomising the world into 'good' objects and 'bad' objects. Klein believed that the infant in the paranoid-schizoid position wants to possess the contents of the mother's body, while at the same time wanting to destroy her. She believed these responses arose from the death instinct.

Klein also included in her object-relations theory other defence mechanisms delineated by Freud, including introjection and denial. To quote from Klein (1986):

Idealization is bound up with the splitting of the object, for the good aspects of the breast are exaggerated as a safeguard against the fear of the persecuting breast. While idealization is thus the corollary of persecutory fear, it also springs from the power of the instinctual desires which aim at unlimited gratification and therefore create the picture of an inexhaustible and always bountiful breast – an ideal breast … The denial of psychic reality becomes possible only through strong feelings of omnipotence – an essential characteristic of early mentality. Omnipotent denial of the existence of the bad object and of the painful situation is in the unconscious equal to annihilation by the destructive impulse. It is, however, not only a situation and an object that are denied and annihilated – it is an object relation which suffers this fate (p. 182).

Managing cyber-interactions in the workplace

We have previously drawn from object-relations theory proposing that cyberspace could be understood as potential space (Whitty 2003; Whitty and Carr 2003, forthcoming). As we have suggested in the past, cyberspace should be understood as a space somewhere outside the individual, but which is still not the external world. Important to the arguments formed in this chapter, we believe that the web should be conceptualized as a potential playground.

It is in such a context that we argue that a new space has been introduced in the workplace. This new space allows for new kinds of play within organizations, between organizations and even inclusive of individuals outside the workplace. Drawing from Winnicott's notion of potential space, meanings are created and re-created within this space. Moreover, playing in such a space promotes the development of self. We would like to extend this to argue that it can promote the development of an organization. If it is agreed that cyberspace can be understood as a potential space, then individuals can play within such a space to develop the growth of themselves and, in turn, their organizations.

Cyberspace provides an opportunity for individuals to work together to engage with material, play with material and hence create knowledge. We believe that it is through this playing that organizations can reap the benefits of cyberspace. One common way people have used their short break-time in the workplace is by chatting round the water-cooler or while making cups of tea, or having cigarette breaks. While this may have been perceived by both the people engaging in this activity and their fellow workers as more play-time than work-time, nevertheless there has been some utility in having these conversations and time out from what is formally constituted as 'work'. These interactions can be a way of sharing information, which leads to creating knowledges. We would like to make the point that in a similar way cyberspace can be a place where this kind of play or break-time can be spent. Of course, people's break-time around the water-cooler is not solely spent on creating new knowledge. It can be simply a way to have a short break, so that one can move back to work with a fresh mind and as a consequence of the short break be more productive. Hence, while some play-time might not be spent directly on work tasks, it can still be a means of increasing an individual's productivity.

Although we do make the claim that cyberspace can be an important and productive place for workers to play in, we do not dismiss the case that electronic bullying can and does take place within the workplace. While cyberspace is a place where new important creative processes can take place, we need to question what happens if an individual strays too close to the borders of reality or fantasy? As illustrated through numerous examples earlier in this chapter, there are many forms of electronic bullying that are starting to emerge within organizations, to organizations, from organizations, as well as between organizations. To give another recent example, Aftab (2004) reports that 'a company executive was being harassed through e-mail messages sent to his family, employees and investors that said he molested his children.' In yet another example, Aftab claims that 'an employee set up a Web site claiming to be another employee and offering to have sex.'

As the examples in this chapter demonstrate, many of these forms of electronic bullying are illegal. This illegal activity has become even more of a concern for employers, given that some places (e.g. the Australian State of Victoria) have written into recent legislation that employers can now be liable for harassment or discrimination claims against an employee unless they take all reasonable steps to prevent it.

When we consider that cyberspace is a new place to play in the workplace, we also need to consider the rules that accompany this new activity. Winnicott contends that *we need to consider the rules of the game, as while play is separated from the ordinary world, it is still constrained by the rules.* We believe that the rules on how to play in cyberspace at work are still currently being devised. As mentioned earlier, legislators and psychologists are still grappling with how to define certain types of cyber-harassment, such as cyberstalking and cyber-terrorism. Despite the lack of consistency in these professionals' definitions (or understanding of the 'rules'), workplaces have managed to develop clear policies in respect to cyber-harassing and discriminatory behaviour. However, these rules are not consistently applied by workers in respect to how they conduct their electronic communications. One reason we would like to offer for this is because *cyberspace is considered to be a different kind of space in the workplace, a place where the rules are still being negotiated and defined.* It would be reasonable to assume that this space is perceived by workers to be a more private space and quite separate from the 'real' world. An employee might see this as a space that is, in a sense, more one's own space where an employer has no right to intrude and effectively spy on an individual. The conceptual optic developed in this chapter would suggest that it is perceived to be a space where people can feel more liberated and free, which could be in stark contrast to the physical office space these individuals work in. This illusion of privacy is perhaps sustained given that work colleagues are not necessarily privy to all the conversations that take place online and the information that is downloaded. This is quite different to the conversations that take place in the workplace either face-to-face or by telephone, where one is accountable for one's actions given that others can witness them. Of course, the reality is that while workers might be sustaining an illusion in respect to cyberspace being a more private space, this is not the case. Others can see colleagues' computer monitors, the computer keeps a trace of where the individual has been surfing on the Internet, those who have access to the server have access to e-mails being sent back and forth, and commonly e-mails are accidentally sent to people they were not intended for. That being said, we nonetheless would argue that people often separate themselves from this reality when they log on into cyberspace. Hence, given the separateness of this space to other spaces, we are not applying old rules to this new form of communication.

It is here that we believe Klein's theory is useful. According to Klein, part of a paranoid-schizoid defensive condition is splitting the world into 'good' objects and 'bad' objects. If we consider, as argued earlier, that one of the objects that occupy cyberspace is the text, we can identify some interesting splitting behaviour that appears to take place here. A type of splitting between good and bad objects has been identified in our empirical work (Whitty 2004). We pointed out earlier in this paper the contradictions in people's attitudes towards Internet and e-mail behaviour in the workplace. It appears that for some, double standards are being applied, where it is acceptable for an individual to talk about sexual matters or to send chain or joke e-mails, while at that same time disapproving of sexual content on the web, offensive e-mails and being sent chain e-mails.

The relationship people have with the objects that occupy cyberspace also needs to be considered. As mentioned earlier, Winnicott believed that objects that occupy potential space can be transitional. However, we need to be clear that it is not the object itself that is transitional. In turn, not all objects in cyberspace will act as transitional objects. Hence, it is how people relate to and use objects in cyberspace that has some important repercussions in the workplace. If we use and play with these objects creatively, then there is the opportunity to create knowledge.

Bollas's view that transitional objects leave a trace within us is an important point to consider when we examine objects in cyberspace. The computer in some ways can be seen as an extension of self, which is perhaps why people feel this is an object that contains private information. Hence, individuals ascribe a very different meaning to their computer than they would to other objects in an office. For example, putting a calendar of naked women on the wall is seen as inappropriate perhaps because this is understood to be a public space.

Conclusions and starting points

We are slowly learning that cyberspace represents a new space – a space that cannot be assumed to obey the 'rules' assumed of behaviour in other spaces. The object-relations optic, developed in this paper, reveals that the manner in which employees have 'engaged' the object called the computer yields behaviour that requires us to revisit and reconsider our definitions and understanding of workplace bullying and violence. Indeed, the conceptual lens of object-relations provides us with insight as to why cyberspace and its related objects are an attractive place to 'play' in a creative manner within the workplace itself. The space called cyberspace can be *a seductive place to play*, where gradations of violence, bullying and harassing behaviour may become emergent phenomena. This space can also be a targeted space through which violence and bullying are premeditated behaviours. The 'rules' under which access is provided to employees to be creative need to include an appreciation of how this space can be 'abused' and become a place through which forms of violence and bullying can be perpetrated which are both similar and different in character to those violent and bullying behaviours that are 'offline'.

The advent of cyberspace has, in many respects, blurred the distinction between public and private spaces. Those charged with policy development and legislative responsibilities need to artilculate carefully such a distinction and be open to the manner in which cyberspace is a changing place. As we write, we note that, in Australia, the New South Wales government is instituting new legislation and policy to recognize cyberspace bullying in schools via mobile text-messaging and e-mail (Noonan 2004; see also Burke 2004). Specifically, this proposed new initiative gives school principals the power to take disciplinary action in such a context. Unfortunately, this initiative fails to articulate private versus public space and does not come couched in an educative programme that delineates forms of electronic bullying and cogent rules for the use of cyberspace. The challenge for schools, as with workplaces, is to commence a dialogue that helps everyone better conceptualize cyberspace and at the same time recognizes the potential darker side to this space.

References

Aftab, P. (2004) 'The Privacy Lawyer managing cybercrime, privacy and cyber-abuse risks'. Accessed 5 November 2004 from http://www.aftab.com/in_the_newscybercrimes.htm

Bocij, P. (2004) *Cyberstalking: Harassment in the Internet Age and how to Protect your Family*, Westport: Praeger.

Bollas, C. (1987) *The Shadow of the Object: Psychoanalysis of the Unthought Known*, London: Free Association Books.

Bollas, C. (1992) *Being a Character: Psychoanalysis and Self-experience*, New York: Hill & Wang.

Burke, K. (2004, 3 April) 'SMS bullies face school suspension', *Sydney Morning Herald*, p. 3.

Carr, A. (2001) 'Organisational and Administrative Play: the potential of magic realism, surrealism and postmodernist forms of play', in J. Biberman and A. Alkhafaji (eds) *Business Research Yearbook: Global Business Perspectives*, Saline: McNaughton & Gunn Inc, pp. 543–7.

Carr, A. (2003) 'Organisational Discourse as a Creative Space for Play: the potential of postmodernist and surrealist forms of play', *Human Resource Development International*, 6(2), pp. 197–217.

Carr, A. and Downs, A. (2004) 'Transitional and Quasi-objects in Organization Studies: viewing Enron from the object relations world of Winnicott and Serres', *Special Issue of Journal of Organizational Change Management*.

Deirmenjian, J.M. (1999) 'Stalking in Cyberspace', *The Journal of the American Academy of Psychiatry and the Law*, pp. 407–13.

Driscoll, M. (1999, 8 March) 'You've got mail: "scream"', *The Australian*, p. 15.

Elron Software (2001) The year 2001 corporate web and email usage study. 12 November 2003 from www.elronsw.com/pdf/NFOReport.pdf

Freud, S. (1985) 'Creative Writers and Day-dreaming', in S. Freud *Art and literature*, Harmondsworth, England: Penguin Freud Library, Volume 14. Original work published 1908.

Griffiths, M. (2000) 'Excessive Internet Use: implications for sexual behaviour', *CyberPsychology and Behavior*, pp. 537–52.

Klein, M. (1975) *Love, Guilt and Reparation and Other Works, 1921-1945*, London: Hogarth.

Klein, M. (1986) *The Selected Melanie Klein*, Harmondsworth, England: Penguin Books.

Knight, W. (2001, 20 February) 'Hackers become terrorists under UK law', *ZDNet Australia* (Retrieved, 19 July 2004 from http://www.zdnet.com.au/news/0,39 023165,20205108,00.htm

McGrath, M.G. and Casey, E. (2002) 'Forensic Psychiatry and the Internet: practical perspectives on sexual predators and obsessional harassers in cyberspace', *Journal of the American Academy of Psychiatry and the Law*, 20, pp. 81–94.

Noonan, G. (2004, 4 August) 'Teachers' hands strengthened in discipline fight', *Sydney Morning Herald*, p. 3.

SA Crimes Act (2001, 31 August), Office of the South Australian Attorney-General, s562A.

US Attorney General (1999) *Cyberstalking: a new challenge for law enforcement and industry*. Report from the Attorney General to the Vice President, August. Retrieved 18 July 2004 from http://www.usdoj.gov/criminal/cybercrime/cyberstalking.htm

Whitty, M.T. (2003) 'Cyber-flirting: playing at love on the internet', *Theory and Psychology*, pp. 339–57.

Whitty, M.T. (2004) 'Should Filtering Software be Utilised in the Workplace? Australian employees' attitudes towards internet usage and surveillance of the internet in the workplace', *Surveillance and Society*, pp. 39–54.

Whitty, M.T. and Carr, A.N. (2003) 'Cyberspace as Potential Space: considering the web as a playground to cyber-flirt', *Human Relations*, pp. 861–91.

Whitty, M.T. and Carr, A.N. (forthcoming) 'New Rules in the Workplace: applying object-relations theory to explain problem Internet and email behavior in the workplace', *Computers in Human Behavior*.

Winnicott, D.W. (1997) *Playing and Reality*, London: Tavistock. Original work published 1971.

Wyld, B. (2004, 17 July) 'Fear factory'. *The Sydney Morning Herald* (Retrieved 19 July 2004 from http://smh.com.au/articles/2004/07/16/1089694549469.html

Future Directions

Chapter 14

Where to from here? Countering workplace violence in the new millennium

Vaughan Bowie, Bonnie S. Fisher and Cary L. Cooper

As outlined in Chapter 1, there were a number of key distinguishing themes that we hoped to see represented in this volume. Such issues and foci were indeed strongly represented throughout the book, while at the same time other important issues began to emerge and develop worthy of further investigation and research. While most of these issues are not totally new in themselves, the authors in this volume shed new light on them and raised intriguing questions worthy of future research. These emerging issues and future research priorities are discussed below.

Global nature of workplace violence

Di Martino identified the global nature of workplace violence across all nations, sectors and occupations. The types of workplace violence present and emerging may be partially dependent on the stage of economic, political and social development of the particular country. In many nations the current focus is on preventing overt physical violence and abuse at work, while psychological violence may not be so readily identified or acknowledged or seen as less of a priority for intervention.

There are several avenues for further research to examine fundamental issues concerning the definition and measurement of workplace violence.

To further our understanding of the extent and nature of workplace violence, there is a pressing need to develop theories and test hypotheses about the causal antecedents, including characteristics of the perpetrator and target and organizational factors, and process leading to the onset and execution of violence across different occupations and organizational settings. Further cross-national research is also much needed on the nature and extent of such workplace violence in emerging nations. The exchange of information across countries as to the development and evaluation of responses and interventions to manage and prevent both physical and psychological violence at work are needed to better prepare management, employees, unions and other interested parties for the realities many employees face daily.

Abusive organizations

A common theme throughout many of the chapters of this book was that of the role abusive organizations play in the triggering and escalation of workplace violence (see Grubb *et al.*; Rayner, Wigley, Bowie, Einarsen *et al.*). It is clear from the current research that the growing incidence of workplace violence, including bullying, cannot be explained purely in terms of staff or client personal characteristics (see Rayner). Organizational culture and management styles are increasingly being identified as key factors in the development of workplace violence (Rayner *et al.* 2002). Thus the changing nature of the workplace and the type of embedded organizational practices and culture must also be taken into account if the causal mechanisms that lead to workplace violence are to be more fully understood and incorporated into effective proactive and reactive responses.

Further research needs to be undertaken as to what are the factors that foster or hinder the development of abusive and violent organizational cultures and how to minimize their flow-on effects to employees, clients and surrounding communities. At the same time the development and evaluation of different types of strategies and interventions, both internally and externally for organizations, are needed to minimize organizational abuse and violence.

Growth of psychological violence at work, including bullying

While physical violence at work remains a major concern within particular service and retail industries (or occupations) in some developed countries the rate of physical violence may be plateauing or even decreasing (Budd 2001; Duhart 2001). Perhaps ironically, as identified here by Di Martino, it also appears that psychological violence is spiralling upwards in many countries.

Further research is needed to identify why psychological violence is continuing to grow while at the same time physical violence is plateauing in some Westernized work cultures. There are many unanswered questions whose answers could provide needed insight into the workplace trends. For example, is this current plateauing part of a cyclical phenomenon of rises and falls in physical violence generally or unique to the workplace? Further probing into the relationship between physical and psychological violence is also needed. This area of research is in its infancy stages of understanding, in part because of the lack of data sources that collect information about both physical and psychological violence, but fortunately the research continues to grow and address definitional and measurement issues inherent in this field of study.

Staff-on-client abuse

The chapter by Hockley raised the important issue of staff abuse against those in their care and outlined some responses of a legal nature to minimize such incidents. Staff-initiated violence is usually identified as being aimed at colleagues or others not those in a dependent relationship to a 'carer'. Some staff by nature seem to be sadistic and serial abusers while others become reactive abusers under increasing work-related pressures and personal stress issues (Conlin Shaw 1998). There are a number of other strategies alongside that of legal response that could help minimize abuse by staff including improving the selection, more training and support for staff, as well as changes in the culture and management style of human service organizations.

Further research is required on this sometimes 'hidden' aspect of workplace violence. Especially needed is an understanding of the roles that organizational cultures and management practices may play in triggering, encouraging, condoning or even rewarding such behaviour.

Gender differences in the type of workplace violence experienced by men and women

Overall, the current workplace violence research suggests that gender differences more so than gender similarities characterize workplace violence. For example, results from the National Crime Victimization Survey in the US showed that males are more likely to be robbery victims while at work or on duty than females (Duhart 2001). Females, however, are more likely than males to be victims of sexual assault, rape and stalking in the workplace, especially by someone known to them. Recent research also supports the notion that many workplace violent incidents are the result of domestic violence spilling over into the workplace, more so for females than males. Fisher and Peek-Asa suggested that domestic violence in the workplace poses different safety and security challenges to employers and employees compared to other types of violence against employees, clients or customers.

After examining the scant workplace domestic violence research, Fisher and Peek-Asa concluded that many of these challenges have yet to be researched or addressed by employers, unions or other parties interested in employee safety. The gaps in our understanding of workplace domestic violence include identifying individual-level perpetration and victimization characteristics and organizational-level opportunity factors and their respective causal and interactive effects. Collaborative partnerships between researchers and employers are needed to better understand these relationships and their impacts on the physical, emotional and financial wellbeing of employees and the functioning and operations of the organization. These understandings can then serve as the foundation for the development, implementation and evaluation of innovative proactive and reactive safety and security strategies to workplace domestic violence.

Aid workers and humanitarian organizations

Another issue of growing concern identified in a number of chapters is the impact of workplace violence, including terrorism, on humanitarian aid and peacekeeping workers. Thomas and Wigley both stressed the need for aid organizations to provide psychological support for staff targets of violence, and the opportunity to disclose their emotional vulnerability. They also identified the need to develop, strengthen and support positive leadership within such organizations.

With the growing threat of reactive terrorism and other associated forms of workplace violence against humanitarian organizations and their workers, there is a need for a greater recognition of this problem through research and the development of integrated international responses.

The economic and financial costs of workplace violence

The question of the economic and financial costs of workplace violence as raised by Di Martino and Fisher and Peek-Asa is addressed in this volume in two ways. First by examining the impact of such violence on organizations and communities in monetary terms, both obvious and hidden, and second by outlining ways that the need to reduce such costs can be used as a tool to bring about organizational change that decreases workplace violence and associated financial losses. Such a financial analysis and costing of 'the bottom line' may prove to be a key stimulus for changing organizational practices and work cultures leading to violence at work and its spilling out into associated communities.

As foreshadowed by Di Martino, Bowie, Rayner and other contributors, there is first a need to recognize this socio-economic dimension of workplace violence. The linkages between managerial and company goals at the enterprise level that directly tie in violence-prevention initiatives are yet to be fully explored. Thus there is a need for researchers and practitioners to more accurately document and then estimate the effects that this socio-economic dimension has on the financial profits and goals of the organization. There is a need to outline strategies in which the business profit motives are more closely linked with anti-physical and psychological violence initiatives in the workplace.

Terrorism as an emerging form of workplace violence

A number of contributors identified terrorism as a major potential source of workplace violence (see Wee and Myers, Bowie, Vineburgh *et al.*). Two emerging concerns are evident: how can organizations, especially those providing human services, train and equip their staff to deal with terrorist incidents, and what are the forms of reactive terrorism and how can each be minimized?

Much of the current research on the impact of terrorism and responses to it has focused on large-scale incidents such as September 11 and its devastating short-term and long-term effects both inside and outside the workplace. However, little is known about the impact of terrorism on secondary responders and the ongoing cumulative impact of numerous, limited terrorist incidents. More analysis needs to be undertaken on the effects on human service workers and organizations of 'smaller scale', ongoing terrorist situations such as in Iraq, Sri Lanka, Spain and Northern Ireland. Further research is also needed as to what role organizations may play in triggering or decreasing reactive terrorism and how the ripple effect from abusive organizations may be minimized in its impact upon co-located business, industries and welfare and aid groups.

Polices and programmes to manage workplace violence

One response to the problem of workplace violence is the development of procedures, policies and codes of professional practice which govern and direct the behaviour of service users and customers, employees, managers and organizations. Such frameworks, however, in themselves may be of little practical use or effectiveness and may in fact be a 'smokescreen' to hide ongoing structural violence problems within organizations or merely to rehash the same old information with little meaningful content. Fisher and Peek-Asa, Grubb *et al.*, and Einarsen *et al.* discuss these possibilities.

The challenge for employers and employees is to develop, implement and evaluate anti-workplace violence policies and procedures in a way that is inclusive of all key stakeholders. Information and resources to develop and implement organizational and cultural change must be discussed and incorporated into any such policies and procedures. Published 'successful' case studies are scarce. A first big step forward in this regard is the documentation of 'best practice' case studies in developing and implementing such policies and procedures within a framework of positive organizational change.

Cyber-terrorism

Cyber-harassment as outlined by Whitty and Carr, and its more extreme form cyber-terrorism, are growing threats that can impact upon not only a single worksite but workplaces around the world in a simultaneous manner. At a more localized level it is now possible for workers to be harassed by e-mails and other electronic forms. Also, at an international level it is now no longer necessary to attack with bombs or hijacked planes with their associated risks. Attack can be made through the crippling of key power, transport and security networks by cyber-terrorists. This blurring of the private and the public domains in the 'electronic workplace' and the relative ease with which external intruders can penetrate and cripple and destroy the work cyberspace is emerging as one of the major issues in workplace violence.

Such possibilities of cyber-harassment and cyber-terrorism at the local, national and international levels raise a number of issues and challenges that are only now beginning to be grappled with. This is a growing and crucial area in need of extensive research and technological and policy development to minimize the opportunities for cyber-terrorism and hold the perpetrator(s) accountable.

Countering workplace violence in the new millennium

In 2003 the Organization for Economic Cooperation and Development estimated that the total labour force in its member countries was around 545,923,000. The sheer size of the labour force coupled with the diversity inherent in the personalities of employees as well as that of customers and clients, job-related duties and locations, and organizational characteristics have led researchers to conclude that no one occupation or type of organizational setting is immune from physical or psychological violence, but that some employees are more at risk than others. Thus, with such a range of workplace settings and types of incident no one volume can expect to cover in depth all the major issues related to workplace violence. Collectively and individually, the authors have provided the reader with innovative insights into current and newly emerging workplace violence issues. Their timely contributions are coupled with directions for future research and work-based programmes and policies to address the growing realities of workplace violence.

Among our goals in this volume was to provide an opportunity for a team of international experts to address, identify and discuss emerging workplace violence issues. We are hopeful that their collective scholarship will help in the development of a worldwide agenda to address key workplace violence issues. We are also confident that the authors' various strategies will further stimulate discussion and development of policies and practices to address effectively the physical and psychological safety of the many millions of workers worldwide, thus helping to counter the many faces of workplace violence in the new millennium.

References

Budd, T. (July 2001) *Violence at work: New Findings from the 2000 British Crime Survey*, London: Home Office and Health and Safety Executive.

Conlin Shaw, M. (1998) 'Nursing home Resident Abuse by Staff', *Journal of Elder Abuse and Neglect*, 9(4), pp. 1–21.

Duhart, T. (2001) *Violence in the Workplace*, National Crime Victimization Survey Special Report, Bureau of Justice Studies, US Department of Justice NCJ, http://www.ojp.usdoj.gov/bjs/pub/pdf/vw99.pdf (accessed 27/06/05).

Organization for Economic Cooperation and Development (2003), http://213.253.134.29/oecd/pdfs/browseit/0104071E.PDF (accessed 26/06/05).

Rayner, C., Hoel, H. and Cooper, C.L. (2002) *Workplace Bullying*, London: Taylor and Francis.

Index

absenteeism
  by aid workers 154
  by domestic violence victims 97–8,
    102, 103–4, 106, 108, 109
  and European Union workplace
    violence 24–5
  and fear of workplace violence 39
  and psychological aggression 39, 42
Action Against Terrorism (UN) 178
Acute Stress Disorder (ASD) 129, 132–3
addiction 28–9, 220
  see also alcohol abuse; drug abuse;
    tobacco abuse
advocacy groups, workplace violence
  prevention 180
Afghanistan 123–4, 126, 176
Aftab, P. 258
age discrimination, and psychological
  aggression 53, 55
agencies, health sector 88, 89, 90, 91
agriculture sector, psychological
  aggression 49, 50
aid workers
  aid work entry 122–3, 154–5
  beneficiaries 141, 148–9, 175

and humanitarian organizations
  150–1, 153–5
individual coping strategies
  128, 135–6
inter-personal relationships
  131–2, 142, 149–50
international security policies 125–6
law 125–6, 133
moral dilemmas 122, 127
motivations and characteristics
  122–3, 147–8
neutrality 123–4
and organizations 126–7, 134–5,
  143–5
psychological problems 122, 128–33,
  136, 142, 145, 149–55
psychological support 128, 131–6,
  149, 150–1, 153–5
and reactive terrorism 141, 149, 175
security issues 121–2, 123–8, 129–30,
  133, 150–1, 175–6, 177
training 135, 149, 154
workplace homicides 123–4, 126, 176
alcohol abuse 27, 28–9, 213, 214, 219

individual explanations 169–70
risk factors 38
socio-economic factors 32, 269
as terrorism 23, 168–72, 173–6
typologies 2–3, 79, 80, 164
workplace violence prevention and
intervention
best practice 179, 180, 181, 270
codes of practice 178, 270
guidelines 27–8, 31, 33, 128
international responses 26–34, 179–81
law 27, 30–1, 178
negative inter-personal behaviour
(NiB) 61–2, 65–6
negative organizational behaviour
(NiB) 70–1
programmes 112, 114–15, 179–81, 190
psychological aggression 56–7, 88–9
reactive terrorism 177–81
regulations 23, 27, 32–4, 178

and response critiques 199
staff-initiated violence 88–9, 267
strategies 38
workplace domestic violence 106–15,
116–17
World Health Organization (WHO) 27,
29
World Report on Violence and Health
(WHO) 29
World Trade Center terrorist attack
207, 212, 214, 218
worldwide-web *see* Internet
Wyld, B. 252

Youth, Sport and Protection (YSP) 28–9
Yugoslavia 128

Zadek, S. 180
Zapf, Dieter 233, 234, 238–9
Zorza, J. 106